THE EXTRAORDINARY ENVOY

General Hiroshi Ōshima and Diplomacy in the Third Reich, 1934-1939

Carl Boyd

UNIVERSITY
PRESS OF
AMERICA

University Press of America, Inc.™

P.O. Box 19101, Washington, DC 20036

ISBN (Perfect): 0-8191-0958-4
ISBN   (Cloth): 0-8191-0957-6
LCN: 79-9600

Second Printing, 1982

To my father

and

in memory of my mother

1915-1975

ACKNOWLEDGMENTS

At Old Dominion University a fellowship from the
Research Foundation and a research grant from the School
of Arts and Letters have enabled me to do much of the investigation and writing for this study. My work was greatly
facilitated by a leave from my teaching duties in the
Department of History during the autumn semester 1979. I
am indebted to the university and to my colleagues there--
in particular to Willard C. Frank, Jr., who kindly agreed
to teach a course required for ROTC cadets, an American
military history course which I was originally scheduled
to offer. I am also greatly indebted to Andreas Dorpalen
of Ohio State University, Robert H. Ferrell of Indiana
University, and to Peter Paret of Stanford University for
their encouragement, thoughtful suggestions, and scholarly
examples. It is a pleasure to acknowledge the assistance
of John E. Taylor (Modern Military Branch, Military Archives Division, National Archives) and Key K. Kobayashi
(Japanese Section, Orientalia Division, Library of Congress)
as well as the staff of Old Dominion University Library,
particularly in the Documents, Interlibrary Loan, and
Reference Departments. I would like to thank George Marinos
for his work in developing the previously unpublished
photographs (Figures 1-9) from old and fragile negatives,
and Alfred H. Lewis of the Department of History, Old
Dominion University, for his efficient typing. The editor
of the Journal of Asian History and The Citadel Development Foundation kindly permitted me to incorporate parts
of my work that first appeared in somewhat different form
in their publications. Also, the editor of Modern Asian
Studies has kindly allowed me to incorporate some material
in this longer study from my article on "The Berlin-Tokyo
Axis and Japanese Military Initiative" that is in press at
Cambridge University. Finally, I am obligated to Columbia
University Press for permission to quote extensively from
Deterrent Diplomacy: Japan, Germany and the USSR, 1935-
1940, edited by James William Morley.

Norfolk, Virginia   Carl Boyd
January 1980

v

Acknowlegments

Though the substance of the original edition remains unchanged in this second printing, several small changes and specific corrections have been incorporated. I remain indebted to those people cited on the previous page for their great assistance, and I should like now to add my thanks to Akira Amakawa, Rose-Marie Dorpalen, and Robert T. MacPherson for their extremely helpful and valuable suggestions.

Old Dominion University   Carl Boyd
Norfolk, Virginia
June 1982

vi

CONTENTS

Acknowledgments   v

      Introduction   1
  I. Prelude to Military Diplomacy   5
 II. Intrigue and Influence   19
III. A Year of Struggle   35
 IV. The Expansion and Dominance
               of Military Diplomacy   57
  V. The Warrior-Diplomat   85
 VI. Ōshima and the New Order   127

      Appendix A: German-Japanese Agreement
                   against the Communist
                   International, November
                   25, 1936   157
      Appendix B: Memorandum of a Conversation
                   between Hiroshi Oshima and
                   Heinrich Himmler, January
                   31, 1939   167
      Appendix C: Ōshima's Military and Court
                   Ranks, Major Assignments,
                   and Decorations   169
      Appendix D: The State Secretary to the
                   Embassy in Japan   173
      Appendix E: Ambassador Oshima's Account
                   of His Conversation with
                   Hitler on 27 May [1944]   179
      Appendix F: Excerpts from Ōshima's Reports
                   of His Last Conference with
                   Hitler, 4 September 1944   185
      Appendix G: 8 March [1945] Report from
                   Ambassador Oshima Describing
                   Living Conditions in Berlin   191
      Appendix H: Excerpts from Ōshima's Reports
                   of His Conversations with
                   Ribbentrop, March and April
                   1945, Followed by the "Magic"
                   Diplomatic Summary of 16
                   April 1945   197

Contents

Bibliography   209
Index   239

Illustrations

Figure 1:   Ōshima at a performance of
            the Berlin Philharmonic
            Orchestra, November 1935   14
Figure 2:   Ōshima at Hitler's house on
            the Obersalzberg,
            November 1938   75
Figure 3:   Ōshima at the Reich
            Chancellery with Lammers
            and Keitel, January 1939   110
Figure 4:   Ōshima at the Pergamon
            Museum, February 1939   111
Figure 5:   Ōshima with Göring, Hitler,
            Himmler, and Ribbentrop,
            February 1939   112
Figure 6:   Ōshima with Hitler, March 1939 113
Figure 7:   Ōshima with Ribbentrop, March
            1939   114
Figure 8:   Ōshima with Admiral Nagano at
            the International Military
            Tribunal for the Far East,
            1946-1948   146
Figure 9:   Ōshima at the International
            Military Tribunal for the
            Far East, 1946-1948   147

INTRODUCTION

During the Second World War both the Germans and the Americans attached great importance to the Japanese ambassador in Berlin, Hiroshi Ōshima.[1] Hitler's Propaganda Minister, Paul Joseph Goebbels, wrote in his diary in April 1942 about Ōshima and his recent trip to Romania and Hungary:

> Oshima spoke extremely eloquently in favor of the Axis policies. He behaved very cleverly and tactfully. He made no bones about being pro-German. . . . Oshima is really one of the most successful champions of Axis policies. A monument ought later to be erected in his honor in Germany.[2]

About two years later, on the other side of the Atlantic Ocean, General George C. Marshall, then Chief of Staff of the U. S. Army, wrote in a letter dated 25 September 1944 that

> our main basis of information regarding Hitler's intentions in Europe is obtained from Baron Oshima's message[s] from Berlin reporting his interviews with Hitler and other officials to the Japanese Government.[3]

Ambassador Ōshima's messages fell victim to "Magic"--the code name for the American interception and deciphering of Japanese diplomatic messages exchanged between the Foreign Ministry in Tokyo and Japan's representatives abroad.

In 1978 the "Magic" Summary documents were declassified by the U. S. National Security Agency and later made available to researchers in the National Archives, Washington, D.C. These sophisticated documents are rich sources for the study of the Second World War, and their intelligence data reiterate for today's researcher the significance of Marshall's words in 1944. Indeed, the esteem with which Goebbels seemed to regard Ōshima was surpassed only by Ōshima's importance to the Allies in the "Magic" betrayal of Hitler.

Introduction

Although the conversations Ōshima had with Hitler were
paraphrased in his messages to Tokyo, they capture a di-
mension of Hitler not previously seen by relying on German
documents alone. The scenes during the Second World War of
Hitler offering wide-ranging and frank responses to Ōshima's
often penetrating questions resulted because of a peculiar
trust and a oneness of interests built up over several
earlier years.

How did this unique relationship come about? Why did
Hitler's subordinates advance Ōshima in National Socialist
circles in 1934 and 1935 and scarely acknowledge others in
the Japanese embassy in Berlin? A partial explanation is
supplied through a survey of the setting. Important was a
common backdrop emphasizing dissatisfaction with the international status quo; both societies also experienced the
growth of military and totalitarian tendencies after the
First World War. Of even greater importance, however, is
a detailed examination of Ōshima and his work in Berlin from
1934 until shortly after Hitler's invasion of Poland.

Ōshima approved of the militarism and totalitarianism
evident in the Third Reich when he arrived in Berlin as the
Japanese military attaché in 1934. Ōshima's personal ability
and initiative sub rosa greatly enhanced his importance in
German-Japanese relations. Scenes between the spirited military attaché and National Socialist functionaries soon
followed, the like of which are often enacted in higher
places and by more important people. Ōshima's behavior was
exceptional. He would become Japan's Ambassador to Germany
in 1938 when the military gained greater influence in the
Japanese government. Though many Japanese army officers
admired the German military, Ōshima represented an extreme
military point of view, and he was infatuated particularly
with the armed forces of Hitler's Third Reich.

The present study is the culmination of my research in
the prewar period; it also foreshadows my work on Ōshima,
"Magic," and Hitler after Ōshima's return to Berlin in 1941.
For the special character of the earlier Ōshima-Hitler
association offers the key to their relationship in wartime
Germany. "Magic" turned the later relationship into an
Allied advantage.

NOTES

Introduction

1. Japanese proper names have been inverted for the convenience of most English readers, that is, the personal name followed by the surname. A macron is used over a long vowel in all Japanese terms appearing in Romaji except well-known place names, e.g., Tokyo. However, the practice of the publisher is followed in quoted passages and source citations.

2. Joseph Goebbels, The Goebbels Diaries, 1942-1943, ed. and trans. Louis P. Lochner (Garden City, N.Y.: Doubleday, 1948), p. 181.

3. "'Six Lectures on Cryptology' by William F. Friedman, April 1963," SRH-004, National Archives, Washington, D.C., Record Group 457, p. 179. Marshall's letter was addressed to Governor Thomas E. Dewey of New York, then the Republican candidate for President. Marshall asked Dewey not to reveal in the campaign the fact that American cryptanalysts had broken the Japanese diplomatic code before the attack on Pearl Harbor, for the Japanese were using the same code in 1944. Such a revelation would cause the Japanese to change their code, thus denying vital information to the Allies. This story is told in Friedman's Lecture VI as well as in Forrest C. Pogue, George C. Marshall, 3 vols. (New York: Viking, 1963-73), 3: 470-73.

I

PRELUDE TO MILITARY DIPLOMACY

Germany and Japan, on opposite sides in the First World War, reestablished diplomatic relations in 1920. Each government was represented by professional diplomats during the decade, career civil servants trained in the customs, habits, and formulas of conventional diplomacy. They were scrupulously faithful to the instructions of their Foreign Ministries, and their style of diplomacy was probably suitable for the times when neither government sought anything more than stable and friendly relations with the other. But in May 1934 the exploitive and inordinately ambitious Ōshima arrived in Berlin as the senior Japanese military attaché, and not long afterward the traditional diplomacy of Japanese career civil servants appeared slightly outmoded. For foreign representatives who were openly sympathetic with the ambitions of the Third Reich were most welcome and effective among National Socialist officials.

Germany's three ambassadors in Tokyo for nearly two decades were top diplomats who offered continuity in their distinguished service. In December 1920 Ambassador Wilhelm Solf, Colonial Secretary of State (1911-1918) and briefly Foreign Minister near the end of the First World War, reopened the German embassy in Tokyo. Solf was succeeded by Ambassador Ernst Arthur Voretzsch in 1928. And in 1933 Herbert von Dirksen was transferred as ambassador from Moscow to Tokyo; in 1938 he was appointed Germany's chief representative at the Court of St. James.

The several Japanese counterparts to these three German ambassadors were less experienced. Shigenori Tōgō reopened the Japanese embassy in Germany as second secretary in 1920; Ambassador Masu Hioki arrived the next year. In 1924 Kumatarō Honda became ambassador, but he was succeeded two years later by Haruichi Nagaoka. In 1931 Ambassador Nagaoka was replaced by Yukichi Obata, followed by Matsuzō Nagai in 1933, and Kintomo Mushakoji in 1934. Before appointment as head of mission in Berlin each of these six Japanese ambassadors had held lesser diplomatic positions

5

in various relatively unimportant and small European countries. Furthermore, the Japanese Foreign Ministry's practice of frequently transferring ambassadors had the effect of weakening its representation in Berlin. Certainly a chargé d'affairs could adequately represent Tokyo's interests, and the practice of frequently changing mission chiefs was of no consequence as long as both governments sought only modest goals in their otherwise stable and friendly relations. The dangers became real in National Socialist Germany, however, when frequent changes and prolonged absences of the ambassador at least increased the opportunity for lesser embassy officials to usurp authority.

* * *

The first two Japanese ambassadors to Hitler's government were uncertain about the course of future relations between the governments. Aside from the changing attitudes that the respective governments held toward each other during the formative years of Hitler's East Asian policy, the different Japanese ambassadors were individuals who had varying interpretations of their official and unofficial prerogatives. They also held different personal attitudes toward National Socialism.

Most foreign ambassadors at Berlin were cautious in their initial relations with the new German government; the new Japanese ambassador was no exception. The arrival of Ambassador Matsuzo Nagai coincided "with the beginning of a new epoch in German history," he said in an innocuous statement in September 1933.[1] And though National Socialism was quickly changing the character of the entire society, Nagai seems to have had less difficulty than many other ambassadors in getting along in the new Germany.

For example, members of the diplomatic corps received invitations to attend the annual National Socialist rally at Nürnberg in early September 1933. Representatives of several lesser powers attended the rally where the victory of the party was celebrated. But most foreign representatives of other powers emphasized that it was improper for them to attend a purely political affair; hence, at the outset of the Hitler regime the British, French, Spanish, American, Dutch, Belgian, and several other ambassadors declined to attend.[2]

Nor did the Japanese ambassador attend the rally in 1933, although he attended the rally in 1934 and his successor frequented the gaudy exhibitions. Nagai's reasons for not attending are not clear, but he did not share American Ambassador William Dodd's misgivings. Dodd believed, as his biographer has written, that attendance at the rally "would establish 'a vicious precedent,' allowing the Nazis to trumpet it around the world 'as an endorsement of [both] the present regime and . . . the theory that the Nazi Party is synonymous with the German Government and nation.'"[3] Ambassador Nagai was generally sympathetic in his attitude toward the Third Reich, and he seems not to have been discouraged by Propaganda Minister Josef Goebbels' speech at the 1933 rally on the subject of "the race question and world propaganda."[4] Two weeks later Nagai visited Hamburg as the guest of the Ostasiatische Verein, an association that represented the interests of German merchants in East Asia. At Hamburg he spoke of the parallels between the two peoples and maintained that the Japanese people regarded Germany "with best understanding and warmest sympathy."[5] At an association dinner for Ambassador Nagai, which was attended by the Japanese vice-consular at Hamburg, the Director of the Yokohama Specie Bank, other Japanese representatives, and various Verein and National Socialist officials, the group of Germans and Japanese "burst forth with a 'Siegheil' for Imperial Japan and its exalted ruling house, for the German Fatherland, the Reichs President Field Marshal von Hindenburg, and Reichs Chancellor Adolf Hitler. They then played the Japanese national anthem ["Kimi ga yo"], 'Deutschland über Alles,' and the 'Horst Wessel Lied.'"[6] Thus, Nagai had little difficulty adjusting to the boisterous ritual of National Socialism. He was tactful when choosing to slight its racial theories and to rationalize that they did not apply to the Japanese. For the Japanese "virtues, aims and doctrines," he said in April 1933 to Bella Fromm, a diplomatic columnist for the Vossische Zeitung, were similar to those of the Germans.[7]

Nagai's personal attitude toward National Socialism did not, however, prevent him from clearly stating his views on a troublesome issue in German-Japanese relations. He remarked to a German journalist during his visit to Hamburg that if one were to look at the figures of German-Japanese foreign trade, he would see that "Japan imports much more from Germany than Germany imports from Japan. A healthy development and the expansion of foreign trade will take place only when a mutually favorable balance is established."[8]

Prelude to Military Diplomacy

Though balanced foreign trade was not predicated on close foreign relations, nevertheless, Nagai's remark reflected in good measure the basic concern of the Japanese government with Germany in 1933. It came only eight months after Hitler became chancellor and when neither government had a considered policy to establish exceptionally close relations with the other. The imbalance of trade was common knowledge, and it was the sort of objection, particularly during the depression, that any Japanese ambassador to Germany was expected to raise. But the new German government was in no position to correct the imbalance. For a major concern of Hitler's government was to consolidate its victory and to unite the country under National Socialism. Hitler could not for domestic political reasons press German merchants to increase their trade with Japan at the expense of more established and lucrative trade with China.

The themes of the 1933 and 1934 rallies at Nürnberg represented the National Socialist government's primary concern with domestic policy, and Nagai's attendance at the second rally suggested the growing friendly attitude of the Japanese government. "Sieg des Glaubens," the 1933 theme, was a celebration of the victory of National Socialism eight months earlier. In October Germany announced her withdrawal from the League of Nations. A year later, by which time President Paul von Hindenburg was dead and Hitler was chancellor and president, the rally of the "Triumph des Willens" was a celebration of the rejuvenation and unification of the German people under National Socialism. Nagai represented the strongest foreign nation that accepted the German government's invitation to the rally in 1934. Japan was beginning to feel diplomatic isolation resulting from the 1931 Manchurian incident, independent action by the Japanese army that reduced the Chinese Manchurian province to a Japanese military colony. Condemned as an aggressor by the League of Nations, Japan announced in March 1933 her intention to withdraw from the League. Withdrawal was to take effect in two years; meanwhile, there was nothing to be lost by sending her ambassador to a political rally in a nation that was also dissatisfied with the international status quo.

Nagai appeared contented on the speaker's platform in Luitpold Hall when Hitler's deputy, Rudolf Hess, opened the rally on September 5th. "You are Germany," he declared to Hitler. "When you act, the nation acts; when you judge, the people judge."[9] Ambassador Nagai, who was seated with Julius Streicher, Hermann Göring, Martin Bormann,

and other key National Socialists, seemed not to be dis-
quieted by the political regalia and gaudy exhibitions of
the rally as Hitler clasped Hess's hand and Streicher read
Hitler's proclamation.

Nagai's behavior at the rally was hailed a few days
later when foreign ambassadors at Berlin attended a special
ceremony at Hindenburg's former palace in honor of the
Führer. Nagai, who was standing next to American Ambassador Dodd in the reception line, was warmly thanked by Hitler
for his attendance at the rally and for a speech that the
Japanese ambassador had made in Nürnberg. Dodd recorded in
his diary that nobody misunderstood Hitler's warmness to
Nagai, "it was intended as a rebuke to the French, Italian,
English and Spanish representatives and myself who had declined to attend the show both this year and last."[10] And
shortly before the Japanese ambassador left Berlin on
leave in November 1934, Nagai spoke publicly and again
sympathetically of German problems. He maintained that
the Germans and Japanese had common grievances: "the two
lands were united . . . by their common isolation, in the
demands that each made for equality of rights, and through
an affinity of unfavourable circumstances."[11]

But Nagai seems to have had no special instructions
from his government for the promotion of German-Japanese
relations, and an appraisal of his behavior as a diplomat
is only an imperfect indication of a possible direction
for future relations. His tenure in the Third Reich was
colorful but uneventful in terms of specific political
accomplishments. He became openly friendly to the Hitler
regime during his brief assignment in Berlin, and his
initial attitude probably helped to create favorable conditions for his successor. There seemed to be a desire in
the German government to foster more cordial relations with
Japan. The new Japanese ambassador could play an important
role.

The appointment of Viscount Kintomo Mushakōji as the
new ambassador to Germany was announced in December 1934.
The Japanese Foreign Ministry had recently been carefully
assessing the international situation and Japan's future
role among the powers. Mushakōji's mission to Germany was
complex and difficult.[12] He was to gather information and
to assist the Foreign Ministry in answering three major
questions: 1) Should Japan strive for special relations
with Germany? 2) Should Japan remain cordial but not
closely attached to Germany? 3) Should Japan strive to

strengthen relations with Great Britain and the United States because the Hitler regime was considered dangerous? Those were the weighty questions that guided Mushakōji's mission to Berlin, but for diplomatic and public purposes his rhetoric and attitude were much like his predecessor's.

Mushakōji presented his credentials to Hitler in early February 1935. In the customary exchange of brief speeches, Mushakōji, who spoke German fluently, said that his father was one of the first Japanese students sent in 1870 to Berlin where he studied law for four years. Mushakōji said of himself that he was first at Berlin in 1909 as embassy attaché until 1913. During that time he received an indelible impression of German culture. Near the end of his speech, however, his remarks became a little more pointed. In spite of the political nature of his special instructions from the Foreign Ministry, on the surface Mushakōji's concerns about the future of German-Japanese relations appeared to focus on economic considerations. It was his "most distinguished mission . . . to cooperate actively in the further development of mutual connections, especially of business dealings between Japan and Germany," and he sought Hitler's "good will and support in influential German circles."[13] The general tenor characteristic of his first speech in the Third Reich was not unlike that expressed by Nagai, and later Mushakōji would also elaborate upon the subject of the imbalance of trade between the two countries.

Like Nagai earlier, Mushakōji visited Hamburg as the guest of the Ostasiatische Verein. Again the group of Germans and Japanese "burst forth with a 'Siegheil'" for Hirohito and for Hitler, and the national anthems and the "Horst Wessel Lied" were played.[14] A spokesman for the association welcomed the Japanese ambassador to Hamburg, and emphasized factors that he claimed were common to both nations--they arrived late as major powers in the world, and the military spirit of a samurai was "the spirit of a Prussian officer."[15] He quoted from Rudyard Kipling's Ballad of East and West--"East is East, and West is West, and never the twain shall meet"--and concluded that the essence of German and Japanese contact made it possible "to build a great bridge between East and West. This bridge of understanding," he said, "had to be built for the peaceable and humane solutions of political and economic problems."

The rhetoric of that speech probably did not have any special significance for Mushakōji until the Verein spokesman defined what he meant by Kipling's poetic East. The bridge was to be built "between Germany on the one side and China and Japan on the other side . . . , not only between Germany and Japan, but between the eastern and western worlds." China was the obstacle from Mushakōji's point of view, for it was the East Asian country with which German merchants continued to trade the most, and China was still a principal political and economy enemy of Japan. Moreover, the German military advisory group to the Kuomintang government was of no small concern to the Japanese. The Japanese were not interested in a rapprochement with China as a means of drawing closer to Germany. But it would not have been prudent of Mushakōji to raise these issues as a gambit in his Ostasiatische Verein address.[16]

Rather he seemed concerned about the imbalance of trade. After introductory comments on common points that were becoming by 1935 the standard rhetoric in speeches before German-Japanese audiences (all of which suggested that closer German-Japanese relations ought to follow almost automatically), he spoke candidly and in some detail concerning the topic of foreign trade. "The opposite direction is seen in the trade between Japan and Germany. As the export of Japanese goods to Germany decreased from 30 million Reichsmarks in 1931 to 16 million Reichsmarks in 1933, the imports of German goods to Japan decreased from 144 million Reichsmarks in 1931 to 76 million Reichsmarks. Thus you see," Mushakōji warned, "how imports and exports work hand in hand." He then switched to a note of optimism on how the two peoples could fight the world depression by working together. The Japanese ambassador declared that he had "no doubt that Japan and Germany can be good comrades through this hard but advantageous work since there is no vital point of rivalry between both our countries."[17]

The remarks exchanged between Mushakōji and the Germans at the East Asian association's banquet in June 1935 were in the same cooperative tone of the discussions at the banquet for Nagai in September 1933. Mushakōji's exceptions concerning the imbalance of trade were compelling, but they were not central to his mission in spite of what the ambassador told Hitler and the press. Mushakōji's real mission to Germany in 1935 was to collect information and to assist in answering his government's three major questions on Japan's future foreign policy.

Prelude to Military Diplomacy

Mushakōji reached some tentative conclusions just before he left Germany in July on a ten-month leave to
Japan.[18] He feared further diplomatic isolation for Japan.
The United States and Great Britain had been cool toward
Japan since the Manchurian Incident. Mushakōji was in the
Third Reich only five months, but he felt that Hitler's
government was trying to move toward Great Britain as the
recent Anglo-German Naval Agreement seemed to indicate to
him.[19] Although he thought that Japan needed Germany to
prevent isolation, he was reluctant to recommend an un-
qualified affirmative answer to the first question: Should
Japan strive for special relations with Germany? Extensive
German military assistance to the Chinese was a factor of
some concern to Mushakōji. And though recent British
diplomacy with Germany mollified the reservations of some
Japanese statesmen about the dangerous upstart nature of
the Hitler government, Mushakōji believed that Japan ought
not to rush into a courtship with Germany. The ambassador
was prepared to return to Tokyo with the recommendation that
Japan should strive for special relations with Germany only
to the extent that her efforts were not harmful to relations
with the United States and Great Britain. Mushakōji discussed his careful position with the embassy staff--
Counselor Kōjiro Inoue, Dr. Hiroo Furuuchi, Major General
Hiroshi Ōshima, and Commander Tadao Yokoi.[20] Although most
embassy staff members had some qualms about the cautious-
ness of the ambassador's views, only Ōshima demurred strongly.

It was not a matter of one side being necessarily correct and the other side wrong; rather, it was an understand-
able divergence of points of view. The ambassador's responsibility, breadth, and experience in international relations
were greater than those of the embassy staff members. And
for Ōshima, in particular, there was little to ponder--
Japan ought to strive for especially close relations with
National Socialist Germany irrespective of any negative
repercussions from other countries. Moreover, Ōshima's
advice was not merely an opinion expressed in response to
the ambassador's query; it was for the ambitious military
attaché a statement of conviction. In other times when
militaristic values were perhaps less highly regarded and
less persuasive in Germany and Japan (and when junior
officials could not play a role disproportionate in importance with their rank), traditional protocol would call
for the ambassador to consider different views from his
staff. He would then make a decision in consultation with
other civil authorities in the Foreign Ministry. That

decision would be referred to the cabinet for final approval. But the times, values, and Ōshima were not ordinary. The stage was set for Ōshima's military diplomacy in which his goals were absolute while his means were flexible. One Japanese scholar has observed that

> A 'military diplomat' is like a military leader who must often make arbitrary decisions on the battlefield and carry them out resolutely in order to win. If victorious, his behavior is justified even though he may have ignored instructions from above. Even subversive actions in another country pursued without the knowledge of central authorities could be allowed in some cases.[21]

Although Germany and Japan had several experiences in common during the last half century, their diplomatic relations were very ordinary and at times hostile.[22] Both nations seemed to have a high regard for military force and considerable willingness to use it during their rapid rise to the status of world powers. In the First World War Germany was deprived of her Pacific holdings where her imperialistic ambitions frequently conflicted with Japanese aspirations. In the turbulent years after the war both societies experimented with forms of democracy under the adverse conditions of social, political, and economic unrest. There were calls from German and Japanese activists who rebuked the principles of collective security and advocated the use of military force to satisfy national goals on the international scene. Their arguments had greater appeal among the nationalistic masses as the effects of depression became widespread and the   political systems appeared inadequate to meet the challenge of the times. Militarism, that uncritical call for military power, was a force deeply embedded in the tradition of these two new powers. Moreover, they were dissastisfied with the status quo in the 1930s. Their common alienation and their traditional martial spirit tended to enhance relations. But the military attaché at Berlin, a product of the Japanese martial spirit, was pivotal to the future course. Ōshima was the exceptional figure who would cultivate and attempt to perfect German-Japanese diplomatic relations in the military mold.

Figure 1. Military Attaché Ōshima (right), then major
general, is seen in the first balcony at a performance of
the Berlin Philharmonic Orchestra on the anniversary of
the Reich Chamber of Culture, an organization set up in
1933 to act as censor over cultural life in the Third
Reich.   November 1935.   (National Archives)

NOTES

I: Prelude to Military Diplomacy

1. "Interview mit dem japanischen Botschafter Dr. M. Nagai," Ostasiatische Rundschau 14, no. 18 (1933): 387. Nagai was also minister to Latvia.

2. William E. Dodd, Jr., and Martha Dodd, eds., Ambassador Dodd's Diary, 1933-1938 (New York: Harcourt, Brace, 1941), pp. 24-26, 48, 349; André François-Poncet, The Fateful Years: Memoirs of a French Ambassador in Berlin, 1931-1938, trans. Jacques LeClercq (New York: Harcourt, Brace, 1949), pp. 209-12.

3. Robert Dallek, Democrat and Diplomat: The Life of William E. Dodd (New York: Oxford University Press, 1968), p. 202.

4. Fritz Maier-Hartmann, Dokumente des Dritten Reiches, vol. 2, Die Sammlung Rehse, ed. Adolf Dresler (Munich: Zentralverlag der NSDAP, Franz Eher Nachfolger, 1940), p. 80.

5. "Interview mit Nagai," p. 387.

6. "Der Besuch des japanischen Botschafters Dr. M. Nagai in Hamburg," Ostasiatische Rundschau 14, no. 18 (1933): 405.

7. Blood and Banquets: A Berlin Social Diary (New York: Harper, 1942), p. 105. Bella Fromm was convinced that "Nagai knows very well that this Germany, which he calls 'so congenial to the land of the Rising Sun,' considers the Japanese inferior to the German master-race" (ibid.).

8. "Interview mit Nagai," p. 387.

9. "'The Nazi Plan,' A Documentary Motion Picture Composed of German Film," Prosecution Exhibits Submitted to the International Military Tribunal, National Archives Microfilm Publication T-988, roll 12, frame A/088230.

10. Ambassador Dodd's Diary, p. 164.

11. Cited in Ernst L. Presseisen, Germany and Japan: A Study in Totalitarian Diplomacy, 1933-1941 (The Hague: Martinus Nijhoff, 1958), p. 70, and Arnold Toynbee, ed., Survey of International Affairs, 1934 (London: Oxford University Press, 1935), p. 667.

NOTES

I: Prelude to Military Diplomacy

12. Ōhata Tokushirō, "The Anti-Comintern Pact, 1935-1939,"
trans. Hans H. Baerwald, in Deterrent Diplomacy: Japan,
Germany, and the USSR, 1935-1940, ed. James William Morley
(New York: Columbia University Press, 1976), p. 26.

13. "Überreichung des Beglaubigungsschreibens des neuen
japanischen Botschafters in Berlin," Ostasiatische
Rundschau 16, no. 4 (1935): 88.

14. "Besuch des japanischen Botschafters Graf Mushakoji in
Hamburg, 12. - 14. Juni 1935," ibid., no. 12 (1935): 328.

15. Ibid., p. 329.

16. Ibid., pp. 329-31.

17. Mushakōki's visit in Hamburg did not go unnoticed by
some members of the diplomatic corps. The American consul
general in Hamburg, John G. Erhardt, sent a paraphrased
translation of Mushakōji's address to Ambassador Dodd in
Berlin. Dodd's report to Cordell Hull contained the
following notation: "relative to trade between Germany and
Japan in 1932 (when Germany's favorable balance was RM 62
millions) and the critical comment that he [Mushakōji] had
used foresight in taking the figures for that year, it may
be mentioned in passing that the figures for the year 1934
might have illustrated his point just as well; for during
the latter year German exports to Japan amounted to RM
79.6 millions whereas her imports from Japan were only
valued at RM 21.7 millions" (William E. Dodd to Secretary
of State, 26 June 1935, Office of Naval Intelligence File,
Naval Attaché Reports, 1886-1939, No. 7510-C, U-1-i,
National Archives, Washington, D.C., Record Group 38.

18. Ōhata, "The Anti-Comintern Pact," p. 26.

19. Mushakōji interpreted Anglo-German relations to mean
isolation for Japan, but the American ambassador at the
same time saw the situation differently. More recently a
historian examined Ambassador Dodd's analysis in which the
ambassador exaggerated the identity of interests between
Germany and Japan. "As Dodd analyzed it, the British were
giving Hitler a free hand in the Baltic where he might
provoke a fight with Russia. And this, Dodd began warning
repeatedly at the end of June [1935], was producing a

I: Prelude to Military Diplomacy

German-Japanese entente whereby the two powers would en-
circle the U.S.S.R." (Dallek, Democrat and Diplomat, p.
263).

20. Ōshima was promoted from colonel to major general on
15 March 1935. There was no Japanese rank strictly
comparable to that of brigadier general. See Appendix C.

21. Hosoya Chihiro, "The Role of Japan's Foreign Ministry
and Its Embassy in Washington, 1940-1941," in Pearl Harbor
as History: Japanese-American Relations, 1931-1941, ed.
Dorothy Borg and Shumpei Okamoto with the assistance of
Dale K. A. Finlayson (New York: Columbia University Press,
1973), p. 157.

22. Cf. Bernd Martin, "Zur Vorgeschichte des deutsch-
japanischen Kriegsbündnisses," Geschichte in Wissenschaft
und Unterricht 21, no. 10 (October 1970): 606-15.

II

INTRIGUE AND INFLUENCE

Ōshima's behavior and accomplishments as the Japanese military attaché in Berlin were in sharp contrast to American Ambassador Dodd's opinions about the abilities of service attachés:

> Army and Navy Attachés here, and I think all
> over Europe, are utterly unequal to their supposed
> functions. They simply have never received
> good training, except in drill and tactics.
> They may know a little formal history, but they
> really do not grasp the social and economic
> problems in countries to which they are
> accredited. Nor are they clever enough to
> spy on German military performances. Spying
> is really what governments expect in such fields.[1]

Dodd's disparaging remarks were recorded in August 1934, a few months after Ōshima arrived in Berlin. At no point, however, is Ōshima specifically mentioned in the ambassador's 1933-1938 diary. But another diarist in Berlin viewed Ōshima differently. Bella Fromm noted in June 1934 that

> Colonel Hiroshi Oshima is as slick and smooth
> as an eel . . . , extremely shrewd, intelligent,
> and versatile. . . . He repeatedly emphasizes
> the similarity of National Japan's ideology
> with that of Nazi Germany.[2]

Bias and suspicion affected the assessment of each Berlin diarist during the rapidly changing political conditions of the mid-1930s. But Fromm's very early observation about Ōshima would prove to be not wide off the mark. For it was a strange combination of circumstances that facilitated close official relations between Germany and Japan, and it was Ōshima, more than any other Japanese figure in Germany, who shaped the relationship.

* * *

Japanese military attachés were appointed and controlled by the Army General Staff. Shortly before Ōshima left Japan in the spring of 1934 to assume the duties of his new office in Berlin, General Kenkichi Ueda, Deputy Chief of the General Staff, gave him oral instructions "to watch and [to] investigate . . . the stability of the Nazi regime, the future of the German army, relations between Germany and Russia, and particularly between the armies of the two countries."[3] Though Ueda also instructed Ōshima to collect information and report on Soviet intelligence matters, a section head specifically suggested a way this could most effectively be done. Colonel Minoru Iinuma, Chief of the European-American Section, Department of Intelligence of the General Staff, privately requested Ōshima to sound out German authorities on possible cooperation in obtaining intelligence information on the Soviet Union.[4] His comrade'a personal suggestion probably encouraged Ōshima to seize the initiative and to respond quickly to his sensitive military charge.

Before leaving Japan Ōshima met with the newly appointed German military attaché in Tokyo, then-Colonel Eugen Ott. Both officers were appointed military representatives in the spring of 1934 and both in 1938 were promoted to ambassador within their respective embassies. Ōshima tended for his own reasons in a postwar military tribunal to relegate his initial meeting with Ott to the mere status of a "courtesy visit," but there is evidence suggesting that Ōshima had far-reaching discussions with his opposite number at the German embassy in Tokyo. One historian has written that "Ott found himself promptly on intimate terms with his Japanese counterpart, Colonel Oshima. . . . Both men were intriguing their way up to the top of their respective embassies--spies as ambassadors."[5] And an author who was a member of the German Foreign Ministry also suggested that their meeting had significance, for Ott himself seems to have forewarned his superiors in Berlin about the type of Japanese officer they could expect. Ōshima was described in Ott's reports as "a man who belongs to the inner circle of Japan's military camarilla and therefore is very well informed about everything connected with the militarists and their plans for the future."[6] It is not clear what effect Ott's reports had in Berlin, but it is clear that Hitler's government would have an able and energetic Japanese military attaché.

Ōshima's instructions were on the surface fairly commonplace of any service attaché system in the 1930s, but

the institutional framework and special circumstances in
which they were issued tended to enhance the gravity of
Ōshima's undertaking. In the Japanese service attaché system the military attaché was directly responsible to military authority, that is, to the Chief of the Army General
Staff, and not to immediate civil authority, that is, not
to the ambassador of the embassy to which the military
attaché was assigned. Any competent appointee would carry
out the standard instructions, but the Chief of the Army
General Staff throughout the 1930s, Field Marshal Prince
Kotohito Kan'in, had good reason to expect superior service
from Ōshima. For Kan'in knew that Ōshima came from a prom-
inent military family which had helped to build the new
Japan.[7]

Throughout Japan's struggle for ascendancy, Prince
Kan'in and Ōshima's father, former Minister of War, Lieutenant General Ken-ichi Ōshima, were close associates whose
careers dated from the late 19th century through the Second
World War. Each had served, together on at least one occasion, on important missions abroad when Meiji Japan was
rapidly becoming a world power. A major of artillery in
1896, Ken-ichi Ōshima attended the coronation of Czar
Nicholas II as an aide to the Japanese ambassador, then
Count Aritomo Yamagata, who is often regarded as the father of the modern Japanese army. And during the Boer War
the elder Ōshima accompanied Prince Kan'in on a tour of
Europe. When they dined with Queen Victoria at Windsor
Castle, the venerable old queen was pleasantly impressed
by the Japanese gentlemen, Ōshima with whom she conversed
in German and Prince Kan'in whose foreign language was
"quite good French."[8] Prince Kan'in was again in Great
Britain when he accompanied Crown Prince Hirohito on a tour
of Europe in 1921. The tour was symbolic of the new Japan,
for it was the first time in Japanese history that the heir
apparent to the throne traveled extensively outside of
Japan.[9] Ōshima also visited Great Britain again. In 1929
he was the guest of Field Marshal Sir George Milne, Chief
of the Imperial General Staff. Throughout the following
critical years in Japanese history Prince Kan'in held high
office, and the elder Ōshima, who as an Imperial nominee,
was a member of the Imperial Diet in the 1930s and of the
Privy Council throughout most of the Second World War.
Thus, these two notable figures served in the highest
military, civil, and Imperial circles in modern Japanese
history. In March 1934 Prince Kan'in was confident that
in the appointment of then Colonel Hiroshi Ōshima he would
have in Berlin a promising career officer following a

family tradition of loyal and distinguished service to the Emperor and his army.

Ōshima's educational background helped to prepare him for the appointment in Germany. "He was the scion of a military family which had developed sympathies for Germany in Meiji days," one historian has summarized.[10] But those sympathies were not uncommon in the Japanese army where German influence had been pronounced since the late 1880s.[11] German was an important foreign language in the curricula of the military preparatory schools, the military academy, and the army staff college from which the younger Ōshima had graduated in 1902, 1905, and 1915, respectively.[12] Ōshima studied German for nine years in those military institutions, and, as he stated later, it was the foreign language "most commonly studied in those days by those who wanted to enter the military." He "intently read and studied" Clausewitz's Vom Kreige.[13] But Ōshima's military education was not unlike that of other cadets or officers with similar rank, and his professional credentials did not make him singularly qualified for assignment to the Third Reich.

Neither was Ōshima's military experience abroad after his promotion to major dissimilar to that of other field grade officers.[14] Ōshima initially went to Germany as assistant military attaché in 1921. His tour of duty was uneventful, and he recalled later that he received "an unfavourable impression politically, economically, and militarily."[15] From Germany he went to Vienna in February 1923 as military attaché in the Japanese legations in Austria as well as in Hungary. He seemed as unimpressed with the remnants of Austro-Hungarian society as he was with the Weimar Republic. Two of Ōshima's fellow officers, Captains Hideki Tōjō and Tomoyuki (Hōbun) Yamashita (key leaders in the Second World War), were also in Germany in 1921, and they shared Ōshima's disparagement of the Weimar Republic. But apparently Ōshima's opinions were more deep-seated, for judging from his later behavior and attitudes he actually disapproved of the fundamental nature of republicanism and the Versailles peace treaty restrictions placed on Germany's armed forces.

On the surface, then, it would appear that Colonel Ōshima was well qualified for his appointment to Germany, but not necessarily better qualified than many other Japanese army officers. Knowledge of the language of the country in which the military attaché would serve was an

important qualification for appointment; in this respect only
Oshima was probably better qualified than any other Japanese
living in Germany in 1934.[16] Previous experience in the
country was also desirable, but Oshima's experience was no
more extensive than that of several other army officers.
Thus, the Chief of the Army General Staff was certain   that
Oshima was well qualified and suited for the appointment because of his education, experience, and family background.
Kan'in knew Oshima's father as a distinguished general and
patriot, and he expected the younger Oshima to follow his
family's tradition through superior service in the Berlin
assignment. The extent to which Oshima would seize the
initiative in becoming an able and energetic army representative, however, would not become apparent until he arrived
in Berlin and became acquainted with National Socialist
officialdom.

* * *

Oshima's original instructions, again, were standard:
to collect information concerning the stability of Hitler's
government and on the future of the German army and its relationship with the Soviet army. Such instructions traditionally were carried out by the military attaché who
attempted to establish a strong rapport with various
generals in the host country, or foster close relationships
with their subordinates. The attaché would also observe
military maneuvers and, most importantly, would carefully
read military journals and newspapers, searching out data
concerning economic, scientific, political, and social factors which reflected the host country's potential for waging
war.

From the beginning it was clear that Oshima would excel
in his Berlin assignment; he was extremely eager to pursue
General Ueda's instructions. Shortly after Oshima's arrival
in 1934, an American military attaché in Berlin estimated
that there were as many as 150 Japanese agents in Germany.
They worked under the immediate supervision of the Japanese
military attaché. Though many of these alleged agents were
probably Japanese students in German universities, U.S. Army
Captain Rowan reported to his superiors in Washington, D.C.
that some of the students were of unusually high caliber:
one student at the University of Berlin, for example, was
actually a professor of chemistry at Tokyo University.[17]
It is probable that some of the "special students" mentioned

23

were indeed agents and that they reported directly to Ōshima.
Moreover, the American military attaché learned from the
chief of the German army armaments office that "the Japanese
military attaché visits the Waffenamt three or four times
more than any other military attaché."[18] Ōshima's ready
access to the Waffenamt, a secret National Socialist war
office normally off limits to foreigners, would further
suggest that within a few months after arriving in Berlin
the new Japanese military attaché was able to demonstrate
his promise by keeping his Tokyo superiors informed of
significant developments in the economic base of German
rearmament. By September 1934, when Ōshima attended the
Nürnberg rally, he was convinced that the will of National
Socialism had triumphed and that German military strength
was being rejuvenated. The observation and collection of
intelligence data concerning the Soviet Union, another part
of Ōshima's assignment, provied to be a more difficult task.

The Japanese army had long watched the rise of Soviet
military strength with keen interest. In 1929 Ōshima's
predecessor in Berlin, then-Colonel Yurin Ōmura, hosted a
conference of Japanese military attachés in Europe. The
representative from Tokyo was Lieutenant General Iwane
Matsui, a recent director of military intelligence at Army
General Staff Headquarters. The Berlin conference focused
on the Soviet Union, and topics discussed included sabotage,
espionage, and the employment of White Russians for intelligence purposes.[19] There seems to be little evidence, however, that the Japanese actually collaborated with Germany
on such matters at that time, for the Weimar government's
attitude toward the Soviet Union was considerably different
from Hitler's attitude.

Ōshima vigorously sought access to German information
concerning the Soviet Union in 1934. He was also an
intriguer who tried to enhance his own image in the minds
of his Tokyo military superiors by exploring new possibilities beyond the scope of his original instructions.
Daringly Ōshima became engaged in discussions leading to
the highest level in the German government. Ōshima initiated these discussions through a former business associate,
Dr. Friedrich Wilhelm Hack. Hack, an export-broker of
German arms, had close connections in Japanese military and
business circles.[20] Indeed, in 1922 Ōshima, then assistant
military attaché to the Weimar Republic, first met Hack
during secret negotiations for the purchase of German
weapons.[21] They saw much of each other during Ōshima's
first tour of duty in Europe, in Germany (May 1921--

February 1923) and then, until November 1924, in Vienna, where Ōshima "worked primarily on Russian espionage activities," a Japanese scholar has recently written.[22]

In the early 1920s Ōshima and Hack discussed the shackling of military systems during those eras of party government in Japan and democracy in Germany. In both instances the national military forces were restricted and unable to enjoy their former positions of influence. Ōshima deplored the weakness of the Reichswehr and the failure of the Weimar Republic to deal effectively with such problems as inflation and leftist agitation. He was vehemently anti-democratic and anti-Communist, having personally fought in Siberia against the Soviet Russians a few years earlier when his father was Minister of War.[23] It was these strong political views that blossomed in the Third Reich and helped to make Ōshima, from among many very able Japanese army officers, uniquely suitable for acceptance by Hitler's regime and its officialdom. Hack most likely agreed fully with Ōshima's political views, for they collaborated in schemes violating the spirit of the Versailles peace treaty.

Some ten years later Ōshima had entirely different views about Germany. He observed that in "just one and a half years after Hitler had come to power, I found that everything in Germany had changed and had considerably improved, compared to the time of my last sojourn. I felt that there were things in the new Germany which were worthy of serious consideration."[24] By that time Ōshima's old associate from Weimar days was a confidant in Joachim von Ribbentrop's entourage and a member of his Dienststelle—a separate agency suitable for Hitler's arbitrary conduct of diplomatic negotiations, bypassing the German Foreign Ministry. Gradually, in several clandestine and informal meetings in 1934, Ōshima learned much from Hack concerning specific people and their influence in the growing bureaucracy of National Socialist Germany. The emphasis which Hack placed on the strength of Ribbentrop's anti-Russian and anti-Communist views made him realize that these sentiments could possibly serve as a basis for negotiating some sort of Japanese-German alliance aimed at the Communist International and the Soviet Union.[25]

Hack willingly played the role of intermediary between his long-time Japanese associate, Ōshima, and his new Dienststelle chief. In the spring of 1935, as early as March, Ōshima and Ribbentrop met for the first time.[26] It was immediately obvious, as Ribbentrop testified after the

25

Second World War, "that Japan had the same anti-Comintern attitude as Germany," and the two men, using intrigue to reach higher levels of influence, met secretly, often at Hack's house, during the summer. They discussed Ōshima's proposal for some sort of Japanese-German alliance.[27]

Ōshima's idea of making their common anti-Communist attitudes the subject of a German-Japanese pact became especially important from Ribbentrop's point of view when Hitler asked Ribbentrop if "a closer contact with Japan could be established in some form or other."[28] Hitler's personal ambassador-at-large replied that he had certain personal contacts among the Japanese with whom he would explore the idea. Ribbentrop and his Dienststelle were vying with Foreign Minister Constantin von Neurath and the Foreign Ministry for control of German foreign policy. In ensuing conversations with Hitler on East Asian affairs the immodest Ribbentrop very likely sought to describe his association with Ōshima in a way that would promote his own image as an astute diplomat whose skills were indispensable. Hitler wanted to meet the enthusiastic Japanese military attaché, and in the autumn the Führer, Ōshima, and Ribbentrop met to discuss further Ōshima's original "no-aid" proposal: to conclude "a treaty between Japan and Germany to the effect that if Japan or Germany went to war against Soviet Russia, the other one should not take actions beneficial to Soviet Russia."[29]

Hitler showed interest in promoting German-Japanese relations, and he told Ōshima that it was "Germany's intention to split up the Soviet Union into several small states."[30] Furthermore, there seemed to be a new sense of importance to their mutual interests. For at the recent Seventh Congress of the Communist International, Germany and Japan were strongly denounced as archetypes of the towering menace of fascism.[31] Nevertheless, Hitler wanted to know what Ōshima's superiors in the Army General Staff thought of the proposal for a German-Japanese "no-aid" treaty aimed at the Soviet Union.

Earlier in the summer Ōshima had informed the Chief of the Army General Staff of his informal discussions with Ribbentrop, although he apparently omitted specific details. Ribbentrop was little known in Tokyo, but the Japanese General Staff speculated that he was a very important German official. At any rate, there appeared to be no urgency in the matter because a representative of the General Staff would be in Berlin in December for a previously scheduled meeting with Japanese military attachés

stationed in Europe. General Staff officers reasoned that
their representative could then discuss the matter with
Ōshima and assess the attitude of the Germans. At some
point later, however, additional telegrams arrived from
Ōshima informing his army superiors of his "no-aid" proposal for a German-Japanese treaty made to Hitler himself!
An astonishing picture was revealed. Lieutenant Colonel
Tadaichi Wakamatsu, the General Staff's intelligence officer who was selected to attend the December meeting of
Japanese military attachés, recalled the outline of
Ōshima's messages: "Each country would gather and exchange
information against Russia and if hostilities should occur,
the German and Japanese armies would cooperate." The telegrams gave only the general picture, but one "received the
impression that if Japan desired a military alliance of
some sort, it could be concluded."[32]

News of such secret discussions between Ōshima and the
Führer startled General Staff officers. A proposal for
some sort of anti-Comintern agreement was already being
studied by General Staff officers, and although they were
in favor of the idea of a German-Japanese entente, particularly if it were aimed at a traditional adversary to
Japanese expansion in Asia, they were caught unprepared to
work on a contingency plan of the magnitude envisaged in
Ōshima's scheme. For example, some of the General Staff
and War Ministry section and bureau heads with whom
Wakamatsu conferred before leaving Tokyo in November
observed that Polish-Japanese relations were cordial and
that Polish-German relations were cool. They cautioned,
therefore, against a Japanese military agreement with
Germany, even a "no-aid" agreement, for "it was considered
then that Poland was a pretty fair match for Germany."[33]
But the vast majority General Staff and War Ministry officers sided with the Chief of the Army General Staff.
Wakamatsu conferred with him and later called to mind the
field marshal's opinion: since much of "the world did not
hold a good opinion of Japan as a result of the [1931]
Manchurian Incident, [Japan,] fearing the rise of Communism,
was willing to sign an anti-Comintern pact with anyone."[34]
Thus, Kan'in emphasized the advantages for Japan of a
political agreement with Germany, whereas during the preceding several months Ōshima's discussions, first with Hack,
then with Ribbentrop, and finally with Hitler, played down
political considerations and gradually focused on the military aspects.

The unprecedented activities of the Japanese military

27

attaché in the Third Reich presented the Army General Staff with a dilemma. The Japanese military had long been accustomed to influencing government foreign policy in East Asia. The Manchurian Incident, where independent local action afforded the army headquarters in Tokyo an opportunity to exploit it, was perhaps the most striking example of such influence. But Ōshima's exploits in distant Berlin provided the Japanese military with new opportunities for promoting its self-interest and influence. The General Staff's decision would be a watershed for Japan's European policy in the 1930s, but before it was taken there were many uncertainties in the way.

Ōshima had been in the Third Reich for eighteen months, and through backstairs maneuvering he initiated discussions on a question of momentous import with the German head of government and with other important National Socialist officials. Japanese military extremists in the General Staff were impressed by Hitler's success and his bold rearmament proclamations. Hitler's announcement of the reintroduction of conscription, for example, was soon followed by Ribbentrop's conclusion of the June 1935 Anglo-German naval agreement, by which Germany was permitted to create a new navy up to 35 percent of British naval strength. Japanese militarists were also impressed by the ability of their own representative to launch discussions leading to the Führer himself. They were taken aback by the news from Berlin, but the General Staff anticipated that emissary Wakamatsu could sort things out and report back to Tokyo with information enabling Staff officers to decide upon a definite policy.

NOTES

II: Intrigue and Influence

1. Ambassador Dodd's Diary, pp. 151-52.

2. Blood and Banquets, p. 166.

3. International Military Tribunal for the Far East, Exhibit 3508. (Hereafter cited as IMTFE. See my bibliography for the title of each IMTFE exhibit cited.)

4. Ōhata Tokushirō, "Nichi-Doku bōkyō kyōtei, dō kyōka
mondai (1935-1939)" [The question of strengthening the
Japanese-German anti-Comintern pact, 1935-1939], pt. 1,
Sangoku dōmei, Nis-So chūritsu jōyaku [The triple alliance
and the Japanese-Soviet neutrality treaty], vol. 5,
Taiheiyō sensō e no michi, kaisen gaikō-shi [The road to
the Pacific war: a diplomatic history before the war], ed.
Nihon Kokusai Seiji Gakkai Taiheiyō Sensō Gen'in Kenkyubu
[The Japan Association of International Relations, Committee to Study the Origins of the Pacific War] (8 in 7 vols.;
Tokyo: Asahi Shimbun Sha, 1962-1963), p. 17. Cf. Ohata,
"The Anti-Comintern Pact," pp. 23-24, where it is suggested
that Ōshima was instructed to sound out the Germans. I
render the original Japanese (irai) to mean that Ōshima's
comrade in arms, Colonel Iinuma, made a private request or
personal suggestion, and that Ōshima was the active agent
who seized the initiative.

5. Alfred Vagts, The Military Attaché (Princeton: Prince-
ton University Press, 1957), p. 60. Ott was in Japan from
June to December 1933 as an official observer for the
German army. See IMTFE, Proceedings, p. 34,850.

6. Paul Schwarz, This Man Ribbentrop: His Life and Times
(New York: Julian Messner, 1943), p. 173.

7. Prince Kan'in was Chief of the Army General Staff,
December 1931-October 1940.

8. George Earle Buckle, ed., The Letters of Queen Victoria,
3 vols. (London: John Murray, 1930-1932), 3:547. See also
Times (London) 5 May 1900, p. 12, and the autobiography of a
former British military attaché at Tokyo, F.S.G. Piggott,
Broken Thread (Aldershot: Gale and Polden, 1950), p. 230.
Prince Kan'in had studied at the École de Guerre in the
early 1890s. See Ernest L. Presseisen, Before Aggression:

II: Intrigue and Influence

Europeans Prepare the Japanese Army (Tucson: University of
Arizona Press, 1965), p. 134.

9. For the elaborate activities of the Crown Prince and
Prince Kan'in on their state visit in Great Britain, see
the Times (London) 11 May 1921, p. 10; 12 May, p. 12; 17
May, p. 8; 19 May, p. 12; and 30 May, p. 10. For an
account of the entire voyage and tour, see Futara Yoshinori
and Sawada Setsuzo, The Crown Prince's European Tour
(Ōsaka: Ōsaka Mainichi, 1926).

10. Johanna Menzel Meskill, Hitler and Japan: The Hollow
Alliance (New York: Atherton Press, 1966), pp. 54-55.

11. See Presseisen, Before Aggression, especially pp. 92-96,
114-25, 134-35, and J.M. Grierson, The Armed Strength of
Japan (London: Her Majesty's Stationery Office, 1886),
p. 20.

12. See IMTFE, Exhibit 121. See also "Heigo" [Military
terms and the organization of the Japanese army] (n.p.,
n.d. [Washington, D.C.:   United States Army, 1942?]), pp.
186, 190; Hillis Lory, Japan's Military Masters: The
Army in Japanese Life (New York: Viking Press, 1943), pp.
98, 102-5; Saburo Hayashi and Alvin D. Coox, Kogun: The
Japanese Army in the Pacific War (Quantico, Va.:   Marine
Corps Association, 1959), pp. 23, 199.

13. Hiroshi Ōshima to author, 11 July 1969.

14. Hayashi and Coox, Kogun, pp. 220-41. Japanese army
officers who were lieutenant colonels, colonels, or junior
major generals were eligible because of seniority for atta-
chế duty in major nations in the 1930s. Professor Coox has
compiled biographical data concerning 91 officers whose
names were mentioned in Kogun, of whom 54 were approximately of Ōshima's grade in March 1934. All of the latter
number had graduated from the military academy, almost all
had graduated from the army staff college, and 41 had experience in Europe prior to 1934. At least 20 of those in
Europe in this random and incomplete sample had served
specifically in Germany.

15. IMTFE, Exhibit 3508.

II: Intrigue and Influence

16. Ōhata, "The Anti-Comintern Pact," p. 23.

17. Captain Hugh W. Rowan, assistant military attaché,
American Embassy, Berlin, to Military Intelligence Division,
Office of Chief of Staff, War Department, 17 May 1934, ONI
File, No. 13147-A, U-l-b, NA, RG 38.

18. Ibid. Rowan was convinced that "the Japanese Military
Attaché is being given access to important technical information in possession of the German army" (ibid.). The
growing technical and economic needs of Hitler's armed
forces soon rendered the small armaments office obsolete.
Not long after Rowan's report was filed, Colonel, later
General, Georg Thomas headed a new office for Wehrwirtschaft-
und Waffenwesen. Through an elaborate military economic
staff system, Thomas would become largely responsible for
organizing Germany's peacetime economy toward the requirements of war. See Georg Thomas, Geschichte der deutschen
Wehr- und Rüstungswirtschaft (1918-1943/45) (Boppard am
Rhein: Harald Boldt Verlag, 1966), particularly pp. 2-3,
51-68. Ambassador Dodd returned to Berlin from a two-
month leave in the United States on the very evening of
Captain Rowan's report to the War Department, i.e., 17 May
1934. There is no indication that the ambassador saw the
report and its evidence of a certain amount of resourcefulness on the part of one of his own assistant military
attachés. Dodd seems to have remained oblivious to Military Attaché Ōshima's role in German-Japanese relations.
Well over a year later Dodd reported rather uncertainly the
news of secret negotiations for a German-Japanese anti-
Comintern agreement, for to him it was one of "the perennial
rumors which agitate political minds in Berlin." Dodd said
that "the Embassy was recently asked by a responsible and
interested colleague as to whether it had heard that two
important Japanese were conducting secret negotiations with
v. Ribbentrop." The ambassador observed only that "the
Japanese Ambassador is at present on leave, and the Japanese Embassy is under the Chargé" (William E. Dodd to
Secretary of State, 4 December 1935, ONI File, No. 7510-C,
U-l-i, NA, RG 38). The "two important Japanese" referred
to in this report were Ōshima and Lieutenant Colonel
Tadaichi Wakamatsu--the Wakamatsu visit to Berlin will be
discussed later in this chapter and in chapter 3.

NOTES

II: Intrigue and Influence

19. IMTFE, Proceedings, pp. 28,839-40, and 33,884-94.
Japanese military attachés in the Soviet Union, Great
Britain, France, Poland, Austria, Italy, and Turkey attended
the Berlin conference.

20. Ōshima to author, 7 May 1971. Little has been published on the activities of this mysterious man, Hack, who
was formerly an adviser to the South Manchurian Railway
Company. A succinct account of Hack's efforts in Switzerland to initiate peace negotiations between Japan and the
United States in April 1945 is contained in Robert J. C.
Butow, Japan's Decision to Surrender (Stanford: Stanford
University Press, 1954), pp. 104-8. The recently discov-
ered Hack Papers have been used by Bernd Martin, "Die
deutsch-japanischen Beziehungen während des Dritten
Reiches" in Hitler, Deutschland und die Mächte: Materialien
zur Assenpolitik des Dritten Reiches, ed. Manfred Funke
(Düsseldorf: Droste, 1977), pp. 454-70.

21. John Toland's interview with Ōshima, 17 January 1967.

22. Masaki Miyake, Nichi-Doku-I sangoku dōmei no kenkyū
[A study on the tripartite alliance Berlin-Rome-Tokyo]
(Tokyo: Nansō-sha, 1975), p. 43.

23. Walter Voigt, "Begegnung mit Hauptmann Ōshima in
Sibirien 1918," Das Deutsche Rote Kreuz 7 (February 1943):
32-33. Ōshima was very explicit in publishing his anti-
democratic and anti-Communist views. See, for example, his
following articles: "Japan in der Front der Antikominternmächte," Volk and Reich 15 (1939): 310-12; "Das neue
Deutschland im Spiegel der japanischen Freundschaft / La
nuova Germania nello specchio dell'amicizia giapponese,"
Berlin--Rom--Tokio 1 (15 July 1939): 12-14; "Doitsu gaiko
no rinen" [The idea of German diplomacy], Bungei Shunjū
(January 1940) (Library of Congress, Washington, D.C., Reel
WT [War Trials] 82, Doc. No. 3268); "Katte kabuto no o wo
shimeyo" [After winning, keep the string tight on your
helmet], Bungei Shunjū (April 1940) (LC, Reel WT 21, Doc.
No. 756); "Neuordnung des Fernen Ostens, Neuordnung
Europas," Die Aktion 2 (June 1941): 341-42; and "Japan und
der Dreimächtepakt," Volk und Reich 17 (1941): 293-94.

24. IMTFE, Exhibit 3508. The distinguished American
author, William L. Shirer, wrote that "Ōshima . . . often

II: Intrigue and Influence

impressed this observer as more Nazi than the Nazis" (The
Rise and Fall of the Third Reich: A History of Nazi
Germany [New York: Simon and Schuster, 1960], p. 872).
Apparently the Japanese ambassador in Berlin, Tōgō, often
referred to Ōshima as "a Nazi" (Fromm, Blood and Banquets,
p. 268), and a slightly less political observation was
offered by a wartime senior member of the press section of
the German Foreign Ministry who wrote that Ōshima was "a
convinced Germanophile" (Hans-Georg von Studnitz, While
Berlin Burns: The Diary of Hans-Georg von Studnitz, 1943-
1945, trans. R. H. Stevens [London: Weidenfeld and
Nicolson, 1964], p. 200).

25. I have demonstrated in an article entitled "The Role of
Hiroshi Ōshima in the Preparation of the Anti-Comintern
Pact," Journal of Asian History 11, no. 1 (1977):   49-71,
that the enterprising military attaché was the prime instigator of the Pact.   Hans H. Baerwald in his introduction
to Ōhata's essay on "The Anti-Comintern Pact, 1935-1939,"
cited in full above, endorses my conclusions: "One point
emerges with crystal clarity . . . :   it was Ōshima who
was the prime instigator of the Anti-Comintern Pact.   On
this issue all previous commentaries concerning the origins
of the pact . . . have now been superseded" (p. 4).   The
valuable translation of the Ōhata essay was published on
26 December 1976, regrettably too late to be cited in my
article, though I made extensive use of the original 1963
Japanese edition.

26. Ōshima to author, 21 November 1966.   Ōshima stated that
their first meeting was "at a luncheon held in March or
April 1935."   Actually Ōshima and Ribbentrop met much
earlier in 1935 than stated in most scholarly works dealing
with the subject.   This point is confirmed in the diary of
Bella Fromm, a diplomatic columnist for the Ullstein papers,
for on 6 April 1935 she recorded that "it seems that
Rib[bentrop] and the new Japanese Military Attaché, Oshima,
are pretty thick these days.   Something's brewing . . .
some poison cup is being prepared" (Blood and Banquets,
p. 193).   See also Miyake, Nichi-Doku-I sangoku dōmei,
p. 44, and Ōhata, "The Anti-Comintern Pact," p. 24.   The
Hack Papers reveal only that Ōshima and Hack discussed
German-Japanese collaboration on 17 September 1935 and that
by October 4th Ōshima had prepared a draft treaty for
Ribbentrop.   Martin ("Die deutsch-japanischen Beziehungen,"

II: Intrigue and Influence

pp. 460-61) suggests, however, that presumably the initial
Oshima-Ribbentrop meeting was somewhat earlier.

27. International Military Tribunal, Trial of the Major
War Criminals, 42 vols. (Nuremberg: Secretariat of the
Tribunal, 1947-1949), 10: 240.

28. Ibid. It is not clear when exactly Hitler started to
take interest in Japan. During an interrogation on 29
August 1945 Ribbentrop said that "The Fuehrer once told
me--this really dates back as far as '33--that he would
like to have good relations with Japan." See "Extracts
from a Verbatim Report of an Interrogation of Joachim von
Ribbentrop," Records of the Department of State Special
Interrogation Mission to Germany, 1945-1946, National
Archives Microfilm Publication M-679, roll 3, frame 0154.

29. Ōshima to author, 7 May 1971. See also Ōhata, "The
Anti-Comintern Pact," p. 24, and IMTFE, Proceedings, pp.
34,076-77.

30. Ōshima reminded Hitler of his "fall of 1935" private
statement during their September 1944 conversation about
Japan's proposal for a German-Russian peace. See "Magic"
Diplomatic Summary, SRS 1420, 9 September 1944, National
Archives, Washington, D.C., Record Group 457. (Hereafter
cited as "Magic," RG 457.)

31. For the Comintern resolution of 20 August 1935 attack-
ing fascism in Germany, Japan, Italy, and Poland, see "The
Tasks of the Communist International in Connection with
the Preparations of the Imperialists for a New World War,"
Communist International 12 (20 September 1935): 1,350-56.

32. "Interrogation of Wakamatsu, Tadakazu [Tadaichi], Lt.
General," IPS 453, 9-10 May 1946, National Archives,
Washington, D.C., Record Group 331.

33. Ibid.

34. Ibid.

III

A YEAR OF STRUGGLE

By November 1935, the end of the first year and a half
of Ōshima's extraordinary activities in the Third Reich,
the enterprising military attaché was able to offer his
supporters in the Japanese army a new opportunity for major
changes in Japan's foreign policy. His backers faced a
crucial test of strength during negotiations resulting
eventually in the signing of the November 1936 Anti-Comintern Pact, the first step in the alignment of the Japanese
government with Hitler's government. Thus, Ōshima both
represented and expressed military and totalitarian tendencies in the Japanese army, government, and society, helping
those tendencies to become more influential in 1936.

* * *

Ōshima could work independently of the Japanese
ambassador and other political authorities in the embassy,
for the Japanese service attaché system authorized the
military representative to negotiate and conclude purely
military agreements with the military of the host government. In such cases, as Ōshima testified after the Second
World War, "no participation of the ambassador is toler-
ated."[1] Matters which were of a purely military nature,
however, were so determined by Ōshima himself, and by
German officials. Thus, their criteria for judgement in
totalitarian diplomacy became conveniently broad and
expedient. The General Staff was confident that Ōshima
would take full advantage of all opportunities to advance
military relations with Germany--his original orders in
1934 contained only a private suggestion that he should
sound out German authorities on possible cooperation in
obtaining intelligence information on the Soviet Union.
Yet Ōshima's "no-aid" proposal sent to the General Staff
late in 1935 was clear evidence that his endeavors far
exceeded the letter and spirit of his original instructions.
He also went beyond his special prerogatives as military
attaché, for inevitably political aspects were intertwined
with military considerations. But until early 1936 no one

35

in the Japanese embassy knew about Ōshima's discussions
with the Germans. In the ensuing months Ōshima would,
indeed, exploit every opportunity to enhance relations,
not only between the Japanese and German armies, but between the two governments as well.

The question of how the army should deal with Ōshima
was a delicate matter. It was placed in the hands of the
Chief of the Army General Staff, Field Marshal Prince
Kotohito Kan'in. He trusted Ōshima and, as mentioned
earlier, knew his family well. In November Kan'in personally instructed emissary Wakamatsu, before he left Tokyo
en route to Berlin, to assess the intentions of the German
army and government on the question of concluding an anti-
Communist pact, a political agreement. Kan'in needed more
information before making a decision on Ōshima's proposal
for a "no-aid" military agreement. A German-Japanese
political agreement could offer Japan a new opportunity
for dealing more effectively with her Communist antagonist;
moreover, Kan'in thought the agreement would enhance Japanese relations with the Western democracies. In this view
Kan'in had the support of the Deputy Chief of the Army
General Staff, Lieutenant General Gen Sugiyama, whose
assessment emphasized the disadvantages of Japan's state of
international isolation. Japan needed an ally. Sugiyama
believed that not only might an anti-Comintern agreement
with Germany be of some appeal to Western democracies where
communism was also a threat, but such an agreement could
provide Japan with some military advantages as well. He
estimated that the partial encirclement of the Soviet Union
through an agreement with Germany, coupled with Japanese
military, economic, and political strength in China and
Manchukuo, would reduce the Soviet military threat to
Japan.[2] Kan'in approved of Ōshima's efforts, and he included in Wakamatsu's instructions the specific order to
"inform Ōshima to continue his investigation;" nevertheless,
Ōshima was to seek an anti-Comintern pact with the Germans,
not a military alliance.[3] For the time being at least,
even though Ōshima would emphasize political considerations
in future talks with the Germans, the matter was to be kept
in the General Staff's hands while the military extremists
tried to learn more about the situation in distant Germany.
Thus, Wakamatsu had an additional assignment, one that
offers a clearer picture of the General Staff's lack of
preparation for dealing with the new situation produced by
Ōshima's single-handed diplomacy. After the war Wakamatsu
said that he had been ordered to "find out . . . who
Ribbentrop was, his position, and his relations with the

German Government."[4] General Staff officers were ignorant
of the _Dienststelle_ and did not understand why its chief,
Ribbentrop, was involved in the discussions with Ōshima.

Little was accomplished during the first half of
December when Wakamatsu met secretly with Ribbentrop,
Colonel General Werner von Blomberg (Minister of War), and
Ōshima. He met also with Hack; Hermann von Raumer (another
member of Ribbentrop's _Dienststelle_); Lieutenant General
Wilhelm Keitel, then Head of the Armed Forces Office
(Wehrmachtamt); and Admiral Wilhelm Canaris, head of the
central military intelligence service (_Die Abwehr Abteil-
ung_). In all of these meetings Wakamatsu said that he was
"merely a spectator," for he could only understand German
when spoken, but could not himself speak it very well.
Therefore, Ōshima did all the talking for the Japanese
side. Wakamatsu said later that he was introduced to the
Germans as the "Lieutenant Colonel who had brought the
information that the Japanese General Staff was interested
in forming an alliance with Germany." Ōshima, Wakamatsu's
personal friend, remained completely in charge; nevertheless, Wakamatsu believed "that there was no difference of
opinion between them."[5]

The discussions centered on their desire to conclude
some sort of anti-Comintern pact, and the Germans and
Japanese agreed that their countries ought to unite against
a common Communist enemy. But Wakamatsu felt that there
was no point in further discussion at that level. He had,
indeed, brought the Japanese army's proposal for a political agreement--the Germans seemed to have no major objections. But Wakamatsu was troubled by Ribbentrop's personal
attitude and was unable to understand the role of the
quasi-official _Dienststelle_ in forming German foreign
policy. Why was the German Foreign Ministry not involved
in these discussions? Ribbentrop impressed the Japanese
emissary as being simple and unrealistic: all that really
mattered was the main area of general agreement. Since the
Japanese army agreed in principle, it ought to obtain its
government's approval and authorization for a _pro forma_
agreement as, Ribbentrop could easily assert, Hitler would
do on the German side. (Presumably Ribbentrop already
received Hitler's approval.) But first the Germans wanted
positive assurance directly from the Japanese government.
Thus, Ōshima's key contact among those most closely associated with Hitler in foreign policy matters, Ribbentrop,
was a disappointment to Wakamatsu. As Gordon A. Craig has
written, Ribbentrop "had no real sympathy for genuine
negotiation . . . ; he could see nothing but his own

version of the facts; he had no patience with lengthy
deliberations, being desirous of headlong decisions. . . ."[6]
Wakamatsu was wary of Ribbentrop; he left Berlin in the
middle of December with the understanding that each party
would seek the views of its government.

The stumbling block that these secret talks reached
late in 1935 would not have surprised professional diplomats, for the conversations were initiated by individual,
increasingly influential, parvenues who had modest back-
grounds as diplomatists. Ōshima could perhaps speak with
more authority than Ribbentrop because of the nature of the
Japanese service attaché system and because Ōshima's superiors in the Army General Staff proposed the conclusion
of a political agreement against the Comintern. Ribbentrop
was in a weaker position in December 1935, for he could not
speak for the German Foreign Ministry; nor could War Minister Blomberg speak for the Wehrmacht because of Hitler's
personal influence in the armed forces and his rigorous
objection to allowing the military much voice in the formation of foreign policy. That these particular German
and Japanese parties reached nothing other than agreement
in principle was predictable; that such serious conversations on vital national matters took place at all, particularly outside the proper channels of authority and reached
the head of government on one side, was extraordinary in
1935, even by the standards of these two ambitious and
increasingly reckless nations.

On the German side Ōshima's proposal and subsequent
political discussions reached the highest government level,
circumventing professional diplomats in the German Foreign
Ministry. The German ambassador in Tokyo, Herbert von
Dirksen, claimed that in December he first "got full information from members of the Japanese General Staff, who
kept the Military Attaché of the [German] Embassy informed--
General (Eugen) Ott."[7] Also in December Hitler finally
told Foreign Minister Neurath of the matter.[8] Neurath
argued against the idea--he believed Japan really had
nothing to offer Germany--and he possibly influenced Hitler
against rushing into an arrangement. Though Neurath and
Ribbentrop were vying for weight in determining foreign
policy, by the end of 1935 they both appreciated the political reality of the National Socialist government--ulti-
mately the decision rested with the Führer. But the
sources of power were not so sharply defined in Japan, nor
was power so concentrated.

A little later the Japanese Foreign Ministry learned
something of the negotiations. Before Wakamatsu reached
Tokyo on 15 January 1936, a few junior members of the
Foreign Ministry and of the General Staff apparently held a
secret discussion about Ōshima's negotiations, but the
matter was not referred to higher levels in the Foreign
Ministry. The Japanese Foreign Ministry was not expressly
informed by its own representative in Berlin of Ōshima's
conversations with Ribbentrop until about eleven months
after the talks were initiated. In early February the
chargé d'affaires ad interim, Counselor Kojiro Inoue,
reported to the Foreign Ministry that there were accounts
in German newspapers of Ōshima "informally carrying on
political negotiations with the German side."[9] But Inoue's
report was filed by a minor official before Foreign Minister Koki Hirota or Vice Foreign Minister Mamoru Shigemitsu
saw it.[10] In mid-February, however, Wakamatsu conferred
with Shigenori Tōgō, chief of the Foreign Ministry bureau
in charge of European affairs. He gave Tōgō the same
assessment of the situation in Berlin that he had already
given to his military superiors in the Army General Staff
and War Ministry: the Germans with whom he met "were more
than willing" to conclude an anti-Comintern pact with
Japan.[11] And in mid-March Wakamatsu made a similar report
to Ambassador Mushakoji, who had been on leave from his
Berlin post since July 1935.

Only in late March was the full matter aired specifically with the new Foreign Minister, Hachiro Arita. This
action was taken by the new Minister of War, not by the
General Staff where the military extremists were much more
influential in March 1936. At that time veteran diplomat
Ambassador Kintomo Mushakoji was preparing to return to
Europe where Hitler had just shocked the British and French
governments by scrapping the Locarno Treaty and reoccupying
the demilitarized Rhineland. General Hisaichi Terauchi,
Minister of War in the newly formed Hirota cabinet, invited
Ambassador Mushakoji and chief officials of the Foreign
Ministry to discuss the Ōshima-Ribbentrop negotiations in a
meeting with twenty of his bureau-level army officers.
Only the Chief of Military Affairs, Colonel (Ryōki) Machijiri,
felt that Ōshima's original proposal was wise, and he con-
tended that there was an urgent need to conclude a military
pact with Germany. The majority of the other army officers,
however, agreed that a carefully negotiated political
agreement, an anti-Comintern pact, was more desirable.
That view was also shared by Foreign Minister Arita, Vice
Foreign Minister Shigemitsu, and Ambassador Mushakoji.[12]

A Year of Struggle

Initially, key figures in the General Staff had refused
to pass the matter of the Oshima-Ribbentrop discussions on
to the Foreign Ministry, although inevitably they would
have to since the General Staff was interested in concluding
some sort of political treaty between the two governments.
Field Marshal Prince Kan'in, with the support of his Deputy
Chief, yielded to the precedent Oshima attempted to set in
European totalitarian diplomacy; indeed, he instructed
Oshima to continue negotiations, except along political
lines. Hence, the General Staff seemed to be in no hurry
to consult the Foreign Ministry. But the sequence of events
took charge. First, a partial report and several rumors of
Oshima's talks with the Germans reached the Japanese Foreign
Ministry, and now, in March 1936, they could no longer be
ignored. Secondly, in the immediate aftermath of recent
political assassinations by military extremists, the new
Minister of War was expedient and politic in his maneuvers
to regain political strength in the government and popu-
larity in public opinion. Although Terauchi did not attach
much importance to the substance of Oshima's talks, the fact
remained that the political discussions had not been authorized, or participated in, by members of the Foreign Ministry.
Thus, Terauchi saw an opportunity to help mollify tense
civil-military relations by discussing Oshima's activities
openingly with Foreign Ministry officials.[13]

It appeared for a brief time in late March and early
April 1936 that there was no essential difference of opinion between the Foreign Ministry and the army--a carefully
negotiated anti-Comintern agreement was most desirable from
the point of view of the majority of Terauchi's bureau
chiefs as well as Foreign Minister Arita and his subordinates. But War Minister Terauchi, like his German counterpart, Werner von Blomberg, enjoyed only limited prerogative on the subject, and he did not necessarily represent
the full views of the army or the General Staff. It was,
then, in these uncertain conditions that Foreign Minister
Arita gave Ambassador Mushakoji oral instructions to start
negotiations upon his return to Berlin, for, as Foreign
Ministry bureau chief Shigenori Togo later recalled, "it
seemed to be necessary to make a political agreement of
some kind with Germany."[14] Arita, Shigemitsu, and Togo
assumed that the Foreign Ministry, through its ambassador
in Berlin, would at last take charge of the negotiations.

Such an assumption was woefully inappropriate. In all
probability Terauchi and Arita initially avoided a detailed
discussion of the issue of responsibility for negotiations.

They knew that the enterprising Ōshima had been carrying on
negotiations with Ribbentrop, but they were also acutely
aware that it would be very difficult for them to restrain
him. Japanese army attachés were directly responsible only
to the General Staff, indirectly responsible to the War
Ministry, while the Foreign Ministry had no statutory control over them. Ōshima later explained that he always
"sent information directly to . . . [the Chief of the Army
General Staff] instead of going through the ambassador."[15]
Arita probably chose to interpret the War Ministry's interest in an anti-Comintern pact with Germany, instead of a
military pact, as a sign that the military as a whole, including the crucially important General Staff, was ready to
relinquish responsibility for negotiations to the Foreign
Ministry. Such an intrepretation was opportune, but it was
also a serious misreading of the times, a disregard of the
history of the proposal, and a disastrous underestimate of
Ōshima's ambitions and abilities. For Ōshima enjoyed power;
he also enjoyed a seemingly indispensable connection with
top National Socialists and the new attention that his
self-made role in German-Japanese relations was starting to
receive in the Tokyo government.

General Terauchi and Foreign Minister Arita met a
second time to discuss the proposed agreement with Germany--
Mushakōji was en route to Berlin to resume his ambassadorial
duties at the time. They debated the issue of responsibility for carrying on the negotiations. Military interest was
rekindled, for, as Terauchi explained to Arita, the Army
General Staff feared that the authority of its representative in the negotiations would surely be challenged by the
ambassador. Before, the chargé d'affaires ad interim, who
in any case probably did not know of the matter until early
February, had not interfered during the previous ten months.
No one wanted an open clash between Ōshima and Mushakōji.
Moreover, military arguments for allowing Ōshima to continue
the negotiations emphasized the expediency of taking advantage of his special relationship with Hitler and Ribbentrop.
Such arguments seemed not without merit. Yet Arita would
not abrogate the Foreign Ministry's responsibility by ordering Mushakōji to yield to Ōshima. Instead, in new instructions to Mushakōji he modified the Foreign Ministry's
earlier position. Having just arrived in Berlin on April
30th and still preparing for fresh negotiations, Mushakōji
was suddenly confronted with a perplexing proposition.
Arita's telegram reaffirmed the Foreign Ministry's support
for the idea of a carefully negotiated anti-Comintern pact,
and Arita added that it ought to be "a vague engagement

41

without limiting the matter." However, he instructed Mushakōji to avoid the appearance of Japan's initiating negotiations; indeed, the ambassador was instructed on shun (yokeru) courting German attitudes, but he was at the same time to keep "in touch with leading figures of the German Foreign Office and the Nazi party."[16]

Arita's new instructions appeared to incorporate aspects of two of the more extreme military points of view: 1) Colonel Machijiri's view that Ōshima's proposal for a defensive "no-aid" military pact was urgently needed would be, in fact, an "engagement without limiting the matter," and 2) the General Staff's standpoint that Ōshima's unique position in the negotiations must be preserved. A general agreement on political and military matters now seemed to have at least the tacit approval of Foreign Minister Arita, while it also seemed that the Foreign Ministry did not for the time being wish to be closely associated with such strategic concerns. How better to avoid such an appearance and to keep closely in touch with the National Socialists than by allowing Ōshima to continue the negotiations with Ribbentrop?

The effect of Arita's ambiguous instructions was to shift the question of how to proceed to Berlin where Ōshima had long enjoyed the upper hand. It was a military victory, though there is some evidence that Terauchi felt obligated, as a cabinet member, to follow protocol. In early May Terauchi sent a cable to Ōshima stating that he and Arita had agreed that the Foreign Ministry ought to take over negotiations.[17] But without the General Staff's explicit endorsement of the War Minister's cable, Terauchi knew that Ōshima's behavior was not likely to change. Furthermore, Terauchi was confident that his army comrade in Berlin understood the new War Minister's position in which prudence and tact could be helpful to his relations with other members of the civil government.[18] Mushakōji, not Ōshima, was in a quandary. Though the ambassador was ambivalent about Ōshima and his political diplomacy, he felt compelled to request the military attaché "to continue negotiations as before until such time as Hitler makes a decision regarding the content of the agreement."[19] The General Staff had long anticipated that when it became necessary to consult the Foreign Ministry about the proposal, only Ōshima, on the Japanese side, would have full knowledge and thorough understanding of the long and complex negotiations; therefore, the military attaché would be recognized as the most qualified Japanese negotiator. Vice Foreign Minister

Shigemitsu's concise assessment, though a little overstated, was not wide off the mark: "in Tokyo it was the Army that drove the Government, in Berlin it was Oshima that drove Mushakoji."[20]

Thus, after Mushakōji's return in 1936 the military attaché was permitted to continue as Japan's key negotiator, while the ambassador's role was largely ceremonial. Oshima later recalled that he discussed the conclusion of the Pact with Hitler in at least two meetings in June, the same month when the ambassador made only a courtesy call on the Führer.[21] Hitler was very cordial to Mushakoji, and he was pleased with the ambassador's report from Japan. Mushakoji told the Führer that "the Japanese form of Government had changed inwardly in that--as in Germany--it had now become authoritarian. Japan regarded Bolshevism and the Communist idea as her great enemies."[22] But nothing was mentioned of Oshima, the negotiations, or the Pact.

In early July Ambassador Mushakōji, who was regarded as persona non grata by the Dienststelle group, asked Ribbentrop to prepare a complete German version of the proposed treaty. Its essence had already been negotiated in the Oshima-Ribbentrop conversations, and it was formally drawn up and named "Anti-Comintern Pact" by a Dienststelle East Asian specialist, Hermann von Raumer.[23] (By aiming the Pact ostensibly at the Communist International, which theoretically was not an arm of the Soviet government, Ribbentrop's able specialist sought to avoid an open breach with the Soviet Union.) Instead of taking the draft to the ambassador, Raumer, presumably acting on Ribbentrop's orders, first took the draft to Oshima at Bayreuth, where every summer the Japanese military attaché, like Hitler, attended the Wagner Festival. On July 22nd Oshima and Hitler met, with Ribbentrop and Raumer, in the serene setting of Wagner's family residence in Bayreuth, Villa Wahnfried.[24] Hitler personally edited the draft--according to Togo, who was responsible on the Japanese side for drafting recommended changes, it at first "read like a Nazi manifesto."[25] The proposed treaty was now made up of two parts--the Anti-Comintern Pact with an attached secret protocol. For Oshima suggested to Hitler that certain features most objectionable to the Japanese Foreign Ministry and to the more moderate elements in the Japanese military could perhaps be saved if they were placed in a secret section of the treaty. It was only after this meeting that Oshima had at Bayreuth that Mushakoji was at last given the full German version. The ambassador dutifully sent it to his Foreign Ministry superiors in Tokyo.

A Year of Struggle

By early August the German draft was returned with the Foreign Ministry's objection that overall the proposed agreement was too strongly phrased. Ribbentrop, in London as the recently appointed ambassador to the Court of St. James, flew back to Berlin several times during the next two weeks for discussions with Mushakōji and Ōshima. On August 16th Ribbentrop confidently reported to Hitler that he had, "during the last two weeks, been in negotiation with the Japanese Ambassador and with General Oshima on the question of the conclusion of the Anti-Comintern agreement as well as of the proposed political agreement. The Ambassador informed me that his Government had in principle approved these agreements. . . . The negotiations will probably be resumed at the end of next week or the beginning of the week after."[26] The Japanese Foreign Ministry had been won over by the military. As a Foreign Ministry spokesman wrote at the time, "as long as Bolshevism threatens world peace . . . it is quite possible that . . . [Germany and Japan] will endeavour hand in hand to check this menace. . . . It can be safely asserted that Germany and Japan . . . will find it easy to come to understanding and co-operation with each other."[27]

The effect in the Japanese Foreign Ministry of Ōshima's monoply in the negotiations before August 1936 was to present Foreign Minister Arita with something of a fait accompli. Actually, Ōshima's earlier "no aid" proposal now appeared rather moderate to all Tokyo factions, especially when compared with Hitler's manifesto for splitting up the Soviet Union. A two-part agreement, half secret, was the result of Ōshima's military diplomacy. Arita felt that all that could be expected at this late date in the negotiations was to introduce some toning down measures to the German draft, making it less "propagandistic" and "more businesslike."[28] To this end the Japanese obtained German agreement to the insertion of a qualification--the term "unprovoked attack"-- in the heart of the set of documents, Article I of the Secret Additional Agreement to the Agreement against the Communist International: "Should one of the High Contracting States become the object of an unprovoked attack or threat of attack by the Union of Soviet Socialist Republics, the other High Contracting State obligates itself to take no measures which would tend to ease the situation of the Union of Soviet Socialist Republics."[29] Presumably at the Bayreuth meeting Hitler had changed Ōshima's original non-assistance provision to a statement whereby each nation would be obligated to take up arms against the Soviet Union when it seemed justifiably provoked (no doubt left undefined by Hitler). In that event the other power would pursue a

policy of armed neutrality vis-à-vis the Soviet Union.
Though Hitler acquiesced on this point in August 1936,
significantly, Oshima's original proposal, which he discussed at various times with Hack, Ribbentrop, Hitler, or
Raumer, survived intact after some twenty months of nego-
tiations--neither Japan nor Germany would "take actions
beneficial to Soviet Russia" in the event of war between
the Soviet Union and either Germany or Japan. Senior
Foreign Ministry officials were unable to persuade War
Minister Terauchi and other army leaders that the military
clauses of the proposed treaty should be eliminated altogether; however, the Japanese military did agree that the
military provisions must be of a "strictly defensive
nature."30 (The Japanese military had its own more press-
ing concerns with Communist and Kuomintang forces on the
Asian mainland; it simply did not want to be bound by a
treaty in which it could lose the option of when and where
to fight.)

As published, the preamble of the German-Japanese Anti-
Comintern Pact declared that the aim of the Communist
International was to "subdue existing States by all means
at its command."31 Toleration of this interference in
Japanese and German domestic affairs endangered their
internal peace and social well-being; to continue to tolerate the international menace would also threaten world
peace. Therefore, Japan and Germany agreed to cooperate in
"defense against Communist subversive activities." Bureau
chief Togo claimed to have limited the cooperation to
merely "the exchange of information concerning the destruc-
tive activities" of the Comintern and consultation about
preventive measures to be taken against them.32 Hitler
wanted a more assertive statement with a provision for
periodic "meetings of the Foreign Ministers and other high
officials." Togo maintained, however, that only "a permanent committee" was necessary to facilitate the cooperation
provisions of the treaty--its times for meeting were not
preset in the treaty. Another minor concession was
obtained from the Germans concerning the length of time
that the agreement would remain effective, five rather than
ten years. All in all, the original draft prepared at
Bayreuth appears to have been toned down, but its essence
was not much different from Oshima's original proposal or
from what Oshima's military supporters encouraged during
the previous year.

There was a major campaign to transform Oshima's idea
into national policy in Europe. The majority of the most

powerful members in the Hirota Cabinet had been won over by various arguments favoring the conclusion of the agreement with Germany.

The Five Ministers' Conference was used extensively by the Hirota government because of the growing complexity and increased importance of national security problems after the Manchurian incident and after Japan's withdrawal from the League of Nations. The Five Ministers' Conference, sometimes called the Inner Cabinet, represented the "bureaucratization of the policy-making process," one scholar has observed; it was "the final voice of authority in matters of national policy."[33] In the autumn of 1936 members of the Five Ministers' Conference were the Prime Minister (Kōki Hirota), the Foreign Minister (Hachirō Arita), the Minister of War (General Hisaichi Terauchi), the Minister of the Navy (Admiral Osami Nagano), and the Finance Minister (Eiichi Baba).

From the beginning these five most important ministers agreed in principle that the conclusion of a political pact against the Communist International was a worthwhile goal. These five ministers also shared a commonly held view that perhaps the army ought to have an opportunity to leave its mark on Japanese foreign policy on this occasion just as the navy had done in the conclusion of the 1902 Anglo-Japanese Alliance.[34]

Fearful of diplomatic isolation in the late 1930s, great importance was assigned to strategic concerns in which the authority of the service ministers in the formation of Japanese foreign policy was extremely pronounced. The navy agreed with the army that the Pact ought not to include specific obligations to provide military assistance, but the navy did not endorse the proposed pact until Admiral Nagano was convinced that the navy specifically would benefit--reportedly the proposed agreement with Germany would aggravate the European diplomatic situation to the extent that major naval powers, Great Britain and France, would become amenable to a modus vivendi with Japan in East Asian waters. Thus, the Five Ministers' Conference appeared to reach a convenient consensus in the autumn of 1936. In addition to having gained naval approval, the army was satisfied that the Pact would serve its anti-Soviet strategic planning. The other ministers, relieved to see army-navy agreement, followed the lead of Foreign Minister Arita and accepted his irrational, though politic, position: since the Soviet government and the Comintern claimed that there was no connection between

them, Soviet-Japanese relations would not be injured while
the Japanese government could work against its enemy, the
Communist International. That was a position that the
Foreign Ministry, with a denial of a secret agreement, would
emphasize in its later public explanation of the Pact.[35]
But in September 1936 the Foreign Ministry requested only
that formal signing and publication of the agreement be
postponed for about two months so that Soviet-Japanese
negotiations for a fishery convention would not be unduly
impaired.[36]

On October 23rd the Pact and a secret supplementary
agreement were initialed by Ribbentrop and the only Japanese official in Germany authorized to represent Japan,
Viscount Kintomo Mushakoji, Imperial Japanese Extraordinary
and Plenipotentiary Ambassador. In Berlin on November 25th,
the two ambassadors formally signed the documents for their
governments, not in the German Foreign Ministry building
on the Wilhelmstrasse, but across the famous street in the
Dienststelle building. Oshima was standing directly behind
Mushakoji during the signing ceremony--a British correspondent erroneously reported that the Japanese military
attaché signed the Pact.[37] The same correspondent, however,
quite correctly reported that "the Japanese army, through
General Oshima, took a hand in the negotiation of the
agreement."[38] But the analysis of American journalists
fell just short of designating Oshima as the prime mover.
One author interpreted the agreement as an aggressive
military pact "cloaked in anti-Communist phraseology" and
he claimed that negotiations for the agreement against
"the non-Fascist world" were "initialled secretly on
January 6, 1936."[39] Another article cited January 4th as
the date when negotiations were started; the result was
"a mask for a military alliance."[40] Speculation about the
secret military nature of the Pact was based on the author's
knowledge and interpretation of Wakamatsu's visit: "Late
in November, 1935, Berlin was the convention town for Japanese military attachés stationed in Western Europe."[41]

Part of the speculation in the British and American
presses was of Soviet origin. Ribbentrop sent Hack to
Tokyo in very early 1936. His task was to promote interest
among his many business associates in the proposal that
he and Oshima launched the previous year. Hack's itinerary
included meetings with high ranking Japanese army and navy
officials as well as with the heads of such industrial
firms as Mitsui and Mitsubishi.[42] Hack worked with Oshima's
counterpart in the Germany embassy, Military Attaché Eugen
Ott, and with Richard Sorge, a correspondent in Japan for

47

the Frankfurter Zeitung. Sorge, an unsuspected Communist agent, gained the confidence of Hack and Ott, and, through a strong friendship with Ott, he acquired access to the rich files of the German military attaché. Ott was kept abreast of recent developments in German-Japanese relations; moreover, Hack probably told Sorge and Ott something about the role of Ōshima in the preparation of the Pact. Thus, the Soviet government's espionage apparatus in Japan kept Moscow informed about the progress of the Ōshima-Ribbentrop negotiations. In late 1935 and in January 1936 the Soviet government started to release reports to the world press concerning the Ōshima-Ribbentrop negotiations, "presumably with the hope," as Gerhard Weinberg has noted, "of preventing any agreement."[43] Ōshima, who had "furtive parleys" in Berlin, was portrayed in a January 1936 issue of Izvestia as one of the "Japanese fanatics who hide from their own people and the press the sinister plans they hatch against the U.S.S.R."[44] Ōshima, then, was the focus of Soviet contempt in Moscow's denunciation of the Anti-Comintern Pact.

Ōshima and his supporters initiated a fundamental change in Japan's European policy. The Japanese newspaper Nichi Nichi, though omitting Ōshima's paramount role, observed that "the enthusiasm of the Army was so strongly expressed that the Cabinet was obligated to conclude the agreement as national policy. . . . It is a first step along a new path. It marks the turning point of Japanese policy."[45] Mamoru Shigemitsu, en route to Moscow in November 1936 as the new ambassador, delineated Ōshima's role explicitly:

> Oshima's telegrams and reports were highly regarded by the Army. . . . [General Staff officers] knew little of world conditions. They were answerable to no one for their decisions and it suited them to swallow Oshima's views wholesale. . . . The Axis policy of the Army, which in turn directed the Government, came eventually to be Japan's fixed course.[46]

Thus, Ōshima's outlook, biased by his association with Hitler and other National Socialists, became the basis for the army's appraisal of the European situation. The General Staff and War Ministry continued to accept Ōshima's advice; moreover, they became Ōshima's defenders in government deliberations.[47] Ōshima could be certain that the agreement would be ratified.

Final approval by the Privy Council, of which Ōshima's father was an Imperial nominee, was required since the agreement was in the form of a formal treaty. Hearings

were held in November at which Prime Minister Hirota and
Foreign Minister Arita argued the army's case for ratifi-
cation before a special committee of the Privy Council.
Many of the Pact's advocates probably regarded the deliberations as a bothersome procedure, but by November 25th they
had little difficulty in winning unanimous approval of the
treaty in a plenary session of the Privy Council. Imperial
consent was granted automatically.[48]

The successful conclusion of the Anti-Comintern Pact
was an indication of the considerable extent to which
military concerns outside of Japan's China policy became a
part of the thinking of civil forces in 1936. While it is
true that most members of the Foreign Ministry were surprised early in 1936 by both the content of Ōshima's talks
and the fact that the military attaché was engaged in the
negotiations, nevertheless, many of them did not disapprove
of the general idea of trying to draw closer to Germany.
There were many traditionally pro-German Japanese who
favored Ōshima's adventures, and they reconciled themselves
to the necessity of entering into some sort of agreement
with Hitler's Germany. On the other hand, some Japanese
who were formerly apprehensive about aligning with National
Socialist Germany were impressed by Hitler going "the way
that Providence dictates with the assurance of a sleep-
walker," as he said of himself in a speech just after the
successful March 1936 reoccupation of the Rhineland.[49] In
July they were again impressed and swayed by the example
of Hitler's daring decision to support General Francisco
Franco and his insurgents in the Spanish Civil War. The
year before Spain was designated by the Comintern as a
country where working class unity, as demonstrated in the
People's Front, could likely succeed in the seizure of
power.[50] The Japanese could interpret Hitler's decision to
aid Franco as a forthright effort to check the spread of
their common enemy, Communism. Furthermore, Hitler's style
was a sign of the times. His diplomacy seemed to be successful at every turn, and those Japanese diplomats,
notably Shigemitsu and Togo, who were distrustful of a
heavy reliance on military force, were unfashionable and
being passed by.

NOTES

III: A Year of Struggle

1. IMTFE, Exhibit 3508.

2. Ibid., Exhibit 3492.

3. "Interrogation of Wakamatsu," IPS 453, 9-10 May 1946, RG 331.

4. IMTFE, Exhibit 3492. See also Ōhata, "The Anti-Comintern Pact," p. 25.

5. "Interrogation of Wakamatsu," IPS 453, 9-10 May 1946, RG 331.

6. Gordon A. Craig, "Totalitarian Diplomacy," in Diplomacy in Modern European History, ed. Laurence W. Martin (New York: Macmillan, 1966), p. 83. This essay originally appeared as "Totalitarian Approaches to Diplomatic Negotiation," in Studies in Diplomatic History and Historiography in Honour of G. P. Gooch, C.H., ed. A. O. Sarkissian (London: Longmans, Green, 1961), pp. 107-25. After the Second World War, Herbert von Dirksen, a professional diplomat who was formerly the German ambassador in Tokyo, observed that "Ribbentrop's character is compounded of an enormous ambition and at the same time of a sense that he is neither gifted nor strong enough to live up to his ambition. He suffers under a secret inferiority complex which he compensates by haughty, dictatorial manners. He is always on the alert lest his authority be insufficiently respected. He is extremely wary of being outmaneuvered by a possible competitor or successor" ("Herbert von Dirksen--An Estimate of Ribbentrop," Records of the Department of State Special Interrogation Mission to Germany, 1945-1946, National Archives Microfilm Publication M-679, roll 1, frame 0353).

7. "Herbert von Dirksen--Origins of the Anti-Comintern Pact," Special Interrogation Mission to Germany, National Archives Microfilm Publication M-679, roll 1, frame 0288. See also Herbert von Dirksen, Moscow, Tokyo, London: Twenty Years of German Foreign Policy (Norman: University of Oklahoma Press, 1952), p. 153.

8. Documents on German Foreign Policy, 1918-1945, series C, vol. 4, No. 479, pp. 948-52. (Hereafter cited as DGFP. See my bibliography for the title of each German document

50

III: A Year of Struggle

cited in series C and D.) State Secretary Bernhard
Wilhelm von Bülow knew of the discussions and dismissed
them as not being very serious. See DGFP, C, 5, No. 197,
pp. 271-73; Dirksen, Moscow, Tokyo, London, pp. 170-71;
Erich Kordt, Nicht aus den Akten (Stuttgart: Union
Deutsche Verlagsgesellschaft, 1950), p. 124; and Gerhard
L. Weinberg, The Foreign Policy of Hitler's Germany:
Diplomatic Revolution in Europe, 1933-36 (Chicago:
University of Chicago Press, 1970), pp. 343-44.

9. IMTFE, Proceedings, pp. 35,408-9. The testimony here
is that of Akira Yamaji, a junior secretary (April 1934-
September 1936) in the Second Section, European-Asiatic
Bureau in the Japanese Foreign Ministry. See also ibid.,
p. 35,643, Exhibit 3646, and Ōhata, "The Anti-Comintern
Pact," pp. 26-27. (The European-American Bureau was re-
named the European-Asiatic Bureau in 1934 when a separate
American Bureau was created in the Japanese Foreign
Ministry.)

10. Ōhata, "The Anti-Comintern Pact," p. 27, and
Presseisen, Germany and Japan, p. 85. See also Mamoru
Shigemitsu, Japan and Her Destiny: My Struggle for Peace,
ed. F.S.G. Piggott; trans. Oswald White (New York: E. P.
Dutton, 1958), p. 123.

11. "Interrogation of Wakamatsu," IPS 453, 9-10 May 1946,
RG 331.

12. Ōhata, "The Anti-Comintern Pact," p. 27. Kōki Hirota
retained the Prime Minister and Foreign Minister portfolios
during most of March until Arita accepted the latter post
near the end of the month.

13. The "ni-niroku (2.26) incident" was a full-scale army
mutiny starting on February 26, 1936. Nearly fifteen
hundred ultranationalists, including twenty-four junior
army officers who led the assassination teams, participated
actively in the conspiracy. In particular, the rebels
aimed to remove politically moderate statesmen._ Among the
leading government officials slaughtered were Jotaro
Watanabe, the inspector general of military training;
Finance Minister Korekiyo Takahashi; and Makoto Saito, lord
keeper of the privy seal. Prime Minister Keisuke Okada and
last Elder Statesman Prince Kimmochi Saionji narrowly

III: A Year of Struggle

escaped the assassins. This revolt of the radicals was as
much of a threat to traditional military influence and dominance in recent cabinets as it was to civil authority alone.
It is not suprising, then, that the new Minister of War
acted decisively. As Professor Butow has written, "the
legal farces which had followed in the wake of the earlier
incidents were not now repeated. The army was severely
shaken by the insurrection. The control faction . . .
came to the fore. The trials . . . resulted in sentences
for some 103 men (Robert J. C. Butow, Tojo and the Coming
of the War (Princeton: Princeton University Press, 1961),
p. 69. The highly experienced British military attaché,
in Tokyo on a second tour of duty in 1936, wrote in his
autobiography that "The new Minister of War, General Count
Terauchi . . . restored discipline by drastic action,
including the death penalty for the ringleaders" (Piggott,
Broken Thread, p. 265). Wakamatsu, recently back from his
mission to Berlin, was for a brief time chief judge at one
of the trials following the February mutiny. See
"Interrogation of Wakamatsu," IPS 453, 9-10 May 1946,
RG 331.

14. IMTFE, Proceedings, p. 35,644.

15. Ibid., Exhibit 3508.

16. Ibid., Exhibit 2614. See also Ōhata, "The Anti-
Comintern Pact," p. 29, and DGFP, C, 5, Editors' Note, pp.
1138-40.

17. Ōhata, "The Anti-Comintern Pact," p. 29.

18. Ōshima was not unaware of some of the complexities of
cabinet-level politics, for his father was Minister of War
in the cabinet formed by Terauchi's father, October 1916-
September 1918.

19. Ōhata, "The Anti-Comintern Pact," p. 29. See also Frank
William Iklé, German-Japanese Relations, 1936-1940 (New York:
Bookman Associates, 1956), p. 30. Ambassador Mushakoji was
on leave to Japan from July 1935 until he returned to Berlin
on 30 April 1936. The absence of the mission chief had no
appreciable effect on Ōshima's behavior in negotiations with
the Germans. One can safely assume that Ōshima would not
have consulted the first-ranked ambassador just as he did

III: A Year of Struggle

not, in fact, consult Counselor Inoue, chargé d'affaires
ad interim. See IMTFE, Proceedings, pp. 35,408-9, 35,643,
and Presseisen, Germany and Japan, p. 85.

20. Shigemitsu, Japan and Her Destiny, p. 124.

21. Ōshima to author, 7 May 1971.

22. DGFP, C, 5, No. 362, pp. 603-4. It was during one of
the Ōshima-Hitler meetings in June 1936 that Hitler
declared that Russia had to be split up into its "original
historical sections" (Hans-Adolf Jacobsen, National-
sozialistische Aussenpolitik, 1933-1938 [Frankfurt am Main:
Alfred Metzner Verlag, 1968], pp. 426, 819). Presumably,
however, Hitler made a very similar statement to Ōshima
nearly a full year earlier. See note 28 below.

23. "Extracts from a Verbatim Report of an Interrogation
of Joachim von Ribbentrop," Special Interrogation Mission
to Germany, National Archives Microfilm Publication M-679,
roll 3, frames 0158-59, and "Herbert von Dirksen--How the
Anti-Comintern Pact Was Named," ibid., roll 1, frame 0289.

24. Theo Sommer, Deutschland und Japan zwischen den Mächten,
1935-1940: Vom Antikominternpakt zum Dreimächtenpakt,
Tübinger Studien zur Geschichte und Politik no. 15 (Tübingen:
J. C. B. Mohr, 1962), p. 34. This is the best scholarly
account of Raumer's work on the proposed Pact, especially
pp. 26-42. See also Ōhata, "The Anti-Comintern Pact," p.
29.

25. Shigenori Tōgō, The Cause of Japan, ed. and trans.
Fumihiko Togo and Ben Bruce Blakeney (New York: Simon and
Schuster, 1956), p. 30.

26. DGFP, C, 5, No. 509, pp. 899-900. The military and
political considerations were inevitably mixed, and here in
this summary for Hitler, Ribbentrop refers to Ōshima's "no
aid" military proposal as "the proposed political agreement."

27. Takahiko Tomoyeda, "Germany and Japan," Contemporary
Japan 5, no. 2 (September 1936): 218.

28. IMTFE, Exhibit 3646. It is reasonable to assume that
Hitler sought to make the document more antagonistic toward

III: A Year of Struggle

the Soviet Union since the previous year, as cited in the
preceding chapter, Hitler told Ōshima that he intended "to
split up the Soviet Union into several small states"
("Magic," SRS 1420, 9 September 1944, RG 457). This was a
recurring   theme in Hitler's conversations with Ōshima.

29. DGFP, D, 1, p. 734n. The secret section of the Pact,
including several annexes and notes exchanged when the
agreement was initialed on October 23rd, have infrequently
been published together. They are published in Gerhard L.
Weinberg, "Die geheimen Abkommen zum Antikominternpakt,"
Vierteljahrshefte für Zeitgeschichte 2, no. 2 (April 1954):
197-201; Sommer, Deutschland und Japan, pp. 494-99; and
Ōhata, "The Anti-Comintern Pact," pp. 261-64. The text of
the published agreement, the secret section, and the
apparatus appear together in my Appendix A.

30. IMTFE, Exhibit 3646.

31. An English translation of the published part of the
Pact will be found in Stephen Heald, ed., Documents on
International Affairs, 1936 (London: Oxford University
Press, 1937), pp. 297-99. See also Appendix A.

32. IMTFE, Exhibit 3646.

33. James B. Crowley, Japan's Quest for Autonomy: National
Security and Foreign Policy, 1930-1938 (Princeton: Prince-
ton University Press, 1966), p. 390. See also Yale Candee
Maxon, Control of Japanese Foreign Policy: A Study of
Civil-Military Rivalry, 1930-1945 (Berkeley: University
of California Press, 1957), pp. 115-16.

34. The Saionji-Harada Memoirs, 1931-1940: Complete Translation into English (Washington, D.C.: University Publications of America, [1978], p. 1,635, and Ōhata, "The Anti-
Comintern Pact," p. 35. On the other hand, as Professor
Butow observes, "after 1936, the navy's assignment in the
further expansion of Japan was to become increasingly
important. . . . Interservice rivalry and jealousy--the
navy view that the army had been monopolizing for too long
the center of the stage--also explain the growing naval
desire to share in the glory accruing to the army as a
result of victories on the continent" (Butow, Tojo and the
Coming of the War, pp. 82-83).

NOTES

III: A Year of Struggle

35. "The Foreign Office Statement regarding the Above [Text of the Pact], November 25, 1936," Contemporary Japan 5, no. 3 (December 1936): 517: "It should be pointed out that in connection with, or behind, this agreement there exists no other agreement whatsoever, and . . . that the present agreement is not directed against the Soviet Union or any other specific country." These assertions were elaborated upon in Iwakusu Ida, "The Meaning of the Japan-German Pact," ibid., no. 4 (March 1937): 523, 525-26.

36. Mamoru Shigemitsu arrived as the new Japanese ambassador in Moscow the day the Anti-Comintern Pact was signed and made public on 25 November 1936. He wrote that the Soviet government "at once took counter-measures" of which one was to discontinue negotiations for a new fishery convention. See his work entitled Japan and Her Destiny, pp. 125-26. The Soviets refused to conclude a new convention, but signed on 28 December 1936 a protocol extending for one year the provisions of the Convention of 1928.

37. Times (London), 28 November 1936, p. 11.

38. Ibid.

39. Philip J. Jaffe, "America and the German-Japanese Pact," Amerasia 1, no. 1 (March 1937): 22. See also Raymond Leslie Buell, "German-Japanese Pact Arouses Democracies," Foreign Policy Bulletin 16, no. 6 (4 December 1936): 1-2.

40. Albert Parry, "Japan and Germany Join Hands," Asia and the Americas 37, no. 1 (January 1937): 43.

41. Ibid. See also American Ambassador Joseph C. Grew's diary entry for 3 December 1936 in his Ten Years in Japan (New York: Simon and Schuster, 1944), p. 191.

42. Martin, "Die deutsch-japanischen Beziehungen," p. 461n.

43. Weinberg, The Foreign Policy of Hitler's Germany, p. 344.

44. Cited by Ignatius Phayre in "Germany and Japan: The Inner Story," Saturday Review 162, no. 4236 (12 December 1936): 750.

III: A Year of Struggle

45. Cited by Hugh Byas, New York Times correspondent in Tokyo, New York Times, 26 November 1936, p. 26.

46. Shigemitsu, Japan and Her Destiny, p. 124. Wakamatsu also suggested that Oshima's views were highly regarded by Army General Staff officers--"Interrogation of Wakamatsu," IPS 453, 9-10 May 1946, RG 331.

47. "Orthodox Japanese administrative theory places great emphasis on the ringisei, a system whereby reports and proposals are expected to be initiated at the bottom of a bureaucratic pyramid and then to be pumped upward through the chain of command until, when they reach the top, they represent the consensus of the institution which the seniors can do little to influence and are expected to represent" (James William Morley, introduction to Chihiro Hosoya, "The Tripartite Pact, 1939-1940," trans. James William Morley, in Deterrent Diplomacy, p. 184). Nevertheless, "in the navy, as in the army, the locus of power rested far below the level of those who nominally held the rank and authority which should have placed them in the decision-making category" (Butow, Tojo and the Coming of the War, p. 83).

48. See Presseisen, Germany and Japan, pp. 104-6, and Iklé, German-Japanese Relations, pp. 35-38.

49. This fragment from Hitler's speech at Munich on 15 March 1936 is quoted in Alan Bullock, Hitler: A Study in Tyranny (rev. ed.; New York: Harper and Row, 1962), p. 375. At Bayreuth, on the same day he met with Oshima, Hitler also made the decision to aid Franco and his insurgents in the Spanish Civil War.

50. See, for example, the Comintern resolution of 20 August 1935: "The Offensive of Fascism and the Tasks of the Communist International in the Struggle for the Unity of the Working Class against Fascism," Communist International 12 (20 September 1935): 1337-49 (then published simultaneously in English, Russian, German, French, Chinese, and Spanish), and G[eorgi] Dimitrov (Secretary General of the Comintern), "The People's Front of Struggle against Fascism and War," ibid. 13 (December 1936): 717-24, published originally in Pravda, 7 November 1936.

IV

THE EXPANSION AND DOMINANCE

OF MILITARY DIPLOMACY

The Anti-Comintern Pact was symbolic of the new rapprochement with the Third Reich, which would culminate in the tripartite alliance of Germany, Italy, and Japan in 1940. First, however, the struggle between Japanese military and civil diplomats became more intense. Military influence and Ōshima's work behind the scenes proved to be more effective, at least in the short run, than the policy advocated by the Foreign Ministry and the activity of most of its professional career diplomats.

* * *

After the conclusion of the Pact the Japanese Foreign Ministry regained a certain amount of control in European policy matters. Foreign Minister Arita wanted to remedy Japan's state of isolation by concluding additional anti-Comintern pacts. In fact, shortly before the Pact with Germany was concluded, Tokyo showed some effort to negotiate similar anti-Comintern agreements with the British and Dutch. The overtures of Japan's Ambassador to Britain, Shigeru Yoshida, and the soundings of Iwao Yamaguchi, chargé d'affairs of the Japanese legation in Amsterdam, revealed that the two European governments were not very interested. Indeed, most Western democracies, contrary to Arita's expectations, grew even more wary of Japan and Germany after the consummation of the Anti-Comintern Pact. The Japanese Foreign Ministry was simply unable to translate Western democratic dislike and disapproval of the aims of the Communist International into some sort of Western alignment with totalitarian powers in an anti-Comintern movement. In effect, the success of Ōshima's military diplomacy with Hitler's Germany made it increasingly difficult for the Foreign Ministry to reconcile and fulfill its policy goals with non-fascist nations.

Military Diplomacy

An alliance with Italy seemed more promising. Just after the Japanese concluded the 1936 Pact with Germany, Mussolini and his Foreign Minister, Count Galeazzo Ciano, informed the Japanese Foreign Ministry that Italy would consider negotiating a similar pact with Japan. Serious negotiations, however, were delayed for nearly a year because of the change of Japanese cabinets in February and again in July, the change of Japanese ambassadors in Rome, and the outbreak of the Sino-Japanese war. But with the concurrence of the Japanese military, in the autumn and early winter of 1937 Foreign Ministry negotiations between Japan and Italy began. They proceeded smoothly for a while. When Ribbentrop, however, then ambassador in London, learned indirectly from Ambassador Mushakōji of the proposed bilateral agreement with Italy, he went to Rome to meet with Mussolini, Ciano, and the recently appointed Japanese Ambassador to Italy, Masaaki Hotta. Ribbentrop proposed to make Italy an equal member of the year-old German-Japanese Pact.[1] Thus, the Japanese Foreign Ministry had seized the initiative in attempts to expand the anti-Comintern group of nations, but its bilateral intentions with Italy were subverted by Ribbentrop. Italy became a member of the German-Japanese anti-Comintern agreement on 6 November 1937, thereby creating the basis for the Berlin-Rome-Tokyo Axis.[2] In February 1939 Manchukuo and Hungary joined the Anti-Comintern Pact--Spain joined two months later. This was the so-called new world order built and protected by the tripartite powers. Japan was represented in all of these negotiations by its Foreign Ministry.

Ōshima's work to enhance German-Japanese relations shortly after the initial anti-Comintern agreement in 1936 focused on intelligence activities, including espionage and subversion associated with the office of the Japanese military attaché. By the very nature of the subject the historian is unable to write with authority, yet it is generally assumed in some secondary literature (always chary of discussing sources) that the Germans and Japanese cooperated in intelligence operations against the Soviet Union. Still, no attempt has been made to describe the extent of these operations or Ōshima's role and involvement.

We have already seen that there was some suggestion made to Ōshima in the spring of 1934 that he should sound out the Germans about cooperating in the collection of secret information concerning the Soviet Union. One result of his initiative was the Anti-Comintern Pact. And we know

also that an American assistant military attaché in Berlin
reported in May 1934 that the Japanese had unique access to
secret information in the Waffenamt. There is additional
evidence, however, that makes it reasonably certain that
German-Japanese intelligence cooperation was extensive and
that Ōshima was intimately involved.

Ōshima apparently had considerable contact with
Wilhelm Canaris long before the Anti-Comintern Pact was
signed.[3] Canaris became head of the Abwehr in January
1935, about seven months after Ōshima arrived in Berlin as
military attaché. The Abwehr was originally set up in 1921
as a small counter-espionage section in the Ministry of
Defense, but Canaris expanded it into an elaborate intelligence organization that served the German air, military,
and naval services.[4] As military attaché (1934-1938),
Ōshima said later that he was "in contact with leading
members of the German" armed forces, and, although Ōshima
was not specific, he admitted that "there was an understanding between the armies of Japan and Germany to collaborate concerning . . . [Soviet] counter-intelligence"
activities. This was some time prior to 1937. The German
role in the collaboration was exclusively handled by the
counter-intelligence section of the Ministry of Defense.
Ōshima stated, furthermore, that "final responsibility"
for the operations on the Japanese side rested with him.[5]

The Abwehr became a department of the Oberkommando der
Wehrmacht (O.K.W.)--the high command of the armed forces
created in Hitler's decrees in early 1938. Wilhelm Keitel,
then lieutenant general, was appointed by Hitler to the
newly created position of chief of the O.K.W., but for
some time before Keitel's appointment Ōshima also had considerable contact with the rising German general. Keitel
wrote that of all the foreign military attachés in Berlin
"only Ōshima was a frequent and welcome visitor at my
office."[6] Records of the details of Ōshima's conversations
with Canaris and Keitel are regrettably unavailable.

Contact between the Japanese military attaché and
German military officers concerned with intelligence matters
was not extraordinary in itself during the 1930s. But the
apparent closeness and the harmonious nature of the contact
were exceptional in Ōshima's case. It can in large measure
be attributed to Ōshima's resourcefulness and effectiveness
in a totalitarian society where the government's political
and militaristic values were similar to his own. Thus,
prior to November 1936 Ōshima boldly exercised in the

59

intelligence field the same sort of independence and initiative we have seen demonstrated in his negotiations resulting eventually in the Anti-Comintern Pact. Orders confirming what he initiated seemed always to follow.

Ōshima received explicit orders from the Chief of the Army General Staff in June 1937 "to study the question of using White Russians in Berlin in order to collect information about Soviet Russia, and for propaganda and counter-intelligence purposes in case of war between Japan and Russia."[7] Implementation of the project involving White Russians was entrusted to Lieutenant Colonel Shigeki Usui from mid-1937 until January 1938 and later to Colonel Manaki.[8] Both officers were on Ōshima's staff. The counter-intelligence aspects of those orders, Ōshima said, were only to be studied in consideration of wartime, and not in any way to be executed in peacetime--a moot qualification in reality. Ōshima claimed that "the Japanese military had previously been using White Russians in Warsaw to gather Russian intelligence and following the signing of the Anti-Comintern Pact . . . [he received orders] to further the exchange of information [with the German military] in regard to the Soviet Union."[9] At that time, June 1937, Ōshima said that he negotiated with the German military and reached an agreement on the exchange of Soviet military intelligence and on joint German-Japanese assistance to any independence movements formed by White Russians. It is not clear with whom in the German military Ōshima reached an agreement since no written document regarding it has survived the Second World War, yet we do have evidence (discussed below) that in the spring of 1938 he and Keitel signed a similar agreement concerning Soviet intelligence.

Another example of Ōshima's collaborative activities can be found in Ribbentrop's memorandum of 5 July 1938. Ōshima reported to Ribbentrop that a former Ukrainian commissar for domestic affairs, who had recently fled from Siberia and who was in Tokyo, "was in a position to give some interesting information about the Ukraine. . . ." Ribbentrop noted also that "General Ōshima had already made the necessary arrangements with counter-intelligence for the interrogation of the Soviet official by a German officer.[10]

In his intelligence work Ōshima was also associated with Heinrich Himmler, Reichsführer SS and, after June 1937, chief of the secret state police. His contact with Himmler was much more substantial than Ōshima was willing

to admit after the Second World War. Ōshima claimed that
he "had no special relations with Himmler either privately
or officially" and that he was visited by Himmler "only
twice"--once in the winter of 1936 and again in March 1941.
But his successor as military attaché, Major General
Torashiro Kawabe, declared that Ōshima and Himmler were
"friendly" and that "they met quite often, although perhaps
not in an official capacity."[11] Kawabe, who before leaving
Tokyo late in 1938 was briefed by Usui about his operations
with White Russians, was also Ōshima's assistant and was
responsible for implementing the project involving White
Russians after December 1938.

Although Ōshima later claimed that he could not remem-
ber seeing Himmler in 1939, Himmler wrote a memorandum on
his conversation with Ōshima on January 31st of that year
(see Appendix B). (And we have a photograph of Ōshima and
Himmler, with Hitler, Göring, and Ribbentrop, taken on 28
February 1939 at the Pergamon Museum--see Figure 5.) When
shown Himmler's memorandum during the trial at Tokyo,
Ōshima declared that the greater part of it "contains matters which I did not know about, and it was impossible for
me to talk about them to anybody. . . . In view thereof,
I must deny the authenticity of this document."

Ōshima's denial cannot be accepted, for the gist of
several paragraphs is partially substantiated by other
evidence. Ōshima appears to have been responsible for an
abortive attempt to ship anti-Communist literature to the
Soviet Union in the autumn of 1938 (paragraph 6, Appendix
B). It was an example of the sort of activity implicit in
Ōshima's June 1937 instructions. Ōshima told Himmler in
confidence "that he had bought a piece of real estate" in
a suburb of Berlin (paragraph 5). Ōshima admitted that he
had in fact "negotiated for the purchase" of the property.
Money for its purchase came from his office, and the house
in Falkensee (25 kilometers west from the center of Berlin)
had facilities for printing anti-Communist literature. But
his assistant at the time, Lieutenant Colonel Shigeki Usui,
made the actual business transaction and directed the
intelligence operations.[12] Ōshima also admitted that he
knew of the activities of a Japanese officer stationed in
Afghanistan (paragraph 4), but that he "had no connection
with his affair, directly or indirectly." If Ōshima were
boastful concerning the details of his attempts to have
Stalin assassinated (paragraph 3), the idea, nonetheless,
was far from bizarre from the perspective of both this
Japanese general and the Gestapo chief.[13] Himmler's

account also tends to support the contention that Ōshima was associated with the Abwehr (paragraph 2). When Himmler's memorandum is viewed as only a part of this section on Japanese intelligence activities, it seems reasonably certain that Ōshima was something less than straightforward, perhaps understandably, in his statements before the Russian justice, Major General I. M. Zaryanov, and ten other members of the International Tribunal for the Far East.

Any Japanese military attaché in Berlin during the mid-1930s would have been an important deputy because of the common attitude towards Communism and the Soviet Union held by the German and Japanese governments. He probably would have received some support from various National Socialist officials who were engaged in similar intelligence activities. But Ōshima's rapport was exceptional. Ōshima quickly developed a relationship with Canaris, Keitel, and Himmler, as he had with Ribbentrop in 1935, in which he was regarded as a comrade in the struggle against a foreign enemy of the Third Reich.

The Japanese army's concern with Soviet intelligence formed a convenient basis for cooperation with the German army. Ōshima and the Army General Staff were forceful advocates of a policy aligning their government more closely with Hitler's, and after 1936 they refused to retreat if their intentions for future German-Japanese relations differed from those advocated by the Foreign Ministry. There was to be no reduction of Ōshima's prerogative and influence. Thus, the real authority and potential effectiveness with Hitler's officialdom of the newly appointed Japanese ambassador (27 October 1937) was significantly undermined before he assumed his new post in Berlin.

On Christmas eve 1937 Shigenori Tōgō, a distinguished career diplomat and a scholar of German literature, arrived in Berlin.* Although Ambassador Tōgō objected to Ōshima's military diplomacy and its goal to strengthen relations with Germany beyond the scope of the Anti-Comintern Pact, his objections were ineffectual before circumstances forced him to relinquish the post in Berlin ten months after he arrived. Ambassador Tōgō had no control over Ōshima. Traditional diplomatic channels were circumvented. Rela-

---

*Here I intend only to introduce Tōgō as ambassador; antagonism between Tōgō and Ōshima will be discussed later in the larger context of relations between the German and Japanese governments.

tions between the two increasingly militaristic states were being formed by a standard alien to Tōgō.

Hitler's earlier views expressed in Mein Kampf were not altogether complimentary to the Japanese whose modern development, nevertheless, had a so-called Aryan origin. But after 1933 political expediency encouraged a change in his attitude. Hitler's impression by late 1937 of the intent of Japanese foreign policy as it was related to Germany played no small part in his own strategic planning. His impression was formed gradually while his own power and ambitions grew. The attitudes of Nagai, Mushakōji, and especially of Ōshima, encouraged Hitler. And their views coincided with the spirit of the Anti-Comintern Pact. With the exception of the issue of German aid to China in the summer of 1937, nothing seemed to stand in the way of ever closer German-Japanese relations, and the articulate and influential spokesman in Berlin for the interests of the Japanese Army General Staff continued to reinforce Hitler's impression of Japan's intentions.

Hitler summoned his four military heads and Foreign Minister to an extraordinary meeting on 5 November 1937. He explained "his basic ideas concerning the opportunities for the development of our position in the field of foreign affairs and its requirements." The only other person present was Colonel Friedrich Hossbach, The Führer's adjutant, who recorded the proceedings five days later.[14] Hitler viewed France and Great Britain as Germany's "two hate-inspired antagonists" and noted that the British position in East Asia was being weakened by Japan. Moreover, in his estimate of foreign reaction to Germany's annexation of Czechoslovakia and Austria, Hitler reasoned that

> the degree of surprise and the swiftness of our action were decisive factors for Poland's attitude. Poland--with Russia at her rear--will have little inclination to engage in war against a victorious Germany. Military intervention by Russia must be countered by the swiftness of our operations; however, whether such an intervention was a practical contingency at all was, in view of Japan's attitude, more than doubtful.[15]

Thus, Hitler envisaged a friendly attitude from the Japanese government. Also, if the essence of Ōshima's position were truly representative of the wishes of the Japanese government, Hitler could expect political and economic support and perhaps even limited military assistance.

With the consummation of the Anti-Comintern Pact, Japanese militaristic and totalitarian sentiments found both a new outlet and a new direction in European affairs. Such sentiments were found primarily among pro-Axis factions of middle-ranking officers in the army and right wing radicals in the bureaucracy. These factions formed a nucleus group of renovationists. They grew in strength after 1936 and sought to bolster German-Japanese relations by changing the ideological, "no-aid" pact against the Comintern and the Soviet Union into a military alliance with the Hitler government. Ōshima, an ardent spokesman for the renovationists in German-Japanese relations, was extremely active in the pro-Axis endeavor.

Very little documentation exists concerning the first attempts to strengthen the Anti-Comintern Pact into a closer alignment with Germany, but it is fairly clear that the initiative came from Tokyo, not from Berlin. The first indication of this is seen in a cable sent by the Italian ambassador in Japan, Giacinto Auriti, to Italian Foreign Minister Ciano:

> About two months ago [November 1937] the Japanese General Staff offered to sign a military alliance with Germany, an offer that was refused by the latter because it feared the unstable situation in the Far East and possible initiatives by Japanese extremists that might precipitate events for which Berlin was not yet prepared.16

Doubtless, there were suggestions from within the bureaucracy of the Japanese Army General Staff for strengthening ties with Germany, but the historical record remains unclear until early 1938.

By then Hitler was ready to explore the possibility of concluding a German-Japanese military alliance. The Führer's plans for expansion in Europe were more clearly formulated than previously, and in his anticipated war with France he would, in fact, unlike Kaiser Wilhelm II in 1914, take measures to avoid a two-front war at the outset. Hitler speculated that a military alliance with Japan, perhaps including the option to utilize the Kwantung army in Japan's

puppet state, Manchukuo, would serve to neutralize the
Russians. Furthermore, Japanese naval strength would serve
as a deterrent against British readiness to assist the
French, or, at least, reduce British effectiveness in a
Franco-German conflict.

Such a fundamental decision by Hitler helps to explain
the removal in early 1938 of those not enthusiastic about
the daring nature of Third Reich foreign policy: the re-
placement of Foreign Minister Constantin von Neurath by
Ribbentrop and the forced retirements of War Minister
Werner von Blomberg and Army Commander in Chief Werner von
Fritsch. Afterwards there followed a reorganization that
placed the Führer in direct control of all German armed
forces. In April Major General Eugen Ott, since 1934
Ōshima's counterpart as military attaché in Tokyo, was
appointed ambassador within the embassy. Also Italy, a
member of the anti-Comintern group since November 1937,
received a new German ambassador. Hitler and his new
appointees were ready to embark upon a more adventuresome
foreign policy, including the serious exploration of possibilities for concluding an Axis military alliance.

Germany started by modifying its foreign policy to
gain Japan's good will. In February Hitler prohibited the
sale of German arms to Chiang Kai-shek's Kuomintang forces
and recalled German military advisers in China. In May
Germany extended diplomatic recognition to Manchukuo.

While such large policy changes were unfolding, the
Germans made preliminary soundings with Ōshima about the
possibility of concluding a military alliance. Ribbentrop
broached the subject with his long-time Japanese associate.
Ōshima enthusiastically reported this news of Ribbentrop's
move and, typically Ōshima was instructed to proceed secretly with the new negotiations. He was to report developments only to the Army General Staff. In this way Ōshima,
as would have been expected, became a fervent spokesman in
Germany for strengthening the German-Japanese Anti-Comintern
Pact. Ribbentrop's suggestion encouraged the Japanese Army
General Staff to renew its earlier interest in such a military alliance with the Third Reich.

Earlier, in November 1937, Ōshima proposed to Keitel
an expansion of their agreement for the exchange and gath-
ering of Soviet military intelligence. It is not clear
what Ōshima's proposal entailed, but in the spring Keitel,
then Hitler's hand-picked man to fill the newly created
post of Chief of the Supreme Command of the Wehrmacht, told

Military Diplomacy

Ōshima that Germany was willing to go well beyond his November proposal for furthering their collaboration in
intelligence operations against the Soviet Union.[17]
Keitel's response to Ōshima was probably another sign that
Hitler envisaged a possible role for the Japanese military
in his own strategic plans.

Ōshima attempted to keep his negotiations with Ribbentrop, German Foreign Minister since February, as secret as
possible, and in early 1938 only a few army officers in
Japan were informed of the matter. Ōshima was confident
that Ambassador Togo would be opposed to such a military
engagement. Togo was well known for his opposition to
many of the policies of National Socialist Germany. Once
again, although the Japanese military realized the ambassador and his Foreign Ministry would eventually have to
become involved, General Staff officers hoped that before
that time Ōshima would progress so far into negotiations
with Ribbentrop that the Foreign Ministry would have no
choice but to accept the proposed military alliance. In
this way, the Foreign Ministry would be forced to instruct
Ambassador Togo to accept, if only with reluctance, Ōshima's
preeminence in diplomatic matters with the National Socialists. The situation, as anticipated by the military, would
be not unlike that which Ambassador Mushakōji had been confronted with two years earlier.

The Japanese military scheme did not work as smoothly
as the Army General Staff had hoped. An open clash developed between Ambassador Togo and General Ōshima—it influenced negotiations. The chief of the Military Affairs
section in the War Ministry, Sadaaki Kagesa, confided in
Yoshitarō Yamada, his associate in the European-Asiatic
bureau of the Foreign Ministry, the fact that Ōshima was
negotiating some sort of military alliance with the German
Foreign Minister. Yamada, realizing the serious implica-
tions of the military attaché's activities, asked Vice
Foreign Minister Kensuke Horinouchi about the accuracy of
the report. Horinouchi, in turn, queried Togo in a cable
to Berlin. Togo, who had been director of the European-
Asiatic bureau in the mid-1930s, was familiar with Ōshima's
improprieties in negotiating the Anti-Comintern Pact.
Thus, Horinouchi's cable to Togo probably caused the ambassa-

dor to investigate Ōshima's current activities.

Tōgō and the entire embassy staff learned of Ōshima's activities in April 1938. The third secretary of the embassy, Katsushiro Narita, recorded the fact that Ambassador Tōgō, who "was strongly opposed to the strengthening of the Anti-Comintern Pact, . . . immediately upon learning of the negotiations . . . presented to the [Japanese] Foreign Minister his views to that effect."[18] Narita's account was confirmed in similar postwar testimony by Yosuto Shudo (commercial attaché), Tadashi Sakaya (first secretary), and Major General Yukio Kasahara.[19]

Tōgō and Ōshima clashed bitterly in their views. Tōgō felt that a German-Japanese military alliance would be of no help in Japan's efforts to end her war with China, and that it would eventually involve Japan in a conflict with Hitler's European adversaries. Ōshima obviously did not share the ambassador's feelings of foreboding. Members of the embassy were divided on the question of the alliance. A schism developed in the embassy staff over the issue of military interference in diplomatic matters. The commercial attaché wrote that

> in March or April 1938 the Naval Attaché of the embassy sent a cable to the Navy Ministry strongly urging Ambassador Tōgō's removal on the ground that he was on bad terms with the German Foreign Minister and that his retention in the circumstances of the time, when it was necessary to promote Japanese-German cooperation, was not in the interest of the country. The cable stated also that the matter had been talked over with the Military Attaché. This became known to us when the content of the cable was transmitted from the Foreign Ministry to Ambassador Tōgō. Upon learning of this the members of the staff were indignant, and, feeling that the conspiracy of [the] Army and Navy to take over the Embassy could not be ignored, moved for the defence of the Ambassador and the Embassy.[20]

Nevertheless, Ōshima continued to handle negotiations and Foreign Minister Ribbentrop continued to ignore Ambassador Tōgō. Tōgō admitted later that by May 1938 "the discord between Ribbentrop and me became impossible to conceal."[21]

Ōshima had long been persona grata to Ribbentrop and

his Dienststelle entourage, and, after he became Foreign
Minister, Ribbentrop continued to regard Ōshima as the fore-
most Japanese spokesman in Berlin. Ambassador Togo's conflict with his National Socialist hosts, especially Ribbentrop, no doubt impeded early progress towards negotiating a
military treaty. Other factors, such as the carrying out
of the change in German policy toward China, helped to
delay a Japanese response to Ribbentrop's suggestion in
January 1938 for a German-Japanese military alliance.

    But in June the Army General Staff sent a courier to
Ōshima with a proposal, in reaction to Ribbentrop's earlier
suggestion, calling for a strictly defensive German-Japanese alliance against the Soviet Union.[22] Based on the
general proposal from the Army General Staff, Ōshima drafted
his own proposal for a defensive anti-Soviet alliance, and
he made it a tripartite arrangement. Though the inclusion
of Italy was discussed by General Staff officers, apparently
no specific tripartite proposal was sent to Berlin. In the
event of a Soviet attack on any one of the signatory powers,
Germany, Italy, and Japan were to hold consultations before
taking any action. In July Ribbentrop responded to Ōshima's
draft. The Germans offered a much stronger counterproposal
for a tripartite pact aimed not only at the Soviet Union,
but at Great Britain and France as well:

> 1. In the event that one of the contracting
> parties is faced with diplomatic difficulties
> with a nonsignatory nation, the contracting
> parties will meet promptly to discuss common
> action to be taken.
>
> 2. In the event of a threat to one of the con-
> tracting parties by a nonsignatory nation, each
> party will be obligated to offer all political
> and diplomatic assistance to eliminate the threat.
>
> 3. In the event that one of the contracting
> parties sustains an attack by a nonsignatory
> nation, the other parties are obligated to give
> military assistance.[23]

Ribbentrop asked Ōshima to send the German draft to
Tokyo by courier for the purpose of maintaining secrecy,
since during secret negotiations for the Anti-Comintern
Pact leaks occurred, presumably because too many people
had access to Ōshima's cables. (Ironically, the leaks of
information, as discussed earlier, probably occurred in

the German embassy in Tokyo through the work of Richard
Sorge and his Soviet spy ring.[24]) Major General Kasahara,
in Berlin with "no particular mission" since January 1938,
was dispatched to Tokyo with Ribbentrop's counterproposal.
Kasahara, who had been told informally "that I was to be
appointed military attaché to the Embassy in Germany," he
said after the war, was also a military diplomatist.[25] For
he argued in favor of the German draft in the Japanese
Foreign Ministry and told the newly named Foreign Minister,
Kazushige Ugaki, stories designed to discredit Ambassador
Tōgō. Kasahara was part of a military conspiracy to help
strengthen ties with the Third Reich by having Ambassador
Tōgō, an opponent to pro-Axis schemes he believed threatening to international peace, replaced by Ōshima.

Military influence in shaping relations with Germany
had become so pronounced that Ōshima's supporters were able
to engineer his appointment as Ambassador to Germany. In
early August Ōshima's courier, Major General Kasahara,
explained details of the alliance proposal to army and navy
authorities, and to Foreign Minister Ugaki (his brother-in-
law) he emphasized informally the advantages of the proposed
alliance and the news that the army already accepted the
plan. The navy approved in general of the plan, Kasahara
told Ugaki, but the navy insisted that Japan ought to avoid
an automatic obligation to go to war, as implied in the
third section of the German draft.[26] More significant in
the present context, however, is Kasahara's report to the
Foreign Minister that Tōgō was not on good terms with German
authorities, and they considered him to be uncooperative.[27]
This was part of the campaign to unseat Tōgō, a project that
became a more urgent undertaking for the army before the end
of August.

On August 26, not long before Kasahara left Tokyo for
Berlin, the Five Ministers' Conference approved in principle, but with significant provisos, the proposal that he
had brought from Germany. Most important, however, was the
decision of the Five Ministers' Conference to have the
negotiations "transferred to the formal diplomatic channel
as soon as possible," Ōshima recalled after the war.
Ōshima's military superiors told him, nevertheless, "that
there would be no harm in communicating [news of the positive decision of the Five Ministers' Conference] to the
Germans in the meantime."[28] A shake-up in the embassy was
at hand.

Foreign Minister Ugaki wanted to keep Ambassador Tōgō

at his Berlin post, but Tōgō was eventually forced to concede his position under intense pressure from various quarters. Naval Attaché Hideo Kojima in Berlin warned his Tokyo superiors that highly ranked German diplomatic officials paid no attention to Ambassador Tōgō. Later Kojima reported that during the crisis over the Sudetenland in September all the ambassadors from nations considered friendly to Germany were invited to Munich—Tōgō alone declined the invitation. But accepting a special invitation, Ōshima flew from Berlin to Munich in Foreign Minister Ribbentrop's private airplane to witness Hitler's victory.[29] Obviously, Ribbentrop favored the appointment of Ōshima, and by August he may have communicated that personal preference to the Japanese Foreign Ministry through German Ambassador Ott in Tokyo. Ernst von Weizsäcker, State Secretary of the German Foreign Ministry, although claiming too much influence for his boss, stated flatly that Ribbentrop "managed to have this soldier—who was an enthusiastic admirer of the German military revival—appointed ambassador in Berlin. This was thought to be a good way of consolidating the Berlin-Rome-Tokyo triangle."[30]

Ōshima recalled the sequence of events in a postwar statement. In September 1938, not long after he received news of the Five Ministers' Conference of August 26th, Ōshima said that he received another "telegram from the General Staff asking whether I had any objection to being appointed Ambassador, an idea which it was said was being suggested in Tokyo."[31] But Ōshima knew much earlier that he was likely to be appointed ambassador, for he told Kasahara so in mid-July before sending Ribbentrop's draft to Tokyo.[32] Moreover, Ōshima's successor as military attaché was selected by September 1st when Major General Torashiro Kawabe, as he later recalled, "was suddenly called to appear at the General Staff Office and was informally notified that I was to be appointed military attaché in Berlin."[33] At the same meeting Kawabe was told that Ōshima was being made ambassador, for it was assumed that as ambassador he could be more effective in efforts to convince members of the Foreign Ministry to support the alliance proposal. Thus, the army probably agreed to transfer the negotiations to "the formal diplomatic channel" because it already expected that Ōshima would replace Tōgō as ambassador. The army would continue to maintain control of the negotiations through its own ambassador, Ōshima.[34]

Tōgō's record of opposition to Ōshima's activities and to efforts to strengthen the Anti-Comintern Pact probably

encouraged Foreign Minister Ugaki to seek a solution by
having Ōshima replace Togo. Togo objected vigorously to
the decision to allow Ōshima to communicate officially with
Ribbentrop before he, the ambassador, was to assume responsibility for the negotiations. (There was the practical
matter of Togo being unable to take over the negotiations
until he was fully informed of the substance of earlier
discussions--predictably, Ōshima was uncooperative.) The
first secretary of the embassy recalled Togo's reaction:

> The Ambassador strongly urged the Foreign Minis-
> ter's reconsideration, insisting that . . . it
> was not proper for a military attaché to be
> charged with matters other than military affairs.
> Within a few days after the dispatch of this
> message, Ambassador Togo received a cable from
> the Foreign Minister requesting his agreement to
> his transfer to Moscow.
>   Ambassador Togo refused to assent to the
> Foreign Minister's request, answering him that he
> would rather remain in Berlin to work on German-
> Japanese affairs, which just then required the
> most careful attention. The response was another
> telegram from the Foreign Minister urging the
> Ambassador's assent, which he then gave.[35]

Togo's own account of his reassignment to Moscow is
similar to the story from the first secretary. Togo wrote
after the war:

> I answered with my objections to a tripartite
> pact, pointing out the difficulties in and dis-
> advantages of cooperation with such a dictator
> as Hitler. The result of my sending this cable-
> gram was that I received shortly afterward a
> request from the Foreign Minister to assent to
> my transfer to the post of Ambassador to the
> USSR. My position was then somewhat peculiar.
> The Moscow post had long been my ambition; and I
> was certainly not, in the usual sense, a success
> in Berlin. It was, however, obvious that my
> removal from Berlin would facilitate the realiza-
> tion of the course of action which I had feared
> and fought; and I felt that by remaining there I
> might be able to exert some restraint upon the
> militarists, and might even be able to sabotage
> the military alliance scheme. I, therefore,
> requested the Foreign Minister to leave me in

71

> Berlin for the time being. A second and more
> peremptory request for my assent came the follow-
> ing day, to which I could only submit.[36]

Thus, Tōgō's refusal to tolerate Ōshima's interference in
diplomacy probably weighed heavily in Foreign Minister
Ugaki's decision to yield completely to military demands
and to nominate Ōshima to be Envoy Extraordinary and Ambassador Plenipotentiary to Germany.[37]

But the army was not the only force behind the shake-
up in the embassy at Berlin. A powerful faction of right
wing radicals--renovationists--also favored the appointment
of Ōshima. Toshio Shiratori, the former minister to Sweden
who on one occasion, at least, helped Ōshima in 1936 during
the negotiations for the Anti-Comintern Pact, led the faction
that sought to link Japanese foreign policy to the interests
of the European fascist governments. The Shiratori faction
numbered about fifty young Foreign Ministry officials in
1938; it helped in the appointment of Ōshima.[38] At about
the same time it sent its own leader to Rome as ambassador.
Shiratori and Ōshima, whose assignments to the Italian and
German capitals were certainly not fortuitous, collaborated
and presented a united front to their Foreign Ministry in
efforts to produce a tripartite military pact.

The decision to promote Ōshima and to transfer Tōgō
was probably inevitable in 1938. Ambassador Tōgō, as stated,
had strongly opposed Ōshima's active role in diplomacy, and
had disapproved of his goal. Tōgō's challenge to military
hegemony in diplomacy emitting from the Wilhelmstrasse,
either with the Dienststelle or Foreign Ministry group,
created a predicament with which the Japanese government
was forced to deal.[39] Significantly, however, it was a
situation in which the military was willing to exert whatever pressure necessary to strengthen its point of view.
Japan found herself alienated from Stalin's government and
the governments of the Western democracies; thus, the idea
of developing closer ties with European Axis powers had a
new appeal, one that was universal, no longer confined to
the traditionally pro-German military circles. With increasing military and totalitarian tendencies in Japanese
society, the promotion of General Ōshima to the rank of
ambassador was viewed by many as a plausible, expedient
solution to the Tōgō-Ōshima impasse. Such a solution,
while being convenient, managed to skirt the fundamental
issue; it was also an indication of the considerable
strength that the more militaristic elements of the Japa-

nese government had gained by 1938.

Ōshima's credentials were strengthened considerably after 1934, particularly after early 1938.[40] Thus, they made his appointment as ambassador appear more appropriate. His rate of military promotion, from second lieutenant to major general in some 29 years, was not extraordinary. Thirteen years in time of peace, a minimum, were required for a Japanese army officer to rise to the rank of major general, but that rate of promotion would have occurred only under ideal career conditions, such as war. While at his post in Berlin, however, Ōshima was promoted to the next higher rank for the first time in his career immediately upon serving the minimum time in grade.[41] Holding the rank of major general for three years, Ōshima was promoted to lieutenant general in March 1938, and soon thereafter he was also invested with the Fourth Court Rank, Junior Grade and decorated with the Imperial Order of the Sacred Treasure, Second Class.

Court ranks were awarded mostly to public servants for meritorious service, and they served to determine precedence. Ōshima's court ranks, ranging from next to the lowest of 16 grades of eight ranks to the sixth from the highest, and spaced rather evenly over a period of some 37 years, suggest steady rather than spectacular recognition. Yet Ōshima became one of a more select group with his higher court rank of April 1938.[42] Although his two orders of decorations (the Rising Sun and the Sacred Treasure) were the most widely held types, few held decorations in the higher categories. The second class decorations in each order were very distinctive awards appropriate for his military and diplomatic ranks of 1938.

The decoration of the Imperial Order of the Rising Sun, Second Class, made less than a month after Ōshima became ambassador, was in recognition of meritorious services rendered during negotiations leading to the Anti-Comintern Pact. The group that arranged the award was the same group that wielded influence sufficient to have Togo transferred and Ōshima appointed in his place. Ōshima's authority in Berlin was disproportionate in importance to his rank and office; by the summer of 1938, when Togo challenged his role in diplomacy, Ōshima's more advanced and impressive military, court, and decorative credentials facilitated the army's arguments for Ōshima's appointment as ambassador.

There was also a certain awareness among members of

the Five Ministers' Conference that the selection of mission chiefs, especially for key foreign posts, ought to be made with a higher purpose in mind: the ambassador ought to be certainly compatible with his host government. Cabinet members in Tokyo felt that the government could not afford at that crucial point in international relations the situation that prevailed during Tōgō's tenure. Beyond that point, there was little consensus among the ministers, and such an equivocal state of affairs provided the most determined, pro-Axis factions in the Japanese government with an excellent opportunity to be decisive. The candidacy of Ōshima was singularly compelling; beyond the fact of his special rapport with German officials, he knew the National Socialist government better than any other Japanese. As Ōshima candidly disclosed later, "I was selected ambassador to Germany in October 1938 because I had many acquaintances among German military officers, to say nothing of Hitler, Göring, and Ribbentrop."[43]

The integrity of Japanese foreign policy toward most of continental Europe was thoroughly eroded by the work of the Shiratori faction in the Foreign Ministry and of Ōshima in Berlin and his military supporters. The cabal of Ōshima's appointment in 1938 is evidence par excellence, whereas the earlier design for the anti-Comintern agreement was more broadly conceived. By arranging to have Ōshima appointed ambassador the army kept its hand on the reins while also adhering to the form of the cabinet decision: on the Japanese side negotiations with the German Foreign Ministry were to be handled by the Japanese Foreign Ministry, not by the Army General Staff and its military attaché in Berlin. The problem remained, however, and the military point of view continued to sway Japan's relations with Germany on the eve of the Second World War.

Figure 2. Ōshima is seen above entering the Berghof,
Hitler's house on the Obersalzberg in Bavaria, to present
his credentials as Japan's newly appointed Ambassador to
Germany, 22 November 1938. Among Ōshima's escorts (right
to left) are Wilhelm Brückner (Hitler's personal aide),
Otto Meissner (State Minister and Chief of the Presidential
Chancellery, 1937-1945), and two unknown German officers
nearest Ōshima. A sentry presents arms on the left of the
picture.   (National Archives)

IV: The Expansion and Dominance of Military Diplomacy

1. Ōhata, "The Anti-Comintern Pact," pp. 39-46.

2. The Italians did not participate in the Secret Additional Agreement to the Agreement Against the Communist International, nor were they invited. Indeed, the Italian government was not officially informed of the secret supplementary agreement. See Weinberg, "Die geheimen Abkommen
zum Antikominternpakt," p. 196, and Miyake, Nichi-Doku-I
sangoku domei, p. 116. Foreign Minister Arita said at a
Privy Council meeting on 22 February 1939 that he understood
"that Italy did not join the secret pact [annexed to the
Agreement Against the Communist International] because she
did not know of its existence" (IMTFE, Exhibit 491).

3. Vagts, The Military Attaché, p. 181. It might be a
common characteristic of any career military officer that
he knows precisely the rank of another officer with whom he
is associated. Throughout the IMTFE Ōshima was careful in
referring to officers by their correct rank at the time for
which he was recalling circumstances. For example, in June
1937 Ōshima received instructions to approach the Germans
with the idea of increasing the exchange of information
about the Soviet Union. When asked with whom he spoke,
Ōshima replied, "Keitel, at that time Lieutenant General."
See Exhibits 488 and 3508; also Proceedings, p. 6,023.
When writing of the same instructions in his affidavit, it
is curious that Ōshima referred to Canaris as "Navy Captain
(later Admiral)." Canaris was promoted to the rank of Rear
Admiral (Konteradmiral) on 1 May 1935 shortly after he became head of the Abwehr. See Rangliste der Deutschen
Kriegsmarine: Nach dem Stande vom 1. November 1935 (Berlin:
E. S. Mittler und Sohn, 1935), p. 69.
    In itself this small observation does not establish a
close relationship between Ōshima and Canaris in late 1934
or early 1935. But when viewed in a larger framework, it
seems to be one of several indications that the two officers
were associated early in their common work. For example, in
his small and austere private office (his "Fuchsbau") at
Abwehr headquarters in Berlin, Canaris worked before a map
of the world on one wall, and on the other walls there were
a few photographs of his predecessors, a picture of a Spanish caudillo with a long dedication to the admiral and a
Japanese painting of a demon's mask. The painting was a
gift from Ōshima. See Karl Heinz Abshagen, Canaris:
Patriot und Weltbürger (Stuttgart: Union Deutsche

IV: The Expansion and Dominance of Military Diplomacy

Verlagsgesellschaft, 1950), p. 113. Ōshima referred to his earlier work with Canaris when in April 1943 he proposed to Hitler that psychological warfare be included in Germany's struggle with the Soviet Union: "The Russian people on the whole seem to be imbued with the idea that the fight against Germany is a war of peoples. Therefore, although the outcome of the war will naturally be decided by force of arms, the formulation of plans for alienating elements within Russia would have no little effect upon the course of the struggle. When I was Military Attaché in Berlin, I carried on joint investigations with Admiral Canaris concerning measures to be taken inside Russia. We arrived at the conclusion that, in view of the diversity of nationalies within the Soviet, the emancipation of these peoples should be made our principal slogan. Wouldn't it be possible for Germany to consider political strategy toward Russia from that viewpoint?" Hitler rejected Ōshima's proposal on the spot: "Your idea sounds plausible enough. However, the fact is that the most effective way to weaken morale is by military offensive on the battle front. There is danger that political schemes would have directly opposite results" ("Magic," SRS 943, 22 April 1943, RG 457). Ōshima persisted to emphasize the advantages of psychological warfare during a four-hour conversation with Ribbentrop on 19 May 1943:

> Oshima: 'Of course these are only my personal views, but some time ago I told Chancellor Hitler himself that he ought to consider some political activity with respect to Russia. You know that since the Russo-German war broke out the Soviet Union has come more completely than ever under Stalin's exclusive control. The utter abandon with which the Slavic race fights for its fatherland--the way that all the Russian people stand shoulder to shoulder--is absolutely amazing. To say that after Germany's drive this year some of the people will turn against Stalin does not make sense, because they are fighting for Stalin and they will continue to fight on for Stalin, and I doubt if you can defeat them.
>
> 'My Military Attachés and I have studied this matter together from every angle and have concluded that you cannot quell a people by force of arms alone. If fighting there must be, then of course it must be, but it is necessary to guarantee independence to the

IV: The Expansion and Dominance of Military Diplomacy

>various nations in our sphere of conflict. . . .   I
>think you should lose no time in giving guaranties of
>independence to the Ukraine and to the three Baltic
>nations. This would cause confusion within the Soviet
>and bring about some results.
>
>'Now take Manchuria. Ever since the incident
>there we have found it more practicable to supplement
>military actions with the milk of human kindness in
>order to win the hearts of the people, and I must say
>we are getting good results. I know, of course, that
>there may be some differences in education and temper-
>ament between the Asiatic and the European people, but
>I think that what I say still holds and I want you to
>please consider it thoroughly.'
>
>Ribbentrop: 'Oh, I understand all that, but both the
>Ukraine and the Caucasus are Bolshevistic through and
>through, and it is impossible to set up a government
>we could deal with there.'
>
>Oshima: 'Well, in the transitory period, why don't
>you put some robot in charge? Then you could gradually
>bring those areas in line with your desires. I believe
>that you should think that over' ("Magic," SRS 988, 6
>June 1943, RG 457).

4. Paul Leverkuehn, Der geheime Nachrichtendienst der
deutschen Wehrmacht im Kriege (3rd ed.; Frankfurt am Main:
Verlag für Wehrwesen Bernard und Graefe, 1960), pp. 9-11.

5. IMTFE, Exhibit 3508.

6. Wilhelm Keitel, Generalfeldmarschall Keitel: Verbrecher
oder Offizier? ed. Walter Görlitz (Göttingen:
Musterschmidt-Verlag, 1961), p. 99.

7. IMTFE, Exhibit 3508.

8. Ibid., Exhibit 3496.

9. Ibid., Exhibit 488, and Proceedings, p. 6,023.

10. DGFP, D, 1, No. 603, p. 887. The day after Ōshima
reported to Ribbentrop, the German Foreign Minister received

IV: The Expansion and Dominance of Military Diplomacy

similar information from the German ambassador in Moscow. See ibid., No. 628, pp. 924-26.

11. IMTFE, Proceedings, pp. 33,771, 33,797.

12. Ibid., Exhibits 488, 3493, and Proceedings, pp. 6,024, 34,331.

13. Himmler apparently sent several captured Soviet soldiers on similar missions after June 1941. See Laslo Havas, Hitler's Plot to Kill the Big Three, trans. Kathleen Szasz (New York: Cowles Book, 1967).

14. DGFP, D, 1, No. 19, pp. 29-39. Present were Hitler, Field Marshal Werner von Blomberg (Minister of War), Colonel General Werner von Fritsch (Commander in Chief of the Army), Admiral Erich Raeder (Commander in Chief of the Navy), Colonel General Hermann Göring (Commander in Chief of the Air Force), Constantin von Neurath (Foreign Minister), and Colonel Hossbach. See also Friedrich Hossbach, Zwischen Wehrmacht und Hitler, 1934-1938 (Wolfenbüttel and Hannover: Wolfenbütteler Verlagsanstalt, 1949), pp. 207-20.

15. DGFP, D, 1, No. 19, p. 36. Emphasis added.

16. Auriti to Ciano, 21 January 1938, as cited in, Mario Toscano, The Origins of the Pact of Steel, 2nd ed. rev. (Baltimore: Johns Hopkins Press, 1967), p. 7. See also Miyake, Nichi-Doku-I sangoku domei, pp. 143-48.

17. Ōhata, "The Anti-Comintern Pact," p. 50.

18. IMTFE, Exhibit 3614.

19. Ibid., Exhibits 3619, 3620, and 3618. Major General Kasahara was dispatched to Germany in January 1938 as an officer attached to the Army General Staff. He seems to have had no specific mission at the time, although technically he was one of the assistant attachés at the embassy. He stayed in Berlin to study the German language and the political situation before his possible appointment as military attaché.

IV: The Expansion and Dominance of Military Diplomacy

20. Ibid., Exhibit 3619.

21. Ibid., Proceedings, p. 35,656.

22. Ōhata, "The Anti-Comintern Pact," p. 50.

23. Gendaishi shiryō (Documents on contemporary history),
vol. 10, Nit-Chū sensō III (The Sino-Japanese war, III)
(Tokyo: Nisuzu Shobō, 1966), p. 173. Cited also in, Ōhata,
"The Anti-Comintern Pact," p. 51.

24. More recently the Soviet government has authorized the
publication of evidence of some of Sorge's activity about
this time--see Doc. No. 12, Telegram from a Soviet Military
Officer in Japan to the General Staff of the Red Army, 3
October 1938, in which Ramzai, Richard Sorge's code name,
wrote that "I have learned from the Military Attaché [at
the German Embassy in Tokyo] that after the Sudeten question
has been settled the next problem will be the Polish
[question]" V. M. Falin, et al., ed., Soviet Peace Efforts
on the Eve of World War II (September 1938--August 1939):
Documents and Records, 2 pts. (Moscow: Novosti Press,
1973), 1: 51. In ibid., 2: 279, note 8, however, Sorge's
work is made more clear still: "With reference to the
possibility of Japan taking part in a war against the Soviet
Union, R. Sorge reported in his telegram of September 14,
1938 that Japanese involvement in a possible European war
would depend on the extent to which that war was directed
against the USSR. He also noted the mounting resolve of
the Japanese "'to begin war against the USSR whenever the
USSR should be involved in a European war.'"

25. IMTFE, Exhibit 3618.

26. Ōhata, "The Anti-Comintern Pact," p. 59.

27. IMTFE, Exhibit 3618.

28. Ibid., Exhibit 3508; see also Exhibit 3493.

29. Ibid., Exhibit 3614-A; see also Proceedings, pp. 35,391-
92, 35,401-2. Ōshima confirmed his use of Ribbentrop's
private airplane in a letter to the author on 7 May 1971.

IV: The Expansion and Dominance of Military Diplomacy

30.   Ernst von Weizsäcker, Memoirs of Ernst von Weizsäcker, trans. John Andrews (Chicago: Henry Regnery, 1951), p. 201.

31.   IMTFE, Exhibit 3508. Ōshima's postwar affirmation does not reveal the exact date of the army's September telegram sounding him out about the ambassadorship in Berlin. However, at the end of August, Councilor Uzuhiko Usami recalled later, Tōgō was told by the Foreign Ministry that "arrangements should be made for official negotiations through diplomatic channels . . . ; the army was notifying Military Attaché Oshima to that effect" (ibid., Proceedings, p. 33,754). We know (Exhibit 3646) that Tōgō was appointed Ambassador to the Soviet Union on October 15th and (Exhibit 3523) that the Foreign Minister asked the Prime Minister "to obtain the Emperor's approval" for the appointment of Ōshima "to the post of Japanese Ambassador to Germany," a matter "already arranged with Your Excellency informally." This was before September 16th. Thus, it is likely that the army compelled Foreign Minister Ugaki to agree to Ōshima's appointment to ambassador in Berlin before Tōgō was asked to agree to reassignment to Moscow. (A good account of Ugaki's diplomacy and his resignation at the end of September is in David J. Lu, From the Marco Polo Bridge to Pearl Harbor: Japan's Entry into World War II [Washington, D.C.: Public Affairs Press, 1961], pp. 36-40. Still very good is John M. Maki's older work, Japanese Militarism: Its Cause and Cure [New York: Alfred A. Knopf, 1945], pp. 219-20. See "Magic," SRS 1622, 30 March 1945, RG 457 for indications of the reemergence of Ugaki in the affairs of state. He was known as a political moderate.) War Minister Itagaki broached the matter of Ōshima's appointment to Ugaki as early as July. See The Saionji-Harada Memoirs, pp. 2,154, 2,205, and 2,213, covering diary entries from late June to 7 August 1938. There is also the suggestion, though only by inference, that in mid-July Ōshima believed he was going to be named Ambassador to Germany, for he "dispatched Major-General Kasahara Yukio to Japan with the German plan, on the assumption that Kasahara would be made the new military attaché in Germany" (Ōhata, "The Anti-Comintern Pact," p. 51).

32.   IMTFE, Proceedings, p. 35,435.

IV: The Expansion and Dominance of Military Diplomacy

33. Ibid., pp. 33,773-74. Though Major General Kasahara returned to Berlin briefly in late 1938, he went back to Tokyo where he became chief of the European section in the Army General Staff.

34. Ōhata, "The Anti-Comintern Pact," p. 70.

35. IMTFE, Exhibit 3620.

36. Ibid., Exhibit 3646. Emphasis added.

37. Ibid., Exhibits 3523 and 3523-A-C. These letters concern the proceedings of the Emperor's appointment of Ōshima as ambassador. In early October Prince Konoye held the Prime Minister and Foreign Minister portfolios concurrently. Togo arrived in Moscow as the newly appointed ambassador on October 29th.

38. Ōhata, "The Anti-Comintern Pact," p. 70. Ambassador Grew recorded in his diary (3 December 1936) "that Shiratori, Japanese Minister to Sweden, who is very close to the Japanese military, may also have had a hand in the affair" resulting in the Anti-Comintern Pact. See Grew, Ten Years in Japan, p. 191. There is a good discussion about the Shiratori faction in Usui Katsumi, "The Role of the Foreign Ministry," in Pearl Harbor as History: Japanese-American Relations, 1931-1941, ed. Dorothy Borg and Shumpei Okamoto with the assistance of Dale K. A. Finlayson (New York: Columbia University Press, 1973), especially pp. 140-44. "Magic" produced an interesting and sophisticated assessment of Shiratori later in the War. After reporting that "last June [1944] the Tokyo radio announced that a 'Committee for the Study of a Postwar International System' had been established under the leadership of Toshio Shiratori," a footnote read: "Shiratori, who served as Ambassador to Italy in 1938-1940, has consistently espoused Japanese imperialism and denounced liberalism and political parties. He has been credited with having sponsored the Japanese end of the Anti-Comintern Pact of 1936 and with having worked with German Ambassador Ott in concluding the Tripartite Alliance. When Shiratori was associated with the Foreign Office in 1932, Ambassador Grew observed that he 'seems to act independently of his superiors; . . . he is apparently supported by the military, with whom he seems to be in entire sympathy'" ("Magic," SRS 1442, 1 October 1944, RG 457).

IV: The Expansion and Dominance of Military Diplomacy

39. The expression "the Wilhelmstrasse" has traditionally been used in works on German diplomacy and foreign affairs to refer to the Foreign Ministry. Here, however, clarification is needed, for Togo's tenure as ambassador in Berlin covered a period during which Ribbentrop took over direction of the Foreign Ministry. Moreover, the Dienststelle was in a building that faced the Foreign Ministry across the Wilhelmstrasse.

40. See Appendix C for the statistics of Ōshima's career and credentials.

41. Many factors were involved when the record of any major general was reviewed for purposes of possible promotion to lieutenant general; the three-year time in grade regulation was not consistently followed. For example, Major General Tomoyuki Yamashita was promoted in less than two years. I have investigated the promotions of 32 major generals in the decade. The average time each spent in the rank of major general before being promoted to lieutenant general was exactly the same as in Ōshima's case—three years.

42. There were 304,062 holders of court rank at the end of 1938. There were 5,530 persons of the rank with which Ōshima was invested in April; there were 3,693 persons with ranks higher than Ōshima's and 294,838 with lower ranks. See The Japan Year Book, 1940-41 (Tokyo: Foreign Affairs Association of Japan, 1940), p. 10.

43. Ōshima to author, 21 November 1966.

V

THE WARRIOR-DIPLOMAT

In spite of the increasingly militaristic posture of
the Third Reich and Japan late in 1938, relations between
the two governments started to cool after Ōshima became
ambassador. The intransigence of the Japanese government,
as Ōshima interpreted it, was shockingly apparent to him
and became strongly suspected by the German and Italian
governments. He sternly disapproved of the failure of the
three governments to form a solid military alliance. The
great lengths to which Ōshima went in attempts to change
the trend of deteriorating relations reveal peculiar char-
acteristics of this warrior-diplomat.

Although Ōshima's attitude and previous work in the
Third Reich facilitated his appointment as ambassador, it
is curious to note that the appointment was a source of
discord within his own family. Ōshima's father admired
much in the Second Reich of Wilhelm II; nevertheless, he
disapproved of his son's infatuation with National Socialist Germany. He was full of mistrust about the sort of
ambassador his son would make. The elder Ōshima's suspi-
cions in 1938 were well-founded, and the ambassador's behavior in Berlin until Hitler invaded Poland was to become
the object of major concern in the highest echelon of Japanese national authority.[1]

* * *

National Socialist officials warmly welcomed Ōshima as
the official diplomatic representative of the Japanese government. In November 1938 Ōshima and four other newly
appointed representatives from Belgium, Albania, Manchukuo,
and the Dominican Republic were taken by special train to
present their credentials to Hitler in his Berghof retreat
near Berchtesgaden (see Figure 2). Ōshima, the first of
the representatives to be received by Hitler, expressed
delight about being able to continue his work in Germany at
a time characterized "by the formation of ever closer con-

85

nections between Germany and Japan and by the growing sympathy and understanding that Japan finds in the German
people."[2] Hitler praised the spirit of the Japanese people,
who had made "such a remarkable advancement in the last
decades," and he asserted that common action against Communism was a further indication of the "spiritual kinship"
of the German and Japanese people.[3] Hitler cleverly quoted
an old Japanese proverb which stressed the importance of
wary watchfulness after success: "katte kabuto no o wo
shimeyo"[4] (After winning, keep the string tight on your
helmet).[4] Ōshima, who was "much impressed by the Führer's
knowledge and insight," congratulated him on the annexation
of Austria and the Sudetenland.[5]

The tenor of their conversation was much more felici-
tous than Hitler could have expected it to be with former
Ambassador Togo. The Führer knew Ōshima and approved of
his outlook and work during recent years. He had good
reason to believe that in Ōshima, he had a Japanese ambassador who was favorably predisposed to the policies of the
Third Reich. Moreover, he was one upon whom he could rely
to represent sympathetically German views before the Japanese government.[6] For in 1938, as Ōshima explained later,
he considered it his "primary task to bring the proposed
treaty between Japan, Germany and Italy to fruition."[7] But
Hitler misinterpreted the Konoye Cabinet's promotion of
Ōshima to ambassador as an indication that the entire Japanese government was approaching an attitude toward the
Third Reich which had been held by Ōshima for years.

Hitler believed that success in fulfilling new foreign
policy objectives after he removed Austria and Czechoslovakia
from his flank depended in part upon the Soviet attitude.
A military alliance with Japan could conceivably nullify
any Soviet interference with his aims of gaining continental domination and Lebensraum in the East. If there were
the likelihood of a Japanese attack from Manchukuo, the
Soviet government would be less likely to take the military
initiative in checking National Socialist expansion in
eastern Europe.[8] Hitler was obviously selective in what he
chose to believe about Japan and her capabilities and intentions.[9] But many of his misapprehensions and miscalcula-
tions stemmed from Ōshima.

In matters of foreign affairs Ōshima's ideas, ambitions,
and perspectives since 1934 grew increasingly like those of
Hitler's government. In the second half of the decade there
developed gradually a divergence of views between Ōshima

and several members of Japanese cabinets. But by no means
was the difference over German-Japanese relations strongly
and consistently marked during his tenure as military
attaché. Those years were relatively placid ones prior to
the crisis over Czechoslovakia._ The official commitments,
for which on the Japanese side Ōshima was largely responsible, involved increasingly cordial diplomatic relations, military
understandings and intelligence collaboration, and the Anti-
Comintern Pact. In late 1938, however, the decisiveness
and speed with which Hitler seemed to be moving towards a
European war caused members of the Five Ministers' Conferences to reflect more soberly than ever upon the future
course of German-Japanese relations.

Ōshima's attitude toward the Third Reich assisted
Hitler, in light of recent developments in the relations
between the two powers, to view with optimism the possibility
of transforming the Anti-Comintern Pact into a military
alliance. But Hitler was to discover that Ōshima as ambas-
sador-official representative was less effective in shaping
German-Japanese relations than he was as attaché-intriguer.

* * *

Negotiations for an alliance progressed steadily, if
slowly, until about the time Ōshima was promoted. During
the summer, as we have seen, Ōshima and Ribbentrop affably
conferred on points upon which the military attaché could
competently state the Japanese military viewpoint. In
October and November, however, when further negotiations
obviously entailed more than the army's point of view,
Ambassador Ōshima started to represent the Foreign Ministry's position in a way designed to manipulate the policy
of his own government and, thereby, bring about the conclusion of the tripartite pact.

The Five Ministers' Conference in late August approved
in principle the German draft taken to Tokyo by Ōshima's
courier, Major General Kasahara. But the provisos to
Tokyo's approval were probably not emphasized, or included
at all, in the army's report to then Military Attaché
Ōshima; in any event, Ōshima operated on the assumption
that the Soviet Union was the main target of the proposed
tripartite pact and other nations could be considered secondary targets.[10] However, the new Foreign Minister who
assumed office on October 29th, Hachiro Arita, clarified

87

the matter with cabinet members--former Foreign Minister
Ugaki, Prime Minister Fumimaro Konoye, Navy Minister
Mitsumasa Yonai, and Finance Minister Seihin Ikeda: the
decision of the Five Ministers' Conference on August 26th
was to make no country other than the Soviet Union the
treaty's target.[11]

Alliance negotiations were temporarily suspended during
the diplomatic reshuffle, but in early November Ribbentrop
and Friedrich Gaus, chief of the Treaty Bureau in the German
Foreign Ministry, gave Ōshima a revised tripartite draft
(October 27th) to transmit to Japan's Foreign Minister.[12]
Mussolini had already agreed in principle to the draft when
Ribbentrop was recently in Rome, but, for reason of domestic
politics, he asked Ribbentrop to postpone the official conclusion of the treaty until the spring of 1939.[13]

But for the Japanese government the main stumbling
block in the most recent German draft remained the same--
the identity of the powers against whom it was directed.
The Konoye Cabinet appeared to stand firm on the issue at
the first Five Ministers' Conference after Arita became
Foreign Minister. All five ministers agreed on November
11th that Great Britain and France would become targets of
the alliance only if they joined the Soviet Union in an
attack on any of the tripartite powers or if France, for
example, established a Communist government.[14]

Both Ambassador Ōshima and Foreign Minister Arita
realized that there was a fundamental difference between
their attitudes about strengthening the Anti-Comintern Pact.
Ōshima's essential responsibility was to obey instructions
from the Foreign Ministry, though occasionally they were
ambiguous and lent themselves to different interpretations.
Nevertheless, Ōshima disobeyed instructions from his
civilian chief; more often he deliberately evaded their
intent by interpreting them in a manner that would not
alter the direction of the policies that he and Ribbentrop
had so carefully charted during the preceding four years.

Soon Arita sent Ōshima the decision of the Five Ministers' Conference of November 11th. His reaction was predictable. Ōshima protested vigorously in a telegram to the
Foreign Minister, charging that not to name Britain and
France as secondary targets contradicted the policy decided
upon at the Five Ministers' Conference of August 26th.
War Minister Itagaki defended Ōshima in another Five Ministers' Conference in early December when he claimed that
the effect of the decision of November 11th was really the

same as the decision of August 26th--Great Britain and
France were actually secondary targets whether or not they
joined the Soviet Union.

Itagaki was probably being driven to a more extreme
position by younger military radicals in the Army General
Staff and his own ministry. Kumao Harada, secretary to
elder statesman Prince Kimmochi Saionji, observed what he
called a "suspicious thing" in December: "the lower echelons of the Army and the Navy are taking it as though the
same joint military action is to be taken against England
and France as with the Soviet. . . . Since they have been
in contact with Ambassador Oshima in Germany, Oshima relayed
this to Ribbentrop."[15] Itagaki was not unfamiliar with the
imminence power lower echelons could focus on an objective,
for as a colonel in the Kwantung army in 1931 he was
chiefly responsible for carrying out the Manchurian incident. At that time the War Minister in Tokyo, as Robert
Butow was observed, "personally aided the Kwantung army by
acting as a buffer between it and the cabinet. He thereby
minimized the danger that the cabinet would implement decisions which might be detrimental to the intentions of the
Kwantung army."[16] As War Minister eight years later, Itagaki
knew full well what was expected of him. Also, Major General Kasahara, formerly Oshima's courier, returned to Tokyo
in December with news that Oshima had already proposed to
Ribbentrop a tripartite alliance that named Great Britain
and France as well as the Soviet Union as targets. This
was done, it was claimed, as a result of Oshima's interpretation of Itagaki's report of the decision reached by the
Five Ministers' Conference in late August.[17]

Oshima and his army supporters created a dilemma late
in 1938 from which the Konoye Cabinet seemed unable to
escape. Even though the four most powerful ministers other
than War Minister Itagaki agreed that the proposed military
pact was strictly anti-Communist, and it always had been,
they could not convince the army; nor would Ambassador
Oshima correct his explanation made to Ribbentrop. The
Konoye Cabinet became stalemated, afraid that the cabinet
would fall and unable to decide on new instructions to
Oshima. In early January 1939 the entire cabinet resigned.

While further instructions to Oshima were held up by
the Konoye Cabinet, Ribbentrop asked Oshima to go to Rome
to encourage Mussolini to join before March. The Italian
Foreign Minister recorded the meeting in his diary on
December 15th:

> I accompanied General Oshima, Japanese Ambassador
> in Berlin, to the Duce. His visit has the recom-
> mendation of Ribbentrop, as Oshima, like him, is
> zealous for the transformation of the Anti-Comin-
> tern Pact into a Pact of Triple Alliance. . . .
> When he began to speak, I realized why Ribbentrop
> is so fond of him. They are the same type: en-
> thusiasts who see things in simple terms—I am
> tempted to say wishful thinkers. He attacked
> Russia and said that Japan intends to dismember
> her into so many small states that all thought of
> revenge will be vain and ridiculous. He also said
> that Japan wants to eliminate British interests
> entirely from China and from the Pacific in gen-
> eral. He shed a lurid light on the position of
> the English in India.[18]

Shiratori, who had helped to arrange Ōshima's appointment
as ambassador in Berlin, arrived in Rome at the end of
December as the new Ambassador to Italy. Ciano noted on
the 31th that "the new Japanese Ambassador . . . is pretty
outspoken and energetic. He talked about the Tripartite
Pact, and immediately revealed himself as a partisan of the
strengthening of the system.[19] Shiratori and Ōshima would
meet more than once before Germany invaded Poland eight
months later. They frequently pooled their resources in
efforts to convince their government to accept Hitler's
version of the proposed tripartite pact.

The new Japanese government was headed by Kiichirō
Hiranuma. It was formed on 5 January 1939. Arita accepted
the Foreign Minister portfolio because Hiranuma assured him
that he, the Prime Minister, was "opposed to the strengthening of the Axis anti-Comintern Pact to the extent of
waging war against England and France. Should the Army
coerce us (into carrying out the foregoing), I shall resign
together with you."[20] Other ministers carried over from
the Konoye Cabinet included Itagaki as War Minister and
Yonai as Navy Minister. The fifth member of future Five
Ministers' Conferences was the new Finance Minister, Sōtarō
Ishiwata.

Arita, who was Foreign Minister when Ōshima negotiated
the Anti-Comintern Pact in 1936, was keenly aware of the
pattern of military diplomacy, especially as it applied to
the Third Reich. But he anticipated trouble from Shiratori
in Rome as well as from Ōshima in Berlin. He was also aware
of the source of some of the power Ōshima and Shiratori

enjoyed--the middle levels of the Army General Staff and
the War Ministry. Therefore, he held several discussions
with various military section chiefs; they apparently convinced him that some compromise was essential in order to
hold together the Japanese government and to encourage long-
standing friendship between Japan and her anti-Comintern
allies in Europe. At the Five Ministers' Conference of
January 19th Arita received approval of his proposal for
adding two secret items of understanding to the agreement:
1) Japan would restrict her military aid obligation to
occasions when the Soviet Union alone or in concert with
other countries launched an unprovoked attack on one or
more of the contracting parties, and 2) Japan wanted European Axis agreement that all contracting parties would explain to the outside world that the treaty was merely an
extension of the 1936 Anti-Comintern Pact. Japan did not
want to arouse unnecessarily such countries as Great Britain,
France, and the United States. Arita felt that Ōshima would
disapprove of these absolutely essential secret items of
understanding. He expected Ōshima to attempt to undermine
their import by interpreting them from the most provocative
pro-Axis point of view. Therefore, as a safeguard against
further compromise, Arita decided to instruct Ōshima not by
telegram but by sending a special mission to Berlin. Minister Nobufumi Ito of the Foreign Ministry headed the mission which included Colonel Eiichi Tatsumi of the Army General Staff and Rear Admiral Katsuo Abe.[21] Arita assumed
that by including military representatives the Ito mission's
joint statement of the government's position would be persuasive to the former military attaché.[22] He hoped that
this apparent unanimity would eliminate the opportunity
often used by Ōshima to evade cabled instructions origi-
nating in the Foreign Ministry alone; he also expected this
direct approach to serve as a check on Ōshima's future
negotiations. On January 26th the mission received a draft
text of the treaty and detailed instructions dated and
approved by the Five Ministers' Conference on the preceding
day. The instructions emphasized flatly that there could
be no modification made to the restrictions Japan placed on
her own military aid obligations.

Arita explained in a cable to Ōshima that the Hiranuma
Cabinet agreed in principle to the text of the most recent
German proposal, but it desired certain modifications.
Therefore, in the interest of secrecy it would be impossible
to communicate by cable the complex details of the changes
(Arita's pretext). He told Ōshima that it was necessary to
send the Ito mission with instructions and the full draft

text of the defensive agreement the Japanese government
called a Treaty of Consultation and Mutual Assistance.[23]
Ōshima was annoyed and frustrated, for the Ito mission was
traveling by sea and was not scheduled to arrive until the
end of February.

Meanwhile, especially during the first month of the
Hiranuma Cabinet, the prospects for the treaty changed
drastically in Europe. The Japanese ambassadors at Berlin
and Rome and the governments of Germany and Italy were on
one side favoring the immediate conclusion of a comprehensive tripartite military pact; the Japanese government
favored a carefully negotiated pact limited in scope.
Ōshima was in an awkward and embarrassing position. The
limitations of his ability to sway the Japanese government's attitude started to become clear to the Germans and
Italians in early 1939.

On December 23rd Mussolini told Ciano of his intention
to adhere to the proposed tripartite pact. By New Year's
eve he decided definitely to sign it as quickly as Ribbentrop's proposal of October 27th could be readied. In a
brief telephone conversation informing Ribbentrop of the
Duce's decision, Ciano was assured by the German Foreign
Minister "that by the end of the month everything can be
ready, even on the Japanese side."[24] Ciano wrote Ribbentrop
on January 2nd that "the Duce . . . suggests the last 10
days of January as the period for signing. He is leaving
it to you to decide the place where the solemn ceremony
shall be held and to organize the appropriate procedure and
also, as before, to make all arrangements with General
Oshima."[25] Mussolini decided to sign the pact much more
quickly than Ōshima had anticipated.

Ribbentrop and Hitler were "extremely glad that the
Duce has now decided to sign the pact in the near future,"
the German Foreign Minister wrote on January 9th in his
reply to Ciano.[26] On the assumption "that agreement on the
final version will quickly be reached between us as well as
with Ambassador Oshima . . . ," Ribbentrop continued, "I
would like to propose to you that we choose January 28 for
signing the pact" in Berlin.[27] But agreement with Ōshima
was not the real issue--it was his government that caused
concern among the pact's advocates. The proposed date for
signing was distressingly near. Ōshima knew that the new
Hiranuma Cabinet was not prepared to accept the present
version of the pact and that further negotiations would
require more time.

Under much pressure, a disconcerted Ōshima attempted
to explain his awkward position to the Germans and Italians.
The State Secretary of the German Foreign Ministry, Ernst
von Weizsäcker, noted in a secret memorandum that

> when the Japanese Ambassador again hinted to me
> yesterday [January 12th] that the agreed date of
> January 28 proposed for the formal signing was
> after all extremely soon, I made it quite plain
> to him that the Foreign Minister attached the
> greatest importance to the observance of this
> time and requested him to do what he could toward
> concluding the matter by the appointed date.
> Mr. Oshima then explained to me that the
> final version of the text, which was the point at
> issue, was on its way to Japan by courier and
> would arrive there on the 20th. In view of the
> generally known procedure of the Japanese Govern-
> ment, he, Oshima, could not with the best will in
> the world guarantee that he would receive the
> requisite instructions within the short space of
> the 6 or 7 days which still remained.[28]

A few days earlier Ōshima offered similar explanations to
the Italian ambassador in Berlin. And Ōshima added that in
his work "to press his government to make every effort to
conclude the agreement as soon as possible," he was going
to "transmit to Tokyo only the variations existing between
the old [27 October 1938] and the [January 6th] texts."[29]
But no reply came from the Japanese government.

Ōshima's explanations did little to deter the growing
impatience of the Germans and Italians, and finally the
date originally set for the formal signing in Berlin was
postponed on January 24th.[30] As Ribbentrop and the Italian
ambassador in Berlin assessed the Japanese situation, "it
is a matter of a new government in Tokyo, diverse from the
one that had, in the beginning, initiated the project:
thus it must--more nipponico--examine ex novo every aspect
of the question. Moreover, the secret council must be
consulted, etc., etc."[31] The explanation that Hiranuma's
new government would have to re-examine the entire issue
was annoying to the pact's European proponents, yet they
continued to be optimistic about concluding the tripartite
pact in early 1939.

Their optimism was fed by reports derived from Japanese military circles. The German ambassador at Tokyo

dispatched a secret telegram to Ribbentrop on January 28th
in which he reported that Japanese "Army circles have informed the [German] Military Attaché in strict confidence
that they anticipate a military alliance between Germany,
Italy, and Japan in about 2 months and that the alliance
will be officially directed against Russia, though it also
contains secret protocols against other powers."[32] The
German and Italian governments, having quickly reached agreement in the last month, now seemed to be obligated to wait
for the Hiranuma Cabinet to arrive at the position long
favored in Japanese military circles.

    Never before during his long career in the Third Reich
did Ōshima seemingly have so little influence on the direction of German-Japanese relations. Ōshima was not accustomed to being ineffectual, and he feared the development
of a major setback. Ōshima pressed Arita to communicate
via cable at least an outline of the instructions being
carried by the Itō mission, but his entreaty was denied.[33]
It was as much a commentary on his determination as on his
abilities as a military diplomat that Ōshima continued with
unabated vigor. He enthusiastically performed many of the
public and more mundane duties of an ambassador while he
continued secretly to solicit support for the pact.

    For example, starting February 15th Ōshima made a
three-day official visit to Hamburg as the guest of the
Ostasiatische Verein. The visit, like those of his predecessors Nagai, Mushakoji, and Togo, was largely symbolic of
his office. Like Hitler a few days earlier, Ōshima placed
a wreath at former Chancellor Otto von Bismarck's tomb. On
the 16th he was shown the newly launched battleship Bismarck
and visited a seminar on the language and culture of Japan
at the Hanseatic University.[34] The rhetoric in both the
German and Japanese speeches at the associations's banquet
was predictably cordial. Ōshima, for example, pledged his
"entire personality" to the goal of continued economic
cooperation between Germany and Japan, two nations already
"under the common banner of the Anti-Comintern Pact." He
ended the exchange with a toast to the "mighty Fatherland
and its highly gifted Führer."[35] Ōshima's flurry of public
activity during the first two months of the Hiranuma Cabinet also included attendance at the New Year's reception
of the diplomatic corps on January 12th (Figure 3); opening
the Exhibition of Ancient Japanese Art at the Pergamon
Museum on February 28th, the day after the Itō mission
arrived in Berlin (Figures 4 and 5); and attendance at
Hitler's reception for members of the diplomatic corps on

March 2nd (Figures 6 and 7).

But in less public ways Ōshima also continued his pro-Axis work while awaiting the arrival of the Itō mission. He conferred with Heinrich Himmler at the end of January, as we have seen in the previous chapter. Also in January he sought the consolation and advice of his newly appointed Japanese colleague to Mussolini's government, Ambassador Toshio Shiratori. They met at San Remo on the Italian Riviera "to talk over the progress in the negotiations for the Tripartite Pact," Ōshima recalled in February 1946.[36] Shiratori, having recently arrived from Tokyo, probably had a more realistic appraisal of the political situation in Japan than Ōshima, who had not been in Japan since the spring of 1934. There were strong factions in the Japanese government that favored a rapprochement with Great Britain and the United States.[37] Those factions were reluctant to conclude a comprehensive tripartite pact for fear of jeopardizing relations with the Western democracies. But Shiratori assured Ōshima of his cooperation and support in efforts to influence their government in Tokyo.

In another effort to persuade the Japanese government to sign the proposed pact, Ōshima sought the support of his Japanese colleagues throughout Europe. He arranged a conference held at Paris in the last week of January. But Ōshima became ill and was unable to attend. In his place he sent "a trusted member of his staff," Counselor Uzuhiko (Yoshikiko) Usami, to meet the Japanese diplomats.[38] At the conclusion of the meeting on the 29th, Usami found that only Ambassador Shiratori favored the immediate conclusion of the pact.[39]

Again, Ōshima sought to convince his colleagues by personal contact. On February 6th he went to London to ask Ambassador Mamoru Shigemitsu for his backing; on the way back to Germany Ōshima conferred with Ambassador Saburo Kurusu in Brussels.[40] Both senior career diplomats declined to advocate the immediate conclusion of a general military alliance with the German and Italian governments.[41] Thus, Ōshima grew more apprehensive about what might be in store for his cherished pact.

Before the Itō mission arrived Ōshima made still another attempt to gather support from among his Japanese colleagues in European capitals. Earlier he had failed in London and Brussels, and his emissary was unsuccessful in Paris; only Shiratori openly endorsed the tripartite proposal. Ōshima called Japanese ambassadors and ministers to a conference in Berlin. Apparently he issued the invitations at about the same time he requested permission from the Foreign Ministry in Tokyo to hold such a conference. Ambassador Togo made the journey from Moscow to Berlin before he learned that Foreign Minister Arita had denied permission for the conference.[42] It seems that only the Japanese representatives from the Soviet Union, Poland, Sweden, Italy, and Switzerland arrived in Berlin before it became clear to all heads of Japanese missions in Europe that the conference was unauthorized by the Foreign Ministry.[43] The conference, therefore, was not held officially. Before returning to their host capitals, probably several of the mission chiefs, like Togo, "merely had dinner with Ambassadors Oshima and Shiratori . . . and later called on Minister Ito, who was sick in his hotel room."[44]

The purpose of the Ito mission was to instruct the Japanese ambassadors, not to take the negotiations out of their hands. Earlier, on February 25th, Ito and his emissary colleagues disembarked from the passenger liner Conte Verde at Brindisi in southeastern Italy. They proceeded to Rome for a brief conference with Shiratori, and then boarded a train to Berlin where they arrived the evening of the 27th.[45] Ambassador Shiratori, with Counselor Tamao Sakamoto and Second Secretary Mikizo Nagai of his staff, also went to Berlin to support Oshima in the ensuing heated discussions.[46] It was essentially a situation in which Ito, supported by two military officers, confronted Oshima and Shiratori with the Hiranuma Cabinet's position and instructions. As German Ambassador Ott cabled to Ribbentrop ten days earlier, Ito was "sent to Europe with the special task of indoctrinating recalcitrant heads of missions.[47]

Oshima and Shiratori delayed carrying out the Foreign Minister's instructions, for they knew that the Axis governments would not accept Tokyo's provisos. Italian Ambassador Bernardo Attolico reported that it was at a dinner he had with Hitler, Ribbentrop, and Oshima in early March when Ribbentrop said he would reject any compromise from a hard and fast military alliance; moreover, "Oshima is in complete agreement with him."[48] Oshima later recalled his point of view: "to present this proposal to Germany as it was would not only cause Germany to doubt Japan's sincerity, but I was also sure that she would not accept it."[49] Negotiations had always been in terms of a complete military commitment, Oshima claimed. In the summer of 1938, as Oshima stated after the war, Ribbentrop

> told me that if a military alliance were to be
> concluded, it would be a complete one, not a
> halfway alliance. . . . Hitler was against such
> halfway pacts, and therefore we could talk only
> about a complete defensive alliance in virtue of
> which the contracting parties should without
> reservations enter into the war with the adver-
> sary which attacked one of the contracting
> parties.[50]

Announcing the military pact as a mere extension of the
Anti-Comintern Pact would weaken its deterrent effect.
Furthermore, Ōshima claimed that it had always been understood that the pact would be aimed at the Soviet Union as
well as France and Great Britain.[51] The ambassadors were
unwilling to follow Arita's instructions, and Ōshima used
as his supporting argument an earlier situation that he had
helped to create with very questionable authority.[52] A
British scholar has recently observed that Ōshima "and
Shiratori functioned less as ambassadors than as traditional
go-betweens, by neglecting their roles as communicators between governments and reformulating the positions taken on
both sides to make them more acceptable to the other side."[53]
But in balance, Ōshima was much more selective and careful
about reporting his Foreign Minister's views to the Germans,
distorting them if necessary to make them acceptable, than
he was in reporting the German point of view to his superiors in Tokyo.

On March 4th the insubordinate ambassadors requested
revised instructions deleting the two secret items of understanding.[54] This was the sort of tactic long employed by
Ōshima: to telegraph back to Tokyo requesting clarification
or revision or redrafting of instructions with which he
personally disagreed. His supporters in Tokyo would argue
in their representative's behalf, claiming that the government ought to trust and rely upon the judgment of its official representative in distant Berlin. For only Ōshima, as
an incomparable expert on the Third Reich, could fully
appreciate the situation. Invariably Ōshima's tactic caused
frustration and confusion in the Tokyo decision-making process. The result was usually new, compromising, and more
confusing instructions which at least gave Ōshima more lati-
tude for interpretation.

The Japanese government attempted to hold fast. Arita
delivered an address on foreign policy before the House of
Representatives of the Imperial Diet at about the time that

97

the cable from Ōshima and Shiratori arrived:

> Britain, the United States and France apparently
> regard the alignment of Japan, Germany and Italy
> as a combination of totalitarian states in antag-
> onism to the democracies, but this is entirely
> mistaken. . . . Japan is banding together with
> Germany and Italy against the Comintern, but that
> is all and there is nothing beyond that. The
> existence of the tripartite Anti-Comintern Pact
> will never mean the antagonism of its signatories
> to the democracies.[55]

As far as Arita was concerned, these observations were not
simply politic expressions designed to quiet apprehensions
in some Japanese and Western circles. But pressure from
middle grade army and navy officers in Tokyo would soon
force him to modify Foreign Ministry instructions to the
two recalcitrant ambassadors.

In long and difficult sessions of the Five Ministers'
Conference of March 13th and 22nd the army and navy argued
that compromise out of deference to the request from Ōshima
and Shiratori would be wise in this instance; furthermore,
without modifying the Japanese position, even if only
slightly, the German and Italian governments might reject
the entire proposal. Thus, on March 25th Arita cabled new
instructions.[56] First, the ambassadors were ordered to
make every effort to carry out their original instructions
dated January 26th. If the Germans and Italians refused to
accept the two provisos, then the ambassadors were authorized to propose minor compromises: Japan would agree to
fight as an Axis ally when the Soviet Union was involved.
But in cases involving other nations, although the basic
principle of the treaty was to provide military assistance,
circumstances made "it in fact impossible for the empire
to . . . [provide military assistance] at present or in the
near future." Furthermore, Ōshima and Shiratori were authorized to propose the immediate conclusion of the treaty,
in which case all of its sections would remain secret. As
an alternative proposal, the treaty could be published but
only with prior agreement concerning the following statement:

> 'Although every section of the treaty is valid,
> since the real threat to the empire in the current
> world situation is the subversive activity of the
> Comintern, the latter constitutes the principal

and sole target of the treaty as far as the empire
is concerned.'[57]

Thus, the substance of the original instructions held.
Under no circumstances would Japan promise military aid to
its allies unless the Soviet Union initiated the attack.
And Japan hoped to avoid further estrangement with the
Western democracies through secrecy or by publishing the
treaty with the statement emphasizing its anti-Comintern
purpose. No additional compromise could be made.

The government appeared able to hold out against Ōshima
and Shiratori because the Emperor became involved. The
Prime Minister and Foreign Minister had kept Emperor
Hirohito informed of developments in negotiations with the
Germans and Italians and of the behavior of Ambassadors
Ōshima and Shiratori. Prime Minister Hiranuma reported to
the Emperor shortly after the draft of the new instructions
was completed in mid-March. The Emperor wanted to know
what action the government was prepared to take if Ōshima
and Shiratori did not obey the latest instructions and
continued to erode and misrepresent Tokyo's position in
negotiations. Hiranuma's verbal assurances that the government would be firm with the ambassadors were not satis-
factory, and, in an almost unprecedented move, the Emperor
requested that the senior cabinet ministers submit to him a
written explanation of the government's position. The carefully brushed signatures, not merely registered stamps or
seals, of Hiranuma, Itagaki, Yonai, Arita, and Ishiwata
appeared on the document dated 28 March 1939.

> 1. On March 25, 1939 the foreign minister
> issued new instructions to Ambassadors Ōshima and
> Shiratori concerning the strengthening of the
> Anti-Comintern Pact. These modified instructions
> were issued with special consideration to the
> ambassadors' requests in spite of the fact that
> the government's previous instructions had not
> been carried out. In the light of this situation,
> should the ambassadors raise objections to the new
> instructions and fail to act in accordance with
> them, our government shall take whatever action
> is necessary to insure the smooth continuation of
> the negotiations, such as recalling the two am-
> bassadors and appointing other delegates to re-
> place them.
>
> 2. We shall have to break off negotiations

> if a compromise cannot be reached with Germany
> and Italy within the limits of the restrictions
> imposed in the instructions issued by the foreign
> minister on January 26 and March 25, 1939.[58]

Here, then, was an incisive statement signed upon Imperial
demand by the five most important ministers in the government.[59] The statement represented the highest level of
national authority in Japan.

An amazingly accurate report of this secret audience
soon appeared in Kuomintang newspapers at Shanghai, and it
was repeated in the British press. Hirohito was "described
as having assumed 'more authority and power than any other
Emperor since the Japanese government was centralised.'"
The Emperor desired "to prevent Japan from entering into a
military alliance with Germany and Italy."[60]

When Ōshima received the new instructions of March
25th, he went to Rome to confer with Shiratori. The two
ambassadors chose to interpret the fact that there was a
slight difference between the new instructions and the
original instructions brought by the Itō mission as an
indication that Tokyo would continue to make concessions.
This was because the conclusion of the military alliance
was considered absolutely necessary. Making no attempt to
negotiate within the limits of the original instructions,
they moved straight to the alternative proposals in the new
instructions. Although those instructions stipulated that
it was impossible for Japan to provide military assistance
in an Axis war against any nation except the Soviet Union,
Ōshima maintained that actually the Hiranuma Cabinet meant
that Japan was unable to provide an effective level of military assistance in a European Axis war with Great Britain
and France. He returned to Berlin to tell Ribbentrop on
April 3rd that Japan would be obligated to participate in
hostilities and was prepared to offer some military assistance; in Rome Shiratori told Foreign Minister Ciano that
"in case of a European war Japanese aid would be limited."[61]

The ambassadors violated Imperial prerogative in their
distortion and disregard of government instructions, but
the Hiranuma Cabinet was divided and could not agree on
recalling the ambassadors or discontinuing the negotiations.
Foreign Minister Arita told the Emperor that the government
should rescind the unauthorized commitment to participate
in European hostilities made by the rebellious ambassadors,
but do do so would cause grave difficulties with the army.

He suggested that the government might define the term
"participation" in a fairly innocuous way; Prime Minister
Hiranuma offered a similar suggestion to the Emperor.[62]
Thus, the Emperor reluctantly followed Arita's recommendation that action not be taken against Ōshima and Shiratori
for exceeding their authority. But Hirohito severely
reprimanded War Minister Itagaki for supporting the ambassadors.[63] Because of the government's inability or unwill-
ingness to go against the army's wishes, the only way to
avoid an open split and fall of the cabinet was to continue
the agonizing and abortive deliberations. Meanwhile, confusing memoranda, telegrams, and instructions were drafted
and redrafted. And the final touch by Ōshima and Shiratori,
whose interpretations were always welcomed by their host
governments, was crucial.

Throughout the late spring and summer of 1939 the government failed to formulate an explicit policy on whether
Japan would become a belligerent or provide military assistance during a war that did not involve the Soviet Union.
The balance of political forces in the government was
extremely precarious; therefore, Itagaki and the other
ministers alike opted for the prolongation of the unproduc-
tive debates. And the instance of Imperial assertiveness
in March had the effect of making some of the Japanese
prime movers of the tripartite pact a little more circum-
spect; War Minister Itagaki, in particular, felt restrained
by Imperial sympathy for the Foreign Minister's position.
He did not, through his own resignation, wish to have the
army held responsible for the fall of the Hiranuma Cabinet.
Moreover, such a resignation would probably have led to the
recall of Ōshima and Shiratori.

The Axis dictators were becoming uneasy about the
Hiranuma Cabinet and its reluctance to conclude the tripartite military alliance. The rapid succession of events
caused the European scene to start to move away from Japan.
In March Hitler's aggression resulted in the disappearance
of the Czechoslovakian state and German annexation of Memel;
Hitler then presented the Polish government with stiff
demands concerning Danzig and the Polish Corridor. Britain
and France reacted by creating a defensive military alliance
with Poland. Undeterred, in the first half of April Hitler
issued general directives for Fall Weiss (Operation White),
the attack "to destroy Polish military potential and to
create in the East a situation corresponding with the requirements of German defense."[64] Then Hitler sent Hermann
Göring to Rome. In a conversation with Mussolini on April

The Warrior-Diplomat

16th, Göring broached the idea of extending

> feelers cautiously to Russia through certain in-
> termediaries with a view to a <u>rapprochement</u> so as
> to cause Poland anxiety over Russia. . . . The
> Duce welcomed this idea most warmly. . . . [How-
> ever, he believed] that a <u>rapprochement</u> between
> the Axis Powers and Russia <u>was naturally</u> depend-
> ent on the attitude Japan would adopt. If Japan
> had no objections to such matters, this <u>rapproche-</u>
> <u>ment</u> could . . . be effected with comparative
> ease.[65]

Mussolini's highly favorable reaction was gratifying to
Hitler, for with care it could be turned into an expression
of Italo-German solidarity related indirectly to Hitler's
concern about Poland. From a German point of view, the
alliance value of Italy in a bilateral arrangement increased
significantly as Hitler methodically prepared for war. Confronted with the intransigence of the majority in the
Hiranuma Cabinet and, on the other hand, with Mussolini's
cooperative attitude during these pivotal months in German
foreign policy, Hitler started to abandon hope of working
out a tripartite arrangement in time to serve his needs.
Mussolini was also turning away from the Japanese. As the
Italian Foreign Minister admitted on April 25th, the Duce
"considered Japanese participation [in an alliance with
Germany and Italy] more harmful than useful."[66] Finally,
on May 23rd Hitler explained to eight of his senior generals
and admirals his "decision to attack Poland at the first
suitable opportunity." In the same meeting he described
Japan's attitude on the tripartite proposal as "a weighty
question."[67]

Meanwhile, army and pro-Axis pressures remained intense
in Japan; the result was that the Hiranuma Cabinet started
to give way. This happened in spite of Imperial assertiveness. April saw more long and difficult sessions of the
Five Ministers' Conference (14th, 21st, 25th, 27th, and
28th). They concerned the commitments to participate in
hostilities made by the ambassadors in Berlin and Rome. As
a last resort it was decided that Hiranuma himself should
send a cable directly to Hitler and Mussolini explaining
the government's point of view. His draft message was
revised in the Five Ministers' Conference of April 28th,
but finally on the evening of May 4th it was sent to the
Führer and Duce via the German and Italian ambassadors in

Tokyo. The vital clauses revealed some yielding to the army:

> 'I can assure you that Japan would be firmly and unshakably resolved to stand by Germany and Italy, even if one of these two Powers were attacked by one or more Powers without the participation of the Soviet Union, and she would also render them political and economic assistance and even such military assistance as was in her power.
> 'Whilst Japan is prepared to accept the principle of military assistance to Germany and Italy in accordance with the terms of such an agreement, in the meantime, in view of the situation in which she finds herself, Japan is not in a position at present nor will she be in the near future, to render them effective military assistance in actual practice. It goes without saying that Japan would willingly provide this support, if a change in circumstances made it possible.
> . . .
> 'Furthermore, as a result of the international situation with which she is faced, Japan would be forced to exercise the utmost circumspection in respect of the interpretations (explication) she would give when this agreement was published.'[68]

Hiranuma wanted to assure the Axis dictators that Japan would not remain neutral, but Arita and Yonai convinced the majority in the Five Ministers' Conference that such a statement was too dangerous and should be deleted.[69] In spite of this, Hiranuma made essentially the same pledge to the Germans that Ōshima made months before: Japan would render effective military aid. However, the Prime Minister emphasized that such assistance was impossible then in 1939 or soon thereafter. Again, the Japanese insisted upon a very careful public explanation of the pact.[70]

Before discussing Hiranuma's message with Hitler at Berchtesgaden, Foreign Minister Ribbentrop quite predictably gave Ōshima an opportunity to voice his opinion. Ribbentrop was in Munich, on his way to meet Ciano in Milan, when he telephoned Ōshima to ask for his interpretation of Hiranuma's message. Would Japan declare war even if she were unable to give military assistance to the Axis powers? Ōshima replied in the affirmative.[71] The Vice War Minister, Lieutenant General Hideki Tōjō, gave Ambassador Ott in Tokyo

103

a similar interpretation--neutrality on the part of Japan
was out of the question. But if the alliance did not
materialize soon, Ott reported to the German Foreign Ministry, Japanese army officers close to War Minister Itagaki
expected the resignation of the Hiranuma Cabinet, a crisis
the army wanted desperately to avoid.[72]

Ōshima reinserted the very point that Arita and Yonai
had deleted from the Prime Minister's message of May 4th.
They were deeply disturbed and provoked by this latest in a
long series of acts of insubordination. The incident probably encouraged them to remain intransigent during the next
two months and to refuse to acquiesce or to compromise with
the pro-Axis extremists. In this attitude they had the
support of the Emperor and the Vice Navy Minister, Admiral
Isoroku Yamamoto.

Hitler could not wait. In Milan on May 6th and 7th
Ribbentrop and Ciano forged the Pact of Steel.[73] The two
Foreign Ministers signed the treaty in Berlin on May 22nd;
on the next day Hitler explained to his military that Poland
was to be invaded as soon as possible. But Hitler had
little hope that the Hiranuma Cabinet would give him what
he thought Mussolini would--Italy agreed to aid Germany as
an ally "with all its military forces on land, at sea and
in the air."[74] Though doubtful about the chances of success,
the Germans continued to negotiate with the Japanese, for
the Italo-German pact was only one part of Hitler's diplomatic preparation for war. It seemed to provide Germany
with an ally in the forthcoming war against the Anglo-
French-Polish alliance, but it did nothing about the Soviet
Union.

Ribbentrop, in particular, was anxious to conclude a
military agreement with Japan. A few weeks before the
signing of the Pact of Steel, Mussolini asked Ciano "to
make a public announcement of the bilateral pact which he
has always preferred to the triangular alliance," the
Italian Foreign Minister recorded in his diary. "Ribbentrop,
who from the bottom of his heart has always preferred the
inclusion of Japan in the pact, at first hesitated" to agree
to the announcement about the bilateral agreement. But he
yielded after Hitler, who was "reached by telephone, gave
his immediate approval."[75] "Better a bird in hand than two
in the bush," the Germans thought.[76]

On May 13th Ribbentrop returned to Berlin from important conferences in the south.[77] Ōshima was anxiously

waiting to confer with the German Foreign Minister, for he
feared that the Italo-German agreement would prejudice his
efforts to conclude a tripartite pact. That was not the
case, Ribbentrop assured Ōshima. Every possibility of
divergences between Japan's European allies had been eliminated through the Pact of Steel. This, Ribbentrop explained
to Ōshima, was a natural relationship between neighboring
countries surrounded by a system of hostile British and
French alliances. Japan could either join the Pact of Steel
or form a parallel tripartite pact. Ōshima agreed with
Ribbentrop that it was "indubitably in Japan's interests to
reinforce this superiority by her accession, and not to
convey the possible impression to the Western Powers that
they could count on Japan's neutrality in a conflict with
Germany and Italy."[78] They agreed to make still another
attempt to persuade the Hiranuma Cabinet, "so that the
Three Power pact can be secretly initialled at the same
time as the Italo-German pact is signed," Ribbentrop cabled
to Ott.[79]

On May 15th both Ōshima and Ribbentrop dispatched to
Tokyo the proposal of the text and the relevant papers.
(Appendix D is the set of documents Weizsäcker sent to Ott
for his personal information.) Article III of the proposed
tripartite pact was much more mild than Article III of the
Pact of Steel (see note 74 above). Nevertheless, implicit
in the vital clause was the assumption that if one signatory
were involved in a war, all signatories would automatically
become belligerents. Ribbentrop's actual interpretation of
Article III left no doubt about Japan's obligation: "If the
pact is signed, the only definite consequence laid down will
be that, in the event of an attack on one of the partners,
the other two partners will also ipso facto be in a state of
war with the aggressor."[80] The limitations contained in a
formal statement that Ōshima was to make to Ribbentrop before signing the pact (Paper No. 4, Appendix D) were, in
fact, of no consequence. Ribbentrop also told Ambassador
Ott to exercise "particular caution . . . in dealing with
officials of the Foreign Ministry in Tokyo."[81]

Ribbentrop kept Ott fully informed so that he could
work more effectively behind the scenes in efforts to influence the Hiranuma Cabinet. In June State Secretary
Weizsäcker cabled Ambassador Ott. He explained some of
Ribbentrop's suggestions for possibly promoting German-
Japanese interests at the expense of Japan's relations with
the Western democracies. For example, in conversations with
the Japanese Ott was urged to emphasize points that would

heighten Japanese misgivings about trade relations with the United States.[82] Similarly, the former Commander in Chief of the German Fleet, Admiral Richard Foerster, was given a special assignment. In Japan as part of a press delegation, Admiral Foerster was to try to convince his Japanese colleagues that they ought not to overestimate Anglo-American naval strength.[83] In June, however, shortly before Foerster was scheduled to leave Japan, Ott was instructed to find some plausible grounds that the admiral could use to extend his visit. Foerster, a retired admiral who would later become the president of the Deutsch-Japanischen Gesellschaft, was known to be strongly in favor of the tripartite proposal, and he agreed readily to exercise his influence with Japanese naval circles in behalf of the proposed pact.[84] Admiral Foerster argued tactfully that only a perfectly clear military alliance among the three Axis powers would ensure American neutrality. After meeting almost daily with various Japanese navy officers for over two weeks, the German Foreign Ministry, Ott, and the admiral "agreed that there was nothing more left for him to do."[85] Foerster was to reach Berlin with a full report on his mission by the end of July.

While Admiral Foerster's arguments may have been effective among certain naval leaders largely from the middle echelons, the top officials such as Admirals Yamamoto and Yonai remained reluctant to alienate the United States, Great Britain, and France. Navy Minister Yonai's views were fixed earlier in April and May. He explained to American Ambassador Grew that "Japanese policy has been decided. The element in Japan which desires Fascism for Japan and the consequent linking up with Germany and Italy" has been "'suppressed.'"[86] By May 15th Grew "was given categorical official assurances that there would be no general alliance, although there would be some arrangement by way of strengthening the Anti-Comintern Pact with applicability only to Soviet Russia."[87] But the navy consistently refused the automatic entry into war if the Soviet Union were not a participant. And that, as it turned out, was the only definite consequence of Article III that Ribbentrop insisted upon.

Ōshima and Shiratori continued to work together in efforts to convince their government to conclude the tripartite pact.[88] Time was running out, they felt, for rumors of a new turn in German-Soviet relations were abundant in July. The Japanese army was nervously "watching Germany's alleged rapprochement with Russia," Ott reported

to Berlin on July 5th.[89]   And on July 19th Ōshima sent
Counselor Usami to the German Foreign Ministry for information concerning the rumors. Under State Secretary Ernst
Woermann replied that all these reports were "pure fabrica-
tion."[90] Usami told Woermann that Ōshima had already assured his superiors in Tokyo that the rumors were unwarrant-
ed.   Nevertheless, in late July and early August Ōshima
and Shiratori pressed Foreign Minister Arita for a "yes"
or "no" answer.

War Minister Itagaki took a strong stand, demanding
the immediate conclusion of the treaty without reservations
concerning Japan's state of belligerency in hostilities
against the Western democracies. And he threatened to resign by August 15th if the government did not agree to sign.
Itagaki's threat to resign, Ott believed, represented "a
drastic step in the internal struggle for power by the Army
against court, financial, naval and Foreign Ministry circles,
who are threatening to gain the upper hand."[91] Lieutenant
General Kazumoto (Ryōki) Machijiri, a newly promoted chief in the War Ministry, met with the Italian and German ambassadors jointly
on August 10th. Ambassador Ott reported that "General
Machijiri requested, almost entreated, concessions before
August 15."[92]

Shortly after Ōshima and Shiratori each cabled Tokyo
with demands for a "yes" or "no" answer, Ōshima went to
northern Italy to discuss the pact with Shiratori at
Cernóbbio. Ōshima made an announcement to the press about
the forthcoming meeting.[93] He tried to convey the impression that his meeting with Shiratori was the final one
on the Japanese side before joint formal announcements of
the pact were made in Tokyo, Berlin, and Rome. This was
one of his maneuvers designed to save face and to suggest
that the pact was essentially a fait accompli. But at the
conclusion of the Cernóbbio meeting Western observers noted
a certain hollowness in the ambassadors' proclamations.
British correspondents in Berlin and Rome speculated that
the meeting and the proclamations were part of the ambassadors' diplomatic move to disguise deteriorating tripartite
negotiations.

The Japanese Ambassadors to Germany and Italy
are, after all, not the Japanese Government, with
whom any decision must rest, and that, in any
case, even if Japan should decide to join in
wholeheartedly with her Western friends, much
discussion and negotiation would be necessary

before a triangular military alliance could be brought into being.[94]

And the fact that the German and Italian presses refrained from commenting on the pro-Axis declarations coming out of the Ōshima-Shiratori meeting led one British correspondent to the conclusion "that enthusiasm for an alliance, which in the past has been eagerly sought by the German Government, may now have waned somewhat."[95] The German government was, in fact, indifferent to Ōshima's efforts to revive the tripartite project on the eve of the signing of the German-Soviet Nonaggression Pact.

The conclusion of the German-Soviet Nonaggression Pact on 23 August 1939 served as a release for the Japanese dilemma. War Minister Itagaki did not resign on August 15th and the impasse deepened as Navy Minister Yonai sided with the Foreign Minister. The frequently equivocal Finance Minister, Sotaro Ishiwata, joined them after Yonai declared that there was absolutely no chance of a Japanese victory in a tripartite Axis war against the combined forces of Great Britain, France, the Soviet Union, and the United States.[96] Prime Minister Hiranuma also sided with Arita, although he appeared earlier to be less appreciative of Arita's point of view. There is no doubt that the procrastination of the Hiranuma Cabinet made the Germans more determined to find alternatives to the long-awaited military alliance with Japan.[97]

Hitler had grown impatient with Japan's reluctance to commit herself to the Third Reich's policy of European expansion. The Führer had decided to resolve the so-called Poland problem through the use of force; therefore, German diplomacy sought bilateral military arrangements. Mussolini believed that peace would last for several years after the conclusion of the May 1939 Pact of Steel, but in little more than three months Hitler threw much of Europe into war. Unprepared militarily for such a war, Italy declined to intervene and Hitler eventually released Mussolini from the obligations of the Pact of Steel. Thus, in the opinion of the Italian Foreign Minister, Mussolini would not "pass as a welcher" in the eyes of the German and Italian people.[98] Hitler was able to move ahead with the invasion of Poland because Soviet neutrality was assured in the Nonaggression Pact, for in a secret additional protocol the Germans and Soviets divided Poland into two spheres of interest.[99] Much earlier Hitler anticipated the conclusion of the tripartite military alliance, and he expected the military presence in

Manchukuo of Germany's ally, Japan, to act as a deterrent to Soviet interference in a Polish-German war.[100] His pact with Stalin served as an alternative.

The Nonaggression Pact angered many in the Japanese government who rightly considered Hitler's action as a violation of the secret supplementary agreement to the Anti-Comintern Pact (Appendix A). German agreement with the Soviets also created a new and complex European situation which the Hiranuma Cabinet was incapable of dealing with. The cabinet terminated all negotiations and resigned on August 28th. The new cabinet of Nobuyuka Abe, formed in a mood of distrust for the Third Reich and pro-Axis forces in Japan, soon recalled Ōshima and Shiratori. The Abe Cabinet advocated the establishment of a balanced foreign policy.

Emperor Hirohito's assertiveness in March 1939 and Hitler's haste to conquer saved the Japanese nation for the moment. Military schemes to ally Japan with the European Axis powers were weakened and temporarily discredited. Nevertheless, at the end of the decade there remained in Japan considerable admiration for Hitler's boldness, for his unhesitating use of force in European affairs. The success of the German armed forces was impressive. A deceptive lull followed the conquest of Poland, but in April of the new year Denmark and Norway were occupied. In May the Netherlands, Belgium, and Luxembourg were overrun by Hitler's forces. France requested an armistice on June 17th. The large number of fantastic German victories tended to strengthen the political position of pro-Axis forces in Japan; conversely, Hitler's conquests weakened the arguments of those who had been critical of Japanese military initiative in shaping policy toward Germany. The new Foreign Minister in July 1940, Yōsuke Matsuoka, advanced an Axis-centered policy and Matsuoka, not Ōshima, became the chief architect of the Tripartite Alliance of Germany, Italy, and Japan signed on 27 September 1940.[101]

Figure 3. Ōshima at the New Year's reception of the diplomatic corps in the Reich Chancellery, Berlin, 12 January
1939. Hans Heinrich Lammers (center) was Reich Minister
and Chief of the Reich Chancellery, 1937-1945. Wilhelm
Keitel (right) was Chief of the High Command of the Armed
Forces, 1938-1945.   (National Archives)

Figure 4. Ōshima formally opening the Exhibition of
Ancient Japanese Art at the Pergamon Museum, Berlin,
28 February 1939. Ōshima stands on a flight of steps,
nearly 20 meters broad, leading to the marble altar to
Zeus on the Acropolis of Pergamon, an eighth century B.C.
Hellenistic town of Asia Minor. In the background is
part of the reconstructed marble frieze (about 2.3 meters
high) representing the contest of the gods and giants.
The museum opened in 1901. (National Archives)

Figure 5.   Hitler comments about a piece of ancient Jap-
anese art in the Pergamon Museum, Berlin, 28 February 1939.
In the foreground (left to right) are Hermann Göring, Hitler,
Heinrich Himmler, Joachim von Ribbentrop, and Ōshima.

(National Archives)

Figure 6. Hitler, talking with Ōshima, hosts an evening
reception for members of the diplomatic corps in Berlin,
2 March 1939. Ōshima used a slightly different frame of
this picture on the first page of his article published
the following July: "Das neue Deutschland im Spiegel der
japanischen Freundschaft/La nuova Germania nello speechio
dell'amicizia giapponese," Berlin--Rom--Tokio 1, no. 3
(1939): 12-14.   (National Archives)

Figure 7. Ōshima talks with Foreign Minister Ribbentrop
at the evening reception for members of the diplomatic
corps in Berlin, 2 March 1939.   (National Archives)

NOTES

V: The Warrior-Diplomat

1. Piggott, Broken Thread, pp. 324-25, and Major General
F. J. C. Piggott to author, 28 April 1969. Major General
F. S. G. Piggott was the British military attaché in Tokyo
in 1921-1926 and 1936-1939. He and Ken-ichi Ōshima were
friends, and their families had been acquainted in the Meiji
period. His son, Major General F. J. C. Piggott, was a
language officer in Japan during the late 1930s.

2. New York Times, 22 November 1938, p. 6.

3. Ibid.

4. Ōshima tells this story in Bungei Shunjū (April 1940),
"Katte kabuto no o wo shimeyo" [After winning, keep the
string tight on your helmet] (Library of Congress, Reel WT
[War Trials] 21, International Military Tribunal, Doc. No.
756). See P. Ehmann, Die Sprichwörter und bildlichen
Ausdrücke der japanischen Sprache, 2nd ed. (Tokyo:
Deutsche Gesellschaft für Natur- und Völkerkunde Ostasiens,
1927), p. 133, where the Japanese proverb is rendered in
German as "Nach dem Siege (muss man) das Helmband fester
binden."

5. Ōshima, "Katte kabuto no o wo shimeyo," WT 21, IMT Doc.
No. 756.

6. On 15 March 1939 Germany's ambassador in Tokyo commented
upon Ōshima's "preferential treatment" of German views, reporting to his superiors in Berlin that he "was able to
gather from conversations in the [Japanese] Foreign Ministry
that Ambassador Oshima has actually telegraphed repeatedly
in accordance with our interests [in unserem Sinne]" (IMTFE,
Exhibit 596).

7. Ibid., Exhibit 3508; see also Proceedings, p. 33,774.

8. Since at least 1934 Hitler considered the effect in
Europe of Japanese military pressure along the Soviet-
Manchukuo border. See Kordt, Nicht aus den Akten, pp.
122-23, and Sommer, Deutschland und Japan, pp. 20-23.

9. See James V. Compton, The Swastika and the Eagle:
Hitler, the United States, and the Origins of World War II
(Boston: Houghton Mifflin, 1967), especially pp. 176-77,
183-84, 189-90, 205, and 263-64.

NOTES

V: The Warrior-Diplomat

10. Ōhata, "The Anti-Comintern Pact," p. 63; see also IMTFE, Exhibit 3508.

11. Ōhata, "The Anti-Comintern Pact," pp. 70-71.

12. "Interrogation of Oshima, Hiroshi, Lt. Gen.," IPS 247, 1946, National Archives, Washington D.C., Record Group 331. It is probably that Gaus first became involved in this proposal late in 1938, though elsewhere (IMTFE, Exhibit 3508) Oshima's first reference to Gaus and the proposed alliance is in May 1939, a date also cited in several secondary sources; Iklé, German-Japanese Relations, p. 98; Presseisen, Germany and Japan, p. 206; Lu, From the Marco Polo Bridge, p. 52; Leonid N. Kutakov, Japanese Foreign Policy on the Eve of the Pacific War: A Soviet View (Tallahasse: Diplomatic Press, 1972), p. 48; and Ōhata, "The Anti-Comintern Pact," p. 96.

13. Toscano, The Origins of the Pact of Steel, pp. 57-65. See also Galeazzo Ciano, Ciano's Diplomatic Papers, ed. Malcolm Muggeridge, trans. Stuart Hood (London: Odhams, 1948), p. 245. Mussolini told Ribbentrop that a military alliance at that time would be unpopular among Italians because of the struggle between the National Socialists and Catholicism. Toscano suggests that a psychological factor was the real reason for Mussolini's refusal to sign the alliance in 1938. Mussolini proudly regarded himself as a great arbiter in the Munich crisis. Had he concluded the tripartite pact immediately after the crisis in September, Mussolini would have destroyed the advantage he had gained with the French and British.

14. Ōhata, "The Anti-Comintern Pact," p. 74. Ōhata has an excellent account (pp. 71-77) of other details in the German proposal and Japanese counterproposal.

15. The Saionji-Harada Memoirs, p. 2,395.

16. Tojo and the Coming of the War, p. 36.

17. Ōhata, "The Anti-Comintern Pact," pp. 76, 314 (note 95), and Lu, From the Marco Polo Bridge, p. 46. See also IMTFE, Proceedings, pp. 6,055-56, 33,734, 33,752; Exhibits 3508 and 3494.

116

NOTES

V: The Warrior-Diplomat

18. Galeazzo Ciano, Ciano's Hidden Diary, 1937-1938, trans,
Andreas Major (New York: E. P. Dutton, 1953), p. 205.
Emphasis added. Obviously, Ōshima personally favored the
conclusion of a tripartite pact that included Great Britain
as a target. The theme about the dismemberment of the
Soviet Union is one Hitler and Ōshima discussed in 1935 and
1936--see chap. 3, especially notes 22 and 28, as well as
Appendix F.

19. Ciano, Ciano's Hidden Diary, p. 210. If by chance
Ciano had read Shiratori's article--"The Reawakening of
Japan," Contemporary Japan 3 (June 1934): 8-13--he would
have known beforehand that Shiratori was a chauvinist who
belonged very much to the new era. See also chap. 4,
note 38.

20. The Saionji-Harada Memoirs, p. 2,411.

21. Itō was Minister to Poland at the time Ōshima negotiated the Anti-Comintern Pact. Tatsumi, one of the middle
level officers with whom Arita conferred earlier, was chief
of the Europe-America Section of the Intelligence Division,
Army General Staff. Abe later became Naval Attaché to
Italy. In April 1943 he became chief of the Japanese Military Commission of the Tripartite Pact in Berlin. The
most thorough and insightful work available on the military
aspects of German-Japanese collaboration during the war is
Bernd Martin, Deutschland und Japan im Zweiten Weltkrieg:
Vom Angriff auf Pearl Harbor bis zur deutschen Kapitulation
(Göttingen: Musterschmidt-Verlag, 1969). Vice Admiral Abe
was Japan's ranking naval officer in Europe when Germany
collapsed. He stayed behind in Berlin when Ōshima escaped
to the south, not leaving "to follow Admiral Doenitz" until April 20th. He had several conversations with Hitler's
successor, Karl Dönitz, as well as with Ribbentrop's successor, Foreign Minister Lutz Schwerin von Krosigk, before
escaping to Sweden on 5 May 1945. See "Magic," SRS 1632,
9 April 1945; SRS 1644, 21 April; SRS 1648, 25 April; SRS
1650, 27 April; SRS 1655, 2 May; SRS 1656, 3 May; SRS 1657,
4 May; and SRS 1664, 11 May 1945, RG 457.

22. Sommer, Deutschland und Japan, p. 176.

23. The full text of the Treaty of Consultation and Mutual
Assistance, a signed protocol, a secret supplementary pro-

V: The Warrior-Diplomat

tocol, and two secret items of understanding, together with a rationale to guide the negotiations, may be found in Ōhata, "The Anti-Comintern Pact," Appendix 4. Security surrounding the Itō mission was, in fact, very lax, for it was surprisingly reported in the British press that "three members of a secret Japanese mission are now on their way-- in the Italian ship Conte Verde--from Tokyo to present official instructions at a conference of the first importance fixed for the end of this month in Berlin." Although the article included the names of the three emissaries and a few other accurate details, there was no awareness of the sharp differences between Ōshima and Arita. It was too easily assumed in the report that the only purpose of the Itō mission was "to take the final steps for converting the German-Italian-Japanese Anti-Comintern Pact into a formal Three-Power Alliance" (News Chronicle [London], 10 February 1939, p. 2).

24. Galeazzo Ciano, The Ciano Diaries, 1939-1943: The Complete, Unabridged Diaries of Count Galeazzo Ciano, Italian Minister for Foreign Affairs, 1936-1943, ed. Hugh Gibson (Garden City, N.Y.: Doubleday, 1946), p. 4.

25. DGFP, D, 4, No. 421, p. 544.

26. Ibid., No. 426, p. 550.

27. Ibid. A British journalist speculated "that the formalities should be completed and made public before the end of January" (News Chronicle [London], 17 January 1939, p. 2).

28. DGFP, D, 4, No. 542, pp. 697-98. Emphasis added.

29. Attolico to Ciano, 9 January 1939, as cited in, Toscano, The Origins of the Pact of Steel, p. 117. The most recent German proposal was dated January 6th; it was an official draft very similar to the revised draft of October 27th.

30. Ibid., 24 January 1939, as cited in, ibid., p. 122.

31. Ibid., 25 January 1939, as cited in, ibid., p. 123.

32. DGFP, D, 4, No. 543, p. 698.

V: The Warrior-Diplomat

33. IMTFE, Exhibits 497, 3494, 3508, and Proceedings, pp. 6,070-71, 6,075, 6,077, 33,735-36.

34. See "Besuch des japanischen Botschafters in Hamburg," Ostasiatische Rundschau 20, no. 5 (1939): 128. The visits to Hamburg by Ambassadors Nagai and Mushakōji have been discussed in chap. 1. For an account of Tōgo's visit to Hamburg, 17-19 March 1938, see "Der japanische Botschafter, Exa. Togo, in Hamburg," ibid. 19, no. 7 (1938): 160-62.

35. "Besuch des japanischen Botschafters in Hamburg," ibid. 20, no. 5 (1939): 130.

36. IMTFE, Exhibit 497, and Proceedings, p. 6,072.

37. Ciano, Ciano's Hidden Diary, p. 210, and idem, The Ciano Diaries, p. 7.

38. Attolico to Ciano, 25 January 1939, as cited in, Toscano, The Origins of the Pact of Steel, p. 123. Usami joined Oshima's staff on 11 November 1938.

39. New York Times, 30 January 1939, p. 5. The Japanese representatives at the conference in Paris included Ambassadors Mamoru Shigemitsu (Great Britain), Toshio Shiratori (Italy), Saburō Kurusu (Belgium, also Minister to Luxembourg), and Ministers Makoto (Shin) Yano (Spain) and Eiji Amau (Amō) (Switzerland). See also News Chronicle (London), 30 January 1939, p. 1.

40. Attolico to Ciano, 6 February 1939, as cited in, Toscano, The Origins of the Pact of Steel, pp. 125-26. "The Japanese Ambassador to Germany and Mme. Oshima have arrived at Grosvenor House from Berlin," it was reported in the Times (London), 9 February 1939, p. 17. Details of Oshima's trip to London and Brussels are found in IMTFE, Proceedings, pp. 34,066, 34,119-21, as well as in, Oshima to author, 7 May 1971.

41. IMTFE, Proceedings, pp. 33,780-82, 33,786-88.

42. Ibid., Exhibit 3646, and Proceedings, pp. 35,458, 35,661.

43. The Japanese representatives who traveled to Berlin in the last week of February included Ambassadors Shiratori

V: The Warrior-Diplomat

(Italy), Tōgō (Soviet Union), Hideichi Sakao (Poland), and
Ministers Shigeru Kuriyama (Sweden, Norway, and Denmark),
and Amau (Switzerland). See ibid., Proceedings, pp. 34,121-
23. At the time of the earlier conference at Paris, journalists speculated that "the Japanese ambassadors to Warsaw
and Moscow . . . would take part in the next conference"
(New York Times, 30 January 1939, p. 5).

44. IMTFE, Exhibit 3646.

45. The Foreign Ministry instructions carried by the Itō
mission were addressed to Shiratori as well as Ōshima. The
19,000-ton Italian ship Conte Verde became the object of
some controversy in 1943--for over six months the Japanese
and Italian governments negotiated charters for the Japanese use of Italian ships caught in East Asian waters. The
Japanese desperately needed extra military transport ships
and finally agreed to pay about $120,000 per month for the
Conte Verde. The deal was concluded by the Badoglio government, after the fall of Mussolini. At Shanghai, however,
when news of the Badoglio government's unconditional surrender reached the Italian crewmen aboard the Conte Verde, they
scuttled their ship on 9 September 1943 before Japanese
naval authorities had a chance to carry out their plan to
seize the liner. The Japanese refloated the liner, sailed
her to Japan for conversion to a military transport ship,
but she was sunk by American aircraft in 1944. Again refloated in 1949, she was finally broken up by the Japanese
in 1951. Some of this story may be found in "Magic," SRS
1081, 8 September 1943; SRS 1085, 12 September 1943; SRS
1393, 13 August 1944, RG 457.

46. Sommer, Deutschland und Japan, p. 183; IMTFE, Exhibits
497, 3595, 3508, and Proceedings, pp. 6,063, 6,072-79,
33,736, 33,776, 34,942.

47. DGFP, D, 4, No. 547, p. 702.

48. Attolico to Ciano, 28 February 1939, as cited in,
Toscano, The Origins of the Pact of Steel, p. 154.

49. IMTFE, Exhibit 3508; see also Proceedings, pp. 6,069,
33,738.

50. Ibid., Exhibit 776-A; see also Proceedings, p. 34,107.

V: The Warrior-Diplomat

51. Ibid., Proceedings, pp. 6,064-65.

52. The Japanese political scientist, Masao Maruyama, examined Ōshima's argument at the IMTFE. In response to a question concerning his support of the Tripartite Pact of 1940, Ōshima said: "I myself, of course, supported it be-cause it had already been decided as a national policy and was also supported by the Japanese people at large" (IMTFE, Proceedings, p. 34,174). Professor Maruyama notes that "here is a man who, having contributed to the formulation of a certain plan, uses the new environment and the new state of public opinion brought about by the realization of that plan as a basis for defending his actions" (Masao Maruyama, Thought and Behavior in Modern Japanese Politics, ed. Ivan Morris, [expanded ed.; London: Oxford University Press, 1969], p. 104). The chapter in which this citation appears, "Thought and Behaviour Patterns of Japan's Wartime Leaders," translated by Ivan Morris, appears also as a two-part article in Orient/West 7, no. 3 (1962): 33-45, and 7, no. 7 (1962): 37-53.

53. Charles D. Sheldon, "Japanese Aggression and the Em-peror, 1931-1941, from Contemporary Diaries," Modern Asain Studies 10, 1 (1976): 15, note 50.

54. Ōhata, "The Anti-Comintern Pact," pp. 81-82; IMTFE, Exhibit 3508, Proceedings, pp. 6,069, 33,738.

55. News Chronicle (London), 9 March 1939, p. 15.

56. The entire text of the slightly modified instructions of March 25th appears in, Ōhata, "The Anti-Comintern Pact," pp. 83-85.

57. Ibid., p. 84.

58. Ibid., p. 86.   See note 59 below.

59. Cf. Sheldon, "Japanese Aggression and the Emperor," pp. 13-14, where it is suggested that this episode was in April and that the signed document was in very general and vague terms.   See also Maxon, Control of Japanese Foreign Policy, p. 138, where Sheldon's source, The Saionji-Harada Memoirs, is also cited, though Maxon offers no suggestion that the document was vague or dated in April.   I have checked the

V: The Warrior-Diplomat

1963 Japanese edition of Ōhata's essay, "Nichi-Doku bōkyō kyotei, dō kyōka mondai (1935-1939),", p. 112, and agree that Baerwald's translation is splendid. However, I believe that the exact key to the signatures on the document is important, for the key contributes significantly to the importance of the document itself and to this occasion of Imperial concern. Baerwald notes in the text before the body of the document (Ōhata, "The Anti-Comintern Pact," p. 86) that it was "signed by the five ministers" and shortly afterwards in Ōhata's text (p. 87) that it was "signed by all of the ministers concerned." The Japanese term shomei used by Ōhata, much like the English term for signature, does not reflect upon the nature of the thing being signed. But the kanji before the signatures on the reproduced document appear as kao, indicating that the carefully brushed (not stamped) signatures of the five cabinet members denote the great importance attached to the document. On most other occasions of official intrastate and intragovernment business those cabinet members would likely have signed a document with their registered han, stamp, or seal.

60. News Chronicle (London), 27 March 1939, p. 2.

61. Ciano, The Ciano Diaries, p. 58; Ōshima's response is found in Ōhata, "The Anti-Comintern Pact," pp. 90-91.

62. Sheldon, "Japanese Aggression and the Emperor," p. 14.

63. Ibid., pp. 14-15.

64. IMT, Trial of the Major War Criminals, 34: 388. The complete text of Fall Weiss is in Doc. No. 120-C, pp. 388-97, of this volume; cf. DGFP, D, 6, No. 185, pp. 223-28, where parts of this general directive appear.

65. DGFP, D, 6, No. 211, p. 259.

66. Ciano, The Ciano Diaries, p. 72.

67. IMT, Trial of the Major War Criminals, 37: 549-50.

68. DFGP, D, 6, No. 326, p. 421.

69. Ōhata, "The Anti-Comintern Pact," p. 316, note 133.

NOTES

V: The Warrior-Diplomat

70. Iklé, German-Japanese Relations, p. 105.

71. Ōhata, "The Anti-Comintern Pact," p. 95.

72. DGFP, D, 6, No. 339, pp. 442-43.

73. For a thorough analysis of the pretentiously named pact and its significance, see Toscano, The Origins of the Pact of Steel, especially pp. 307-402.

74. DGFP, D, 6, No. 426, p. 562. Article III was the vital clause: "If, contrary to the wishes and hopes of the High Contracting Parties, it should happen that one of them became involved in warlike complications with another Power or Powers, the other High Contracting Party would immediately come to its assistance as an ally and support it with all its military forces on land, at sea and in the air."

75. Ciano, The Ciano Diaries, p. 78.

76. Toscano, The Origins of the Pact of Steel, p. 332.

77. These important conferences on the Obersalzberg, in Milan, and in Munich (May 6th through the 13th) were pivotal in the evolution of German policy toward the Soviet Union, and, therefore, important to tripartite relations. Hitler learned of Mussolini's willingness to conclude a binding alliance at about the same time Stalin dismissed Foreign Commissar Maxim Litvinov. Hitler suspected that the dismissal was because "Litvinov had pressed for an understanding with England and France while Stalin thought the Western powers were aiming to have the Soviet Union pull the chestnuts out of the fire for them in the event of war" (Gustav Hilger and Alfred G. Meyer, The Incompatible Allies: A Memoir-History of German-Soviet Relations, 1918-1941 [New York: Macmillan, 1953], pp. 295-96). See also DGFP, D, 6, No. 325, pp. 419-20. The German Ambassador in Moscow, Friedrich Werner von der Schulenburg, who was en route via Teheran to join Counselor Hilger in conferences with Hitler and Ribbentrop, told the Italian Minister to Iran that he believed Stalin was convinced "to abandon the policy championed by Litvinov in order to reach an understanding with the Rome-Berlin Axis" ([Luigi] Petrucci to Ciano, 8 May 1939, as cited in, Toscano, The Origins of the Pact of Steel, p. 335, note 37). It was with these momen-

V: The Warrior-Diplomat

tous German-Soviet considerations in mind that Ribbentrop
assured Ōshima that Axis views were not injurious to plans
for a tripartite pact.

78. DGFP, D, 6, No. 382, p. 496. This document (pp. 494-
96) is a summary of the several meetings Ōshima and Ribbentrop had between the 13th and 15th.

79. DGFP, D, 6, No. 382, p. 495. Ciano regarded the attempt
by Ōshima and Ribbentrop as being "useless because the Japanese will not make, in six days, the decision they could
not make in six months" (Ciano to Mussolini, 14 May 1939,
as cited in, Toscano, The Origins of the Pact of Steel, p.
362).

80. DGFP, D, 6, No. 304, pp. 396-97.

81. Ibid., p. 397.

82. "Ott, Eugen: Analysis of Documentary Evidence," IPS
324, Doc. No. 4050, 28 June 1946, National Archives,
Washington, D.C., Record Group 331.

83. Iklé, German-Japanese Relations, p. 120; Presseisen,
Germany and Japan, p. 213.

84. "Ott, Eugen: Analysis of Documentary Evidence," IPS
324, Doc. No. 4050, RG 331. See also DGFP, D, 6, No. 462,
623-24. For a report of the activities and addresses given
by Foerster and Ōshima at the 1942 founding ceremonies of
the Hamburg branch of the German-Japanese Association, see
"Gründung der Zweiggesellschaft Hamburg der Deutsch-
Japanischen Gesellschaft," Ostasiatische Rundschau 23, no.
12 (1942): 256-58.

85. DGFP, D, 6, No. 619, p. 858; see also ibid., No. 537,
p. 737, and "Terauchi, Juichi: Analysis of Documentary
Evidence," IPS 18, Doc. No. 4034, 14 June 1946, National
Archives, Washington, D.C., Record Group 331.

86. Grew, Ten Years in Japan, p. 281.

87. Ibid., pp. 281-82.

88. Ōshima's role in tripartite negotiations was always

V: The Warrior-Diplomat

much greater and more important than Shiratori's, but the
two ambassadors met frequently to corroborate their efforts.
Ōshima met with Shiratori in Italy in the middle of January,
early April, early August, and early September. Shiratori
went to Germany for talks with Ōshima in late February, late
April, and in the middle of June.

89. DGFP, D, 6, No. 619, p. 860.

90. Ibid., No. 688, p. 943.

91. Ibid., 7, No. 25, pp. 25-26.

92. Ibid., p. 25.

93. IMTFE, Proceedings, pp. 34,140-41. The Ōshima-Shiratori
meeting was not authorized by the Japanese Foreign Ministry.

94. Times (London), 7 August 1939, p. 9.

95. Ibid.

96. Ōhata, "The Anti-Comintern Pact," p. 109.

97. See Lu, From the Marco Polo Bridge, pp. 54-58, for an
insightful discussion of the German-Soviet rapprochement.

98. Ciano, The Ciano Diaries, p. 135.

99. See James E. McSherry, Stalin, Hitler, and Europe, 2
vols. (Cleveland: World Publishing, 1968-1970), 1: 129-
63, 196-230, for a thorough account of the diplomacy resulting in the German-Soviet Nonaggression Pact.

100. For some recent and very useful accounts explaining
the considerable scope of Soviet-Japanese border clashes in
the late 1930s, see Hata Ikuhiko, "The Japanese-Soviet Con-
frontation, 1935-1939," trans., with an Introduction, Alvin
D. Coox, in Deterrent Diplomacy: Japan, Germany, and the USSR,
1935-1940, ed. James William Morley (New York: Columbia
University Press, 1976), pp. 115-78, as well as, Alvin D.
Coox, The Anatomy of a Small War: The Soviet-Japanese
Struggle for Changkufeng/Khasan, 1938 (Westport, Conn.:
Greenwood Press, 1977).

NOTES

V: The Warrior-Diplomat

101. See Lu, From the Marco Polo Bridge, pp. 106-19, for a
thoughtful account of the negotiations leading to the 1940
Tripartite Pact.   See also Takeshi Haruki, "The Tripartite
Pact and Soviet Russia: An Attempt at a Quadripartite
Pact," in Hogaku ronbun shu [A collection of law treatises]
(Tokyo: Aoyama Gakuin University, 1964), pp. 1-27.

VI

ŌSHIMA AND THE NEW ORDER

Hitler's New Order planned the subjugation of neighbors of the Third Reich and the rule of Berlin over the entire continent. Propaganda Minister Goebbels recorded the true picture of what Hitler intended in his New Order. After a meeting with Hitler in 1943, Goebbels wrote in his diary that

> the Fuehrer deduced that all the rubbish of small nations (Kleinstaaten-Geruempel) still existing in Europe must be liquidated as fast as possible. The aim of our struggle must be to create a united Europe. The Germans alone can really organize Europe. . . . The Fuehrer re-emphasized how happy we can be that there are no Japanese on the European continent. Even though the Italians today give us many a headache and create many a difficulty, we must nevertheless consider ourselves lucky that they cannot be serious competitors in the future organization of Europe. If the Japanese were settled on the European continent the situation would be quite different.[1]

But Ōshima remained unaffected by any policies or theories of the National Socialist government which, if applied and carried out to the fullest, would jeopardize the Axis alliance and his belief in the New Order. In this instance he was, of course, unaware of such secret remarks Hitler made in conference with his ministers. At first Ōshima defined the New Order more broadly than Hitler. He placed the Japanese in the vanguard with the Germans in his geopolitical and somewhat theoretical approach. Later, however, Ōshima assigned Japan an imperial role to play in the New Order of East Asia, and he personally became more closely associated with Hitler's concept of the New Order than his own Japanese concepts. For during the ten years before Soviet and Western armies met on German territory in May 1945, Ōshima lived only one year outside of the Third

Reich. His values and interests were mirrored in Hitler's National Socialist society. Thus, the collapse of the Third Reich also signified the end of Ōshima's world.

* * *

Ōshima was always openly sympathetic to Hitler's government. When it suited his purpose in promoting closer ties with the Third Reich he would deliberately fail to make the distinction between the views of the Japanese government and his own. In this way he subtly left his imprint on German-Japanese relations, often contrary to the will of his government.[2]

Soon after the disappearance of the Czechoslovakian state, Ōshima seized the initiative on 19 March 1939 to declare publicly his personal approval of Hitler's action. He personally drafted a congratulatory telegram sent to Foreign Minister Ribbentrop, and, although it was not approved by the Japanese Foreign Minister, Ōshima spoke for the Japanese government:

> The Japanese government sincerely and heartily congratulates the German government on the unexampled success achieved in the past few days. The Japanese government is filled with the firmest conviction that the decision of the German Reich Chancellor signifies an extremely important step towards the pacification of Europe and the maintenance of world peace.[3]

Ōshima's telegram went beyond the convention of diplomatic protocol between friendly governments; it was an openly partisan statement in which his personal feelings were not disguised.

In spite of the failure of the tripartite anti-Comintern powers to agree upon a military pact in the spring of 1939, they sponsored a new periodical dedicated to the discussion of anti-Bolshevik views and to the promotion of ideas concerning a new world order built and protected by Germany, Italy, and Japan. In the first issue of Berlin--Rom--Tokio (often written in German, Italian, and Japanese) a tract-like statement described the mission of the new nations and emphasized their common purpose and harmonious relations. The statement concluded with a map of

128

Eurasia on which superimposed lines connected the countries
involved in a series of agreements. A list followed:

1. Conclusion of the German-Japanese Anti-
   Comintern Agreement: 25 November 1936

2. Italy's accession to the German-Japanese
   Anti-Comintern Agreement: 6 November 1937

3. Conclusion of the Japanese-Hungarian
   Cultural Agreement: 15 November 1938

4. Conclusion of the German-Italian
   Cultural Agreement: 23 November 1938

5. Conclusion of the German-Japanese
   Cultural Agreement: 25 November 1938

6. Conclusion of the German-Spanish
   Cultural Agreement: 24 January 1939

7. Joining of Manchukuo in the Anti-
   Comintern Agreement: 24 February 1939

8. Joining of Hungary in the Anti-
   Comintern Agreement: 24 February 1939

9. Conclusion of the Italian-Japanese
   Cultural Agreement: 23 March 1939

10. Joining of Spain in the Anti-Comintern
    Agreement: 27 March 1939[4]

This was the theme often repeated in varying forms during
the spring of 1939: a new world order with the tripartite
powers as its nucleus had been established, and it was
growing rapidly as the recent adherence of Manchukuo,
Hungary, and Spain demonstrated.

Ōshima referred to this theme in his description of
the "New Order of Things in Europe and the Far East" published in May 1939.[5] He predicted in his article that the
policy of orderliness would take over Europe and Asia. It
would completely replace what he termed the obsolete systems
of Communism and democracy. There was already abundant
evidence of this in Europe, he declared, as seen in the
obliteration [Auslöschung] of Czechoslovakia, the declaration of autonomy by the Slovak people, and the creation of
the protectorates of Bohemia and Moravia. Ōshima saw other
indications of the success of the New Order in Europe:
General Franco's victory over Communist subversion in

Spain, his membership in the anti-Comintern system, and the
further development of security in the Mediterranean sphere
(as manifested by Albania's union with the Italian Empire).
But Japan's foreign policy since 1931 made the New Order
truly a Weltanschauung. Ōshima admitted that Manchukuo had
been called a Japanese "puppet state," but in 1939 no one,
he declared, could ignore the fact that the state so recently
freed from China was a member of a new and rewarding system.
It was a system in which all people--Japanese, Chinese,
Mongolians, Russians, and Koreans--prospered by peacefully
working and living together. Japan had a similar goal for
400 million Chinese of whom many were still under the
control of the Communists or Chiang Kai-shek's decadent
regime. Thus, according to Ōshima, Japan was a member of
New Order philosophy, an amalgam of ideas and sentiments
about life interwoven with a set of political purposes,
national preferences, and economic principles. In fact,
Ōshima's view of the New Order of East Asia was one in
which Japan's neighbors would be subjugated to the will of
Tokyo.

Ōshima asserted that the policies of the tripartite
powers were well-founded because nothing was a more natural
development than to unite under one order all people with
historical, economic, and cultural ties. As proof of this
assertion he cited Hitler's speech of 28 April 1939. Hitler
made a two-hour speech in response to President Roosevelt's
appeal for peace: "Are you willing to give assurance that
your armed forces will not attack or invade the territory
or possessions of the following independent nations?" Then
the president of the United States named thirty-one countries in Europe, southwestern Asia, and northern Africa.[6]
In a grand display of showmanship Hitler replied that he
had taken the trouble to ascertain from these countries
whether they felt threatened by Germany, and in all cases
the reply was negative.[7] Ōshima was infatuated with Hitler's hypocrisy and found good use for it in his own twisted
interpretation. Ōshima saw this episode as revealing the
character of the "political and economic egoism of the other
side."[8] Germany, Italy, and Japan represented a profound
ideological antithesis, Ōshima insisted. They must continue
to stand together in the fulfillment of a mission in Europe
and Asia.

In July 1939 Ōshima published another article that was
typical of his attitudes about the New Order.[9] His fanat-
ical National Socialist point of view was never before pub-

lished so unmistakably. With some editorial ingenuity a
photograph of Ōshima and Hitler together in front of a
conspicuous mirror appeared on the title page of the article, thus depicting the new Germany in the reflection of
Japanese friendship (see Figure 6). The new Germany, "like
our own symbol of the rising sun," climbed from the depths
of a gloomy world war and national misfortune, Ōshima wrote.[10]
"Self-sufficiency" was the only goal for Germany in the
aftermath of the great war; personal consideration was the
way achievement of the goal was attempted. "But then came
the building of the new Reich, the rebirth of the German
people--economically, socially, and militarily--with a
force and a swiftness which is unrivaled, in my belief, in
the history of all people and all times." The unique
achievement was the work of one man--the Führer. In words
faintly resembling a passage from "Deutschland über Alles"
or from Rudolf Hess's introduction of Hitler at Nürnberg,
Ōshima proclaimed that united faith in Hitler "has brought
afresh the great and phenomenal achievement: today over 80
million Germans--from the Meuse to the Memel, from the North
and Baltic Seas to the Alps frontier--are really 'ein Volk
und ein Reich,' great, strong, and invincible!"

Ōshima predicted that the governments of Japan and of
the new Germany, which were already fighting their common
Communist enemy to the bitter end, would soon reach new
heights in common understanding because of their spiritual
attitude since 1936. This was the nucleus of a great
mission to be carried out with Fascist Italy. Its purpose
was the creation of a new world order.

Into this scene of optimistic expectations for the
future of tripartite relations and the New Order fell news
of the conclusion of the German-Soviet Nonaggression Pact in
August 1939. It was mortifying to many Japanese living in
Germany. One Japanese observer who had just arrived from
Japan felt "righteous indignation. The German lack of a
sense of international justice is beyond words," wrote an
unidentified Japanese university student in his private
diary on 23 August 1939.[11] It was a generally held view in
the Japanese embassy that war with Poland was inevitable.
The embassy had provisions for two years and Japanese nationals bought gas masks at the embassy for five marks each.
Hundreds of Japanese were panic-stricken and many left
Berlin on August 26th when the Japanese ship Yasukuni Maru
sailed a day early from Hamburg to seek safety in the harbor
at Bergen, Norway. The Japanese student remarked with

concern that several of his fellow students were taking
their doctoral examinations when the German-Soviet pact was
signed. Some of them were frightened about the coming war
and they returned early to Japan. Ōshima tried to quiet
the Japanese community in Berlin. On September 29th he
advised students to stay, saying that "there is no need for
those who planned to study for a year or two to leave Germany in a hurry." Ōshima's advice reflected his own confidence in Hitler's leadership of the powerful German armed
forces, but there is no evidence that Ōshima influenced many
Japanese in Berlin. Moreover, there were rumors that the
ambassador himself would be recalled by the new Abe Cabinet.
Shiratori had already been recalled on September 2nd and he
left Rome on the 15th. Most students probably considered
it too dangerous to remain in a country at war with which
the Japanese government was cooling diplomatic relations.

News of successful German-Soviet negotiations was as
shocking to Ōshima as it was to his supporters in Tokyo,
but both he and Shiratori were presumably forewarned by
Ribbentrop during a luncheon conference on June 16th.[12]
The ambassadors reported Ribbentrop's comment to their government in Tokyo where it was regarded as a German bluff.
Ōshima probably contributed to the government's attitude,
for he added in his report that it was "out of the question
that Germany would conclude a pact with Russia."[13]

Ōshima's position became obviously awkward after Ribbentrop telephoned him from the Obersalzberg with news of
his impending journey to Moscow.[14] This was late on the
evening of 21 August 1939. On the next day, while Ribbentrop
was traveling through Berlin en route to Moscow, Ōshima met
the Foreign Minister at the airport. He was assured that in
the view of the German government the nonaggression pact was
not injurious to German-Japanese friendship.[15] Ribbentrop
did not have time to give Ōshima thorough explanations since
he was preparing to fly on to Königsberg with an entourage
of some thirty persons that same evening—the next morning
(the 23rd) Ribbentrop had plans to fly to Moscow. The pain-
ful task of explaining the new course of German diplomacy to
Ribbentrop's friend and comrade fell to State Secretary
Weizsäcker.

Ōshima arrived at Weizsäcker's home at midnight on the
22nd. Weizsäcker wrote a memorandum about the meeting. "It
was a heavy blow for him, though he was Japanese and General
enough not to lose his outward poise. Most people knew him

as a brave man who could hold his drink; but he was a man
of finer sensibility than many realized. His face became
rigid and grey."[16] Ōshima wanted to cable his government
immediately some explanations that would soften the impact
of the news in Tokyo. His concern centered around two
points: (1) the Soviet Union would be relieved of anxiety
in Europe, and, therefore, able to pursue the clash along
the frontier between Outer Mongolia and Manchukuo (the
negotiations between Ambassador Tōgō and Foreign Commissar
Molotov for an armistice were still going on) and (2) ju-
rists in Tokyo would interpret the German conclusion of the
new pact as a violation of the Secret Agreement appended to
the Anti-Comintern Pact.

Weizsäcker obviously anticipated Ōshima's concern, for
he had prepared elaborate explanations.[17] He told Ōshima
that he ought not to be surprised by the pact for in June
Ribbentrop informed him of that possibility if the Hiranuma
Cabinet continued to refuse a tripartite arrangement.
"Polish arrogance might force us into war even in the
course of this week," Weizsäcker told Ōshima at about one
o'clock on the morning of the 23rd. "With such a limited
amount of time available," the Germans were absolutely
compelled to take action. Weizsäcker commended Ōshima for
his understanding and assured him of Germany's most friendly
intentions. Indeed, the new German-Soviet relations could
assist the German government in effecting a normalization
of Soviet-Japanese relations.[18] Weizsäcker concluded his
memorandum with the observation that Ōshima "took notes of
these remarks and in conclusion he assured me of his un-
altered intention to work further for German-Japanese friendship." For Ōshima was a devotee of Hitler and would do anything he could to benefit Hitler's New Order, including the
violation of orders from Tokyo.

On August 25th Foreign Minister Arita ordered Ōshima to
protest solemnly to the German government, informing the
German Foreign Ministry that the pact with the Soviets was
a serious violation of the 1936 Anti-Comintern Pact. Therefore, the Japanese government was immediately breaking off
negotiations for the tripartite agreement.[19] On August 26th
State Secretary Weizsäcker, who had already been informed by
Ott that Ōshima was ordered to hand him a formal note of
protest, listened patiently to the anguished Japanese ambassador. Then, speaking "as a friend and comrade," Weizsäcker
wrote in his memorandum,

> I recommended Ōshima to treat our conversation
> as though it had not taken place and as if he
> had not met me in the Foreign Ministry at all.
> I told him to put his Note in his pocket again
> and to reflect for twenty-four hours how best
> he could get round acting on these instructions
> from his Government, which might perhaps suit
> Japanese requirements in domestic policy, but
> which were not in the well-understood interests
> of our two countries.

> Ōshima took his papers back again and left
> me, intending to reflect on what he should now
> do, but expressing great anxiety as to what
> could be done, as he had received unequivocal
> instructions from Tokyo.[20]

A chagrined Ōshima reflected upon Arita's unequivocal instructions. Ōshima claimed later that he consented to
Weizsäcker's request because he had already protested twice
to Ribbentrop, once in their telephone conversation on August 21st and again at Tempelhof Field in Berlin on August
22nd. Therefore, he "postponed the presentation of the note
until the middle of September, when the war situation in
Poland was somewhat clarified."[21]

Ōshima falsely informed the Japanese Foreign Ministry
that he carried out Arita's instructions, and on September
18th he took the note to Weizsäcker for the second time.
After Ōshima suggested that the note be allowed to disappear
in the German archives, Weizsäcker "accepted it only personally and not officially."[22]

The Germans were in danger of losing the services of
their valuable friend and comrade. It is not surprising,
therefore, that they worked vigorously to keep Ōshima at his
post in Berlin.

One of Ōshima's first reactions to news of the German-
Soviet pact was to tender his resignation, as he hinted to
Ribbentrop during their fateful meeting at the airport on
August 22nd. Weizsäcker immediately telgraphed Ott saying
that "Ōshima's continuance at his post is an asset which we
would not like to forgo."[23] He urged him to do what he
could to ensure "that Ōshima remains at this post." Ribbentrop soon iterated the message to Ott: "I deem it to be
of great importance for the policy I have in mind that
Ōshima remain ambassador in Berlin."[24] Ribbentrop said that

since Ōshima had always been initiated "into the aims of
our policy," he was "better in the position to represent the
Japanese interests in Berlin than a new ambassador. He
still enjoys also the complete confidence of the Führer and
the German army." Both messages from the German Foreign
Ministry contained the subtle suggestion that Ott be dis-
creet about expressing German acclaim for Ōshima lest the
new Japanese cabinet might doubt Ōshima's ability to represent in the first instance its interests rather than those
of Germany.

As Prime Minister of the new cabinet at the end of August, General Nobuyuki Abe also held the Foreign Minister
portfolio throughout most of September. Abe, a former
military attaché in Berlin, and Ōshima were personal
friends.[25] It was General Abe with whom Ott discreetly
voiced the view "that the continued labours of Ambassador
Oshima to foster German-Japanese friendship would certainly
be very valuable."[26] Ott was optimistic in his report of
September 8th, for the Japanese army and leading quarters
of the Foreign Ministry indicated that Ōshima's position
was secure for the present. But the Abe Cabinet, in an
attempt to establish a balanced foreign policy during the
early months of the European war, decided to recall the
activist ambassador in the Third Reich.[27]

The National Socialist prepared for Ōshima's grand send-
off. Ōshima was taken for an inspection tour of the West
Wall fortifications behind the Franco-German border. Later,
on September 20th, he was received by Hitler at Zoppot--
the Führer's field headquarters near Danzig.[28] Hitler and
Keitel explained the course of military events to Ōshima
and his party.[29]

After the announcement of Ōshima's recall, Hitler
received the warrior-diplomat in a farewell visit on October 24th. It was an unauthorized visit which a Foreign
Ministry spokesman in Tokyo explained "had no political
significance."[30] Ribbentrop and other key figures in the
National Socialist government also hosted farewell recep-
tions for Ōshima. He was showered with gifts before leaving
the Third Reich. One gift was a picture of a swastika with
the following dedication on the frame: "To my friend Ambassador Hiroshi Oshima in grateful memory of the years of
untiring devotion to the creation of German-Japanese friendship."[31]

Ōshima and the New Order

Ōshima left Berlin on October 29th in the wake of impressive German military victories and little except courageous determination from Europe's democracies. On 9 November 1939 he arrived in New York where he staunchly denied to the press that the German-Soviet pact strained Japanese relations with Germany.[32] In Tokyo on December 12th he predicted a German victory and claimed that Hitler's armed forces had "superior, entirely new weapons that we have not thought of."[33]

In a sense, the Germans had sent their own spokesman to Tokyo to pave the way for a tripartite military alliance. Ōshima was enormously effective in promoting German-Japanese causes during the last five years, but distance, some Germans rationalized, had perhaps handicapped his ability to influence cabinets in Tokyo. His army supporters had been effective in slowly altering reluctant attitudes in the Japanese governments. A setback was an unfortunate by-product of the German-Soviet pact. Now, with Ōshima in Tokyo, it was hoped that his added voice and weight among pro-Axis forces in the interim cabinets would be sufficient to effect a fundamental change in Japan's foreign policy.

Having failed in his efforts to keep Ōshima in Berlin, Ribbentrop then took steps to facilitate Ōshima's work for German-Japanese friendship after he returned to Tokyo. Ott was instructed to support Ōshima in all respects.[34] German embassy officials in Tokyo were ordered to provide Ōshima with telegraphic and postal services: his telegrams addressed to Foreign Minister Ribbentrop personally were to be coded without changes. Ōshima's letters were to be forwarded unopened by the most reliable and swiftest route. These measures were reportedly taken to insure the continuance of Ōshima's freedom of access to National Socialist officialdom.

The record of Ōshima's work in behalf of stronger German-Japanese relations is not altogether clear during his stay in Japan. During the next year until his reappointment in December 1940 as Ambassador to Germany, Ōshima received very little public attention. He held no government post, and, as the German ambassador in Tokyo at the time of his reappointment recalled after the war, "Oshima kept himself much apart from political activities during his stay in Japan [from December 1939 to January 1941]."[35] Nevertheless, his opinions were occasionally solicited by pro-Axis Japanese as the turn of events in Europe helped to strengthen their voice in the affairs of state.[36]

136

Soon after arriving in Japan Ōshima published a pro-German article in an attempt to sway Japanese public opinion.[37] He displayed his own attitudes toward diplomacy and military force and praised the methods and accomplishments of Hitler and Ribbentrop. Hitler fully understood military force as an instrument of policy, Ōshima explained to the Japanese reader. Repudiation of the Treaty of Versailles and rearmament were necessary in order to regain Germany's freedom in international affairs. Ōshima called Hitler's success in dealing with the earlier Austrian and Czechoslovakian problems the art of "bloodless diplomacy." In the autumn of 1939 the idea of German diplomacy was again to have military force available to back up political efforts to solve the Polish problem, but Britain and France forced the issue, as Ōshima interpreted the outbreak of the Second World War. Thus, Germany was "throwing the world into utter amazement" because Hitler had the foresight and ability to develop military force suitable for implementing "sound diplomatic policies." Ōshima considered Ribbentrop "exactly the right diplomatic assistant who has no equal in the positive diplomacy" of the Third Reich. And Ōshima interpreted Hitler's personal direction of the war from the front in Poland as characteristic of the Japanese samurai spirit. Hitler "depends much upon the Japanese nationality and the character of the Japanese," Ōshima claimed.

He ended the article by urging the Japanese people to evaluate the international situation and to decide how best Japan could prosper. Although he admitted that no one could predict that final victory was certain, there was little doubt in his mind about the direction Japan ought to take.

> The view is prevalent that a modern war is a protracted national total war. Germany, of course, is now well aware of this. And yet she has entered into war; thus we might correctly assume that she is prepared for a protracted war and . . . has confidence in her operations to win the war in a short time. . . . It is dangerous to judge the present war by the standards of past wars. What were operations on two fronts before are now operations on one front, and each country is trying to localize the war. We must constantly watch how the world is moving, make a good study of the war, and quietly ponder upon its results.

Ōshima and the New Order

Ōshima's appeal to the Japanese public was a restatement of
views he had advocated more forcefully in the Third Reich.
He concluded by encouraging everyone to "take this opportunity to lead Japan to greater prosperity in the world."

During Ōshima's absence from Berlin the civilian diplomat Saburo Kurusu served as ambassador. The Germans found
Kurusu ineffective and poorly informed by his own government. In August 1940 Ribbentrop sent a personal envoy from
the Dienststelle to Japan "because the situation [with
regard to a possible pact] was too obscure to be analyzed
from Berlin."38 It is not surprising, therefore, that the
National Socialists were delighted by news of Ōshima's
reappointment. With much fanfare in the National Socialist
press, Ōshima was warmly greeted as a friend of the Third
Reich upon his return to Berlin on 17 February 1941.39

Ōshima served as Japan's ambassador until the collapse
of the Third Reich. He became not only the dean of the
diplomatic corps in Berlin, but also chief of all Japanese
diplomatic representatives and intelligence services in
Europe.40

During his second appointment as Ambassador to Germany,
Ōshima enjoyed more than ever before the trust and confidence of Hitler, Ribbentrop, and many other leading figures
in the German government. He was unique among the foreign
representatives in wartime Berlin, for he had been an open
and unashamed supporter of the National Socialists since
1934. He never wavered. Thus, Hitler and his subordinates
repeatedly confided in Ōshima and revealed extremely sensitive information of strategic import.

For example, in January 1943 Hitler admitted to Ōshima
that "disposing of the Soviet Union" has become a considerable problem for Germany. "It is clear that if, in order
to destroy the striking power of Russia, you Japanese would
take a hand and help us out from the East, it would be very
advantageous in getting this job off our hands."41 In
another of the many private conferences Ōshima had with Hitler during the war, the Führer told him almost two weeks
before the Allied invasion at Normandy that he believed the
Allies were ready to attempt an invasion of the European
continent with about 80 divisions; Hitler said that he had
60 divisions ready to destroy the invaders. He anticipated
that "diversionary actions will take place in a number of
places. . . . After that--when they have established bridgeheads in Normandy and Brittany and have sized up their
prospects--they will then come forward with an all-out

second front across the Straits of Dover."[42] In Ōshima's
last conference with Hitler (see Appendix F) the Führer told
him that he was preparing to launch a large-scale offensive
"after the beginning of November" 1944. Hitler's trust and
confidence in Ōshima were not misplaced, nevertheless, un-
beknown to Ōshima, Japanese reports to Tokyo were being
decoded by American crypotologists and analyzed by Allied
strategists.

Ōshima experienced both fame and hardship in wartime
Berlin. The German government built a new embassy for the
Japanese. In a ceremony on 25 January 1943, Under State
Secretary Woermann handed Ōshima the keys to the new building on the Tiergartenstrasse.[43] It was far and away the
most elegant embassy in Berlin. But Ōshima did not have the
opportunity to enjoy it for long, for soon the war started
to close in around him. On 5 October 1943 he reported to
Tokyo that "the Imperial portraits from the Japanese Legation in Rumania have been sent to Berlin for safekeeping,"
and soon he was also the custodian of the portraits from
the Japanese legation in Hungary.[44] It was the beginning
of a pattern. By the end of the year of 1943, Ōshima was
caring for the portraits formerly enshrined at Sofia,
Bucharest, Budapest, Prague, The Hague, Antwerp, and Hamburg.
"The portraits are stored in our own air raid shelter,"
Ōshima cabled to Tokyo, "and during a raid one of my staff
is specially detailed to keep guard over them."[45] It was
not long, however, until the new embassy building was hit
in bombing raids. By February 1944 large parts of the
embassy were "rendered permanently useless" and the air
raid shelter was converted into living quarters.[46] Gasoline rationing for diplomats occurred in the spring of 1944,
and by August 21st the allotment was reduced--the Germans
allotted 224 gallons monthly for the 60-odd cars belonging
to the embassy and its personnel.[47] By the end of 1944 the
allotment was reduced to about 53 gallons per month, and,
as living conditions in Berlin became desperate, "even that
allowance was cut off" on 1 March 1945 (see Appendix G).

Ōshima was witnessing the end of Hitler's New Order
and the destruction of the city he knew so well. Though he
was unable to get an appointment to see Hitler in the last
days, Ribbentrop was ever at hand. On 5 February 1945 a
member of the German Foreign Ministry wrote about a recent
daylight bombing attack he called "the ultimate apocalypse,
as far as Berlin is concerned." Quite by chance, he saw
Ribbentrop and Ōshima

> wandering about among the ruins, surrounded
> by a crowd of people and being greeted with
> the Nazi salute by those in uniform. Ribben-
> trop was wearing uniform, while Oshima was
> wearing a leather jacket and a deerstalker.
> Both were carrying stout walking-sticks.[48]

Their entire association was based on mutual trust and
candor. It had been nearly ten years since they met secretly through an intermediary, Friedrich Hack from Ribbentrop's
Dienststelle. Together they produced the Anti-Comintern
Pact. Now maybe another turning point was at hand. On 17
March 1945 Ribbentrop approached his "friend for many years,"
as he called Ōshima, with an idea that he had not discussed
even with Hitler or any members of the Foreign Ministry--the
possibility of concluding peace with the Soviets followed by
the formation of a Berlin--Moscow--Tokyo alliance to fight
against the Western democracies (see Appendix H). Ribbentrop was willing to fly to Moscow to negotiate directly with
Stalin, a flight he had made twice in 1939. But by March
19th Hitler disapproved, thus bring an end to an unrealistic
scheme with no prospects for success. Still, it was a
daring suggestion for Ribbentrop to make to the Japanese
ambassador. For if any hint of the subject perchance leaked
out "to outsiders (and this includes Germans)," Ribbentrop
emphasized to Ōshima, he, the Foreign Minister, and Germany
would be caught in a very grave position. But nothing could
be done to avoid unconditional surrender.

Again, Ōshima was obligated to leave Berlin, this time
more ingloriously than in 1939. The Germans assisted the
diplomatic corps in Berlin in all possible ways. On April
7th the head of the Protocol Department of the German Foreign Ministry asked Ōshima to reduce the size of his embassy
staff as much as possible. Thus, Ōshima ordered many staff
members, including a considerable number from former embassies in Paris and Rome, for example, to board a special
train leaving for Badgastein on April 8th. Ōshima's wife
and a lot of Japanese nationals had already made good their
escape from the advancing Soviet army and were safe in
Badgastein, about 75 kilometers south of Salzburg. Ōshima
left Berlin for the last time on 14 April 1945 (Appendix H).

High in the Alps at the resort site of Badgastein,
Ōshima wrote a report on April 26th (transmitted to Tokyo
from Berne on the 28th):

'Most of the diplomats here are representatives
of Axis countries, but the Papal Nuncio has
settled here. . . .

'We have not been able to make contact
with Berlin and are not likely to in the
future, because of the incessant bombing of
the city. Unfortunately, the facilities for
communication and transportation here are quite
primitive. Newspapers usually arrive a day or
two late . . . and we rely almost exclusively
on the radio in order to keep abreast of latest
developments.'[49]

Ōshima knew, however, that news from Allied broadcasting
stations about the impending fall of Berlin was not exag-
gerated--his inability to establish radio communication
with Berlin was ominous evidence.

Most of Ōshima's messages sent to Tokyo during the last
days of the Third Reich were remarkably common in tone. But
one demonstratively pro-National Socialist report reveals
some of the anguish he suffered. "When we left Berlin," he
wrote to his Foreign Minister from the safety of Badgastein
on April 27th,

'it was our intention to accompany the German
Government for, as I had indicated to you, I
had assumed that the German Government intended
to retire to southern Germany. [Words uncertain;
the sense probably is: 'However, as might have
been expected from the character of the Fuehrer,
he decided to show his people the way'] and
would not tolerate the idea of leaving Berlin.
As a result, the other top leaders have also
remained in Berlin and it now appears likely
that they will avail themselves of this opportunity to die the death of heroes at the front.
It is quite probable that they have already
made provision for the continuation of the Nazi
regime in the event that they are killed when
Berlin falls. However, I must confess that at
the present time it is difficult to foresee the
future course of events throughout Germany.'[50]

Ōshima and the New Order

There is also some indication that Ōshima started to
reflect on his role as a military diplomat in the Third
Reich; he started to raise questions specifically about how
his role might be perceived by the victors. Since early
1942 the Western democracies issued various declarations
about their intentions to prosecute and punish German war
criminals. Similar declarations about Japanese war criminals were less numerous; moreover, Ōshima very likely
assumed that the term "war criminals" referred to people
guilty of conventional war crimes as defined in various
conventions signed at The Hague and in Geneva.[51] Nevertheless, Ōshima had an indelible impression of how badly the
vanquished suffered at the hands of the victors of the
First World War, though perhaps not through war trials per
se. Ōshima pondered his own fate while, he admitted,
"'carefully studying the possible treatment we might receive
after being taken into custody by the enemy.'"[52] He even
toyed with the idea of escaping into Soviet-occupied ter-
ritory--a course of action that would have been pure folly.[53]
Ōshima's history of anti-Soviet work was well-known in
Moscow. Indeed, an American intelligence report stated that
in October 1941 Prime Minister Tōjō had wanted to give
Ōshima the Foreign Minister portfolio in his new cabinet,
but he "could not do so because of General Oshima's strongly
anti-Soviet background."[54] It is doubtful that the Soviets
would have allowed Ōshima and his party to travel across
the Soviet Union to Manchukuo before they issued their anticipated declaration of war against Japan. Furthermore,
the Japanese had for some time been fearful that the Soviets
were preparing to attack Japan, as a reading of some of the
"Magic" traffic of 1945 makes clear.[55] Ōshima was confused
in a convulsive struggle to discover alternatives to surrender to the Western allies. All hope was gone after he
learned of Hitler's death and the collapse of his New Order.
His fate was sealed.

Events dealt with Ōshima slowly, for the victors in
Europe still had the task of defeating Japan. A unit of
the U.S Seventh Army took custody of Ōshima and 130 other
Japanese at Badgastein on 11 May 1945.[56] Nearly 200 German
ministerial personnel were also at Badgastein, including
Walther Funk, former Minister of Economics and president of
the Reichsbank. Ōshima was kept in custody at Badgastein
until the end of June when he and about 30 ambassadorial
staff members were flown from Salzburg to LeHavre, France.
There he boarded the U.S.S West Point, a troop transport
converted from the liner S.S. America (II); "this was on

July 4, I am sure," Ōshima told an interrogator in February
1946.[57] He arrived in New York on July 11th with 2,420
Swiss francs and 440 American dollars.[58] The former ambassador spent the remained of July interned near Washington,
D.C.; in early August he was moved to a hotel near Bedford,
Pennsylvania. There the group of Japanese internees received news of the bombing of Hiroshima and Nagasaki and
Japan's decision to surrender. The Japanese at Bedford
showed no emotion over news of Tokyo's unconditional
surrender, one American account declared.

> While jubilant Americans celebrated with
> blaring horns, shrieking sirens and jangl-
> ing bells outside the Bedford Springs Hotel,
> a group of impassive Japanese internees
> inside were told of their country's sur-
> render.[59]

Ōshima summoned about 150 Japanese to the assembly room of
the 19th century luxurious resort hotel and read the following statement:

> 'I am informed by a representative of
> the State Department that according to the
> radio a message has been received through
> the Swiss Government announcing that the
> Japanese Government has accepted the condi-
> tions of the Potsdam declaration. While
> this news was received here by radio and not
> by official communication there is no reason
> to doubt its authenticity.

> 'We are, therefore, commanded by the
> Emperor to lay down our arms. I wish to
> add that I appreciate all the efforts you
> have made in this struggle and I feel
> assured that while your efforts have not
> enabled us to win, you have at least done
> your utmost for the Emperor.'[60]

At about the same time, news of the London Agreement of
8 August 1945 reached the Japanese internees in Pennsylvania.
Included in the London Agreement was the charter of the
International Military Tribunal for the trial of Third Reich
war criminals. The term "war criminals" was expanded to
include a person found guilty of crimes against peace,
namely, "participation in a common plan or conspiracy" for
war.[61] Soon Ōshima learned of the indictment against 24

Ōshima and the New Order

National Socialists, many with whom Ōshima had been closely
associated: Ribbentrop, Keitel, Gōring, and Walther Funk,
"Hitler's purse keeper" who was with Ōshima at Badgastein
a few months earlier.[62] About three weeks after the
International Military Tribunal at Nürnberg received the
indictment on October 19th, Ōshima was shifted again--to
Seattle, Washington, where he boarded a ship for Japan.
He spent a week at his home before being arrested and jailed
in Sugamo Prison on 16 December 1945.[63] Two of his associates were already there, Shiratori and Tōjō, and soon
many of his other associates would join him in Sugamo Prison:
Itagaki, Hiranuma, Tōgō, Shigemitsu, and Hirota.[64] On 29
April 1946, a year after he escaped from Berlin, Ōshima
was charged on seven counts:

Count 1 - The Over-all Conspiracy
Count 27 - Waging war against China
Count 29 - Waging war against the United States
Count 31 - Waging war against the British
           Commonwealth
Count 32 - Waging war against the Netherlands
Count 54 - Ordering, authorizing or permit-
           ting atrocities
Count 55 - Disregard of duty to secure
           observance of and prevent
           breaches of Laws of War.[65]

On 12 November 1948 the Tribunal rendered the verdict in
Ōshima's case: guilty on Count 1 and acquitted on the other
counts--sentence was life imprisonment. But after the occupation of Japan officially ended in April 1952, all of the
convicted war criminals still in Sugamo Prison were eventually released. This was done following the recommendation
of the Japanese government and approval of a majority of
governments represented at the IMTFE.[66] In December 1955
Ōshima was released on parole and in April 1958 he was
granted clemency. Hiroshi Ōshima died at his home in
Chigasaki, Japan on 6 June 1975. The extraordinary envoy
was 89 years old.

The long Tokyo Tribunal gave Ōshima an opportunity to
view practically every facet of Japanese history from 1928
to the disaster of 1945. The Tribunal sat on 417 days and
had conducted 818 court sessions.[67] The fraud of Ōshima's
representation in Berlin was revealed for his colleagues,
countrymen, and world to see. The revelation must have
caused Ōshima some distress, although there is no evidence
that he regretted his role in the past. Since 1934 Ōshima

had represented and expressed military and totalitarian
tendencies in the Japanese army, government, and society
and helped them reach dominance by 1940. He was the key
figure who overall was responsible for building the bridge
between the Third Reich and Imperial Japan. As an intriguer
and warrior-diplomat among the National Socialists, Ōshima
usurped authority while trying to commit his government to
a policy that he personally advocated. Ōshima's case
remains a problem that confronts modern nation-state governments, and the extent to which government can decisively
and effectively deal with such cases is a test of the
virility of centrally constituted authority.

Figure 8. Admiral Osami Nagano, Chief of the Naval General
Staff (1941-1944), dropped off to sleep in the dock at the
International Military Tribunal for the Far East while on
his left a stern-faced Ōshima listens to the proceedings.
As Minister of the Navy, 1936-1937, Nagano was a member of
the Five Ministers' Conference when Military Attaché Ōshima
pushed for the conclusion of the Anti-Comintern Pact.

(Collection of the author.)

Figure 9. Taken during the International Military Tribunal for the Far East, 1946-1948, this autographed picture shows the "Ex-Ambassador" leaving the Ichigaya War Ministry Building, site of the Tribunal, to be bussed five kilometers back to Sugamo Prison in the Toshima district of Tokyo.

(Collection of the author.)

VI: Ōshima and the New Order

1. Joseph Goebbels, The Goebbels Diaries, 1942-1943, ed.
and trans. Louis P. Lochner (Garden City, N.Y.: Doubleday,
1948), p. 357. Elsewhere Goebbels recorded that it was out
of place to offer "any description of the future New Order
in Europe from which the members of foreign nations might
gain the impression that the German leadership intends to
keep them in a state of permanent subjection" (idem, The
Secret Conferences of Dr. Goebbels: The Nazi Propaganda
War, 1939-43, ed. Willi A. Boelcke, trans. Ewald Osers
[New York: E. P. Dutton, 1970], p. 332).

2. Chihiro Hosoya, "Retrogression in Japan's Foreign
Policy Decision-Making Process" in Dilemmas of Growth in
Prewar Japan, ed. James William Morley (Princeton:
Princeton University Press, 1971), pp. 99-101. Here Professor Hosoya offers a concise discussion of the disintegration in the communications system in prewar Japan
between the government and its ambassadors abroad. He
describes Ōshima's case as one of the outstanding examples
of this failure.

3. News Chronicle (London), 20 March 1939, p. 13. It is
curious to note Mussolini's first reaction to news that
Hitler scrapped the Munich agreement. Refusing to release
to the press news brought by Hitler's envoy on March 15th,
the Duce reportedly said: "'the Italians would laugh at
me; every time Hitler occupies a country he sends me a
message'" (Ciano, The Ciano Diaries, p. 43).

4. "Die Sendung der jungen Völker / La missione dei popoli
giovani," Berlin--Rom--Tokio, 1 (15 May 1939): 11. Cf.
Karl Haushofer, Japan baut sein Reich (Berlin: Zeitgeschichte-Verlag, 1941), p. 299.

5. Hiroshi Ōshima, "Japan in der Front der Antikominternmächte," Volk und Reich, 15 (1939): 310-12.

6. Carnegie Endowment for International Peace, "Developments in the European Situation," International Conciliation, no. 351 (1939), p. 294. Hitler's major address before
the Reichstag in response to Roosevelt's message is in
ibid., pp. 297-345. Mussolini, to whom Roosevelt sent a
similar message, replied briefly on April 20th--see ibid.,
pp. 346-47. For the origins and significance of the
president's unusual medley of condemnation and appeal, see

VI: Ōshima and the New Order

William L. Langer and S. Everett Gleason, The Challenge to Isolation: The World Crisis of 1937-1940 and American Foreign Policy (New York: Harper and Row, 1952), pp. 75-90.

7. Hitler's reply was both cunning and stinging. It was the most brilliant oration William Shirer "ever heard from him" (The Rise and Fall of the Third Reich, p. 471). At the time Shirer recorded in his diary that "the sausage-necked deputies below us rocked with raucous laughter throughout the session, which was just what Hitler desired. It was a superb example of his technique of laughing off embarrassing questions" (Berlin Diary: The Journal of a Foreign Correspondent, 1934-1941 [New York: Alfred A. Knopf, 1941], p. 166).

8. Ōshima, "Japan in der Front," p. 312.

9. Hiroshi Ōshima, "Das neue Deutschland im Spiegel der japanischen Freundschaft / La nuova Germania nello specchio dell'amicizia giapponese," Berlin--Rom--Tokio, 1 (15 July 1939): 12-14.

10. All words emphasized are Ōshima's as printed in "Das neue Deutschland im Spiegel der japanischen Freundschaft." Each term was also carefully italicized in the Italian version.

11. "Berurin nikki" (Berlin diary), Records of German and Japanese Embassies and Consulates, 1890-1945, National Archives Microfilm Publication T-179, roll 73. The unidentified Japanese student who kept this diary had contacts in the Japanese government, and he was often at the Japanese embassy in Berlin. He moved about freely in Germany between 6 August 1939 until his return to Japan in September 1940. His insights and analyses are valuable. I use frames 4,708,031-44 (August 6th through 3 October 1939) for an impression of Japanese views in Germany other than those of Ōshima and trusted members of his staff. After October there are very infrequent entries, but one is of special interest. In September 1940 (frame 4,708,048) the author commented upon National Socialist racial theories. German officials told the people of Berlin to treat Poles as they would treat Jews. The Japanese student thought that "this order reveals the German national character; the Germans are, in this instance, worse than beasts by Japanese standards."

NOTES

VI: Ōshima and the New Order

12. IMTFE, Exhibit 2232, and Proceedings, pp. 34,138-39; DGFP, D, 8, No. 11, pp. 8-11.

13. IMTFE, Exhibit 2232. In about June the British ambassador in Tokyo warned Arita of the possibility of a German-Soviet understanding, but "from Berlin the fanatically pro-German ambassador, General Oshima, reported that there was no possibility whatever of such a development and that the idea should be dismissed as British propaganda" (Robert Craigie, Behind the Japanese Mask [London: Hutchinson, (1946)], p. 71).

14. Hosoya Chihiro, "The Tripartite Pact, 1939-1940," trans. James William Morley, in Deterrent Diplomacy: Japan, Germany, and the USSR, 1935-1940, ed. James William Morley (New York: Columbia University Press, 1976), p. 191.

15. IMTFE, Exhibit 3508; DGFP, D, 7, Nos. 183, 186, pp.191, 193-95. Brief accounts of Ōshima's immediate reaction to news of the German-Soviet pact appear in several secondary sources. The best one is Sommer, Deutschland und Japan, pp. 283-85. Others include F. C. Jones, Japan's New Order in East Asia: Its Rise and Fall, 1937-45 (London: Oxford University Press, 1954), pp. 125-27; Presseisen, Germany and Japan, pp. 223-25; Iklé, German-Japanese Relations, pp. 133-34.

16. Weizsäcker, Memoirs, p. 201.

17. DGFP, D, 7, No. 186, pp. 193-95.

18. Ribbentrop apparently was sincere in his hope that he could influence Stalin to normalize Soviet relations with Japan. During his second visit to Moscow in September 1939, Ribbentrop proposed to Stalin that they issue a joint appeal to Japan for collaboration with the new German-Soviet pact of friendship. Stalin reportedly answered: "'Your intentions are good, but the implementations are wrong. I know the Japanese better. They just have suffered a defeat at Nomonhan and had 20,000 killed. Now negotiations are under way to wind up the incident. They have understood my language'" (Erich Kordt, "German Political History in the Far East during the Hitler Regime," ed. and trans. E. A. Bayne (Library of Congress, Manuscript Division, Box 809, Folder D), p. 23.

VI: Ōshima and the New Order

19. DGFP, D, 7, No. 262, pp. 277-78.

20. Ibid., No. 329, p. 335.

21. IMTFE, Exhibit 3508, and Proceedings, pp. 33,743-44.

22. Ibid., Exhibit 506, and Proceedings, pp. 6,124-26.

23. DGFP, D, 7, No. 183, p. 191.

24. IMTFE, Exhibit 507, and Proceedings, p. 6,129.

25. DGFP, D, 7, No. 403, p. 398.

26. IMTFE, Exhibit 498, and Proceedings, p. 6,130. Ribbentrop also told Ott that he could "talk quite openly about it with Prince Kan'in" (Exhibit 507). The Field Marshal Prince did not resign as Chief of the Army General Staff until October 1940 when he was seventy-five years old. His successor was General Gen Sugiyama, War Minister in two cabinets (February 1937--June 1938) when Ōshima worked to strengthen the Anti-Comintern Pact.

27. The new Foreign Minister appointed September 25th, Admiral Kichisaburō Nomura, announced the official recall of Ōshima on October 7th. The admiral stated "that Japan had abandoned the intention of strengthening the [Anti-Comintern] Pact in view of the European situation" (Times [London], 7 October 1939, p. 5).

28. New York Times, 21 September 1939, p. 12, and Times (London), 22 September 1939, p. 7.

29. Ōshima's party included his military attaché, Major General Kawabe and General Hisaichi Terauchi, former War Minister in the Hirota Cabinet. Terauchi headed a mission sent to represent the Japanese army at the Nürnberg rally. Originally scheduled for September 1939 in celebration of peace ("Reichsparteitag des Friedens"), ironically Hitler was obligated to postpone the celebration because of his plans for war. The Terauchi mission was already en route to Europe when the decision was made.

30. Times (London), 26 October 1939, p. 7.

VI: Ōshima and the New Order

31. "Ott, Eugen: Analysis of Documentary Evidence," IPS
324, Doc. No. 4045, 25 June 1946, RG 331). Also the
Germans sent gifts to Prince Kan'in.

32. New York Times, 10 November 1939, p. 8.

33. Ibid., 13 December 1939, p. 1.

34. IMTFE, Exhibit 508, and Proceedings, p. 6,131.

35. "Interrogation of Ott, Eugen," IPS 324, 5 March 1947,
RG 331.

36. Hosoya, "The Tripartite Pact," pp. 205, 230, and 235-36.

37. Hiroshi Ōshima, "Doitsu gaikō no rinen" [The idea of
German diplomacy], Bungei Shunjū (January 1940) (LC, Reel
WT 82, IMT Doc. No. 3268). An English translation appears
in IMTFE, Exhibit 3516-A.

38. IMTFE, Exhibit 2744-A. Ribbentrop's envoy, Heinrich
Georg Stahmer, replaced Ott in 1943 as Ambassador to Japan.
The reserve with which Hitler treated Ōshima's successor is
seen in "Botschaft des Führers an die japanische Nation,"
Berlin--Rom--Tokio 2 (15 December 1940): 14.

39. See, for example, "Botschafter Oshimas Ankunft in
Berlin," Ostasiatische Rundschau 22, no. 2 (1941): 43-44,
and "Botschafter Oshima beim Führer / L'ambasciatore Oshima
ricevulo dal Führer," Berlin--Rom--Tokio 3, no. 3 (1941): 13.

40. Captain Walter E. Seager, assistant military attaché,
American Embassy, Ankara, to Military Intelligence Division,
Office of Chief of Staff, War Department, 18 November 1944,
Records of the Office of Strategic Services, XL2416,
National Archives, Washington, D.C., Record Group 226.

41. "Magic," SRS 874, 12 February 1943, RG 457.

42. Ibid., SRS 1320, 1 June 1944, RG 457. See Appendix E
for the full text of Ōshima's paraphrased account of his
conversation with Hitler on 27 May 1944.

VI: Ōshima and the New Order

43. Ōshima to author, 7 May 1971; "Unterstaatssekretär Dr. Woermann vom Auswärtigen Amt überreicht Exzellenz Oshima den Schlüssel zum Botschaftsgebäude," Ostasiatische Rundschau 24, no. 3 (1943): 57; and Hiroshi Ōshima and Erich Voss, "Der Neubau der Kaiserlich japanischen Botschaft in Berlin," Die Kunst im deutschen Reich 7, no. 1 (1943): 24-40.

44. "Magic," SRS 1124, 21 October 1943, and SRS 1128, 25 October 1943, RG 457.

45. Ibid., SRS 1172, 6 January 1944, RG 457.

46. Ibid., SRS 1204, 7 February 1944, RG 457.

47. Ibid., SRS 1455, 14 October 1944, RG 457.

48. Studnitz, While Berlin Burns, p. 241.

49. "Magic," SRS 1654, 1 May 1945, RG 457.

50. Ibid., SRS 1655, 2 May 1945, RG 457. The information in brackets was added by American cryptologists at the time the message was decoded.

51. See Richard H. Minear, Victors' Justice: The Tokyo War Crimes Trial (Princeton: Princeton University Press, 1971), pp. 6-19, and Solis Horwitz, "The Tokyo Trial," Carnegie Endowment for International Peace, International Conciliation, no. 465 (1950), pp. 477-82.

52. "Magic," SRS 1655, 2 May 1945, RG 457.

53. Ibid. The OSS had a report "that about 600 of the approximately 650 Japanese officials, businessmen and others in Germany propose to hide themselves in eastern Germany. They plan to be overrun by the Russians in the hope that the Russians will permit them to work their way home via Siberia" (OSS Report No. RB-8168, 22 March 1945, NA, RG 226).

54. Seager to War Department, 18 November 1944, OSS File, XL2416, NA, RG 226.

NOTES

VI: Ōshima and the New Order

55. See, for example, SRS 1543, 10 January 1945; SRS 1573;
9 February 1945; SRS 1646, 23 April 1945; SRS 1661, 8 May
1945; and SRS 1713, 29 June 1945, RG 457.

56. "Who's Who in Japan and Japanese Occupied Territories,"
5th ed., 20 May 1945, OSS, Intelligence Division of the Far
Eastern Bureau, New Delhi, OSS File, XL10947, NA, RG 226,
and New York Times, 12 May 1945, p. 4.

57. "Interrogation of Oshima," IPS 247, 1 February 1946,
RG 331.

58. Headquarters, Second Service Command, ASF, Governors
Island, New York to Adjutant General, War Department,
Washington, D.C., 8 May 1946, IPS 247, RG 331.

59. New York Times, 15 August 1945, p. 14.

60. Ibid.

61. Ibid., 9 August 1945, p. 10.

62. Ibid., 20 October 1945, p. 1: "Chubby Walther Funk,
Hitler's purse keeper, broke down in tears today when he
and his cohorts received their copies of the indictment
for the war crimes trials in Nuremberg."

63. "Interrogation of Oshima," IPS 247, 1 February 1946,
RG 331.

64. For examples of some of the attitudes of over 1,000
defendants confined in Sugamo Prison, including the 28
Class A defendants tried at the IMTFE (1946-1948), see
Yoshio Kodama, Sugamo Diary, trans Taro Fukuda (n.p. [Japan],
1960) and my article focusing on Tōjō--"Exaltation and
Hindsight: Tōjō's 'Reflections upon Parting with Lieutenant Colonel Kenworthy, A Man Bearing the Spirit of an
Ancient Samurai,'" Montclair Journal of Social Science and
Humanities 3, no. 2 (1974): 79-96. The IMTFE rendered
verdicts in the cases of 25 of the 28 Japanese indicted--
Shūmei Ōkawa was found mentally incompetent to stand trial,
and Yōsuke Matsuoka and Osami Nagano died during the long
trial. See Figures 8 and 9 for Ōshima's appearance at the IMTFE.

65. Horwitz, "The Tokyo Trial," p. 584.

VI: Ōshima and the New Order

66. The Tribunal was composed of a justice from each of
these eleven countries: Australia, Canada, China, France,
Great Britain, India, Netherlands, New Zealand, Philippines,
Soviet Union, United States.

67. Horwitz, "The Tokyo Trial," p. 584. Also, oral testimony from 419 witnesses was heard, and the Tribunal received
affidavits and depositions from 779 other witnesses. There
were in evidence 4,336 exhibits totaling about 30,000 pages,
and the proceedings numbered nearly 50,000 pages.

APPENDIX A

German-Japanese Agreement against the Communist

International, November 25, 1936[1]

(i) Agreement.

The Government of the German Reich and the Imperial Japanese Government, recognizing that the aim of the Communist International, known as the Comintern, is to disintegrate and subdue existing States by all the means at its command; convinced that the toleration of interference by the Communist International in the internal affairs of the nations not only endangers their internal peace and social well-being, but is also a menace to the peace of the world; desirous of co-operating in the defence against Communist subversive activities; have agreed as follows:

Article I

The High Contracting States agree to inform one another of the activities of the Communist International, to consult with one another on the necessary preventive measures, and to carry these through in close collaboration.

Article II

The High Contracting Parties will jointly invite third States whose internal peace is threatened by the subversive activities of the Communist International to adopt defensive measures in the spirit of this agreement or to take part in the present agreement.

Article III

The German as well as the Japanese text of the present agreement is to be deemed the original text. It comes into

---

1. Royal Institute of International Affairs, Documents on International Affairs, 1936, ed. Stephen Heald (London: Oxford University Press, 1937), pp. 297-99.

Appendix A

force on the day of signature and shall remain in force for
a period of five years. Before the expiry of this period
the High Contracting Parties will come to an understanding
over the further method of their co-operation.

In witness whereof the undersigned, being duly and
properly authorized by their respective Governments, have
signed this agreement and affixed their seals.

Done in duplicate at Berlin on November 25, 1936--that
is, November 25 of the 11th year of Showa Period.

[signed] von Ribbentrop, Extraordinary and
Plenipotentiary Ambassador of the German Reich.

[signed] Mushakoji, Imperial Japanese Extraordinary
and Plenipotentiary Ambassador.

(ii) Supplementary Protocol.

On the occasion of the signing to-day of the agreement
against the Communist International, the undersigned
Plenipotentiaries have agreed as follows:

(a) The competent authorities of the two High
Contracting States will work in close collaboration in matters concerning the exchange of
information over the activity of the Communist
International as well as investigatory and
defensive measures against the Communist
International.

(b) The competent authorities of the two High
Contracting States will within the framework
of the existing laws take severe measures
against those who at home or abroad are
engaged directly or indirectly in the service
of the Communist International or promote its
subversive activities.

(c) In order to facilitate the co-operation of
the competent authorities provided for in
paragraph (a) a permanent committee will be
set up. In this committee the further
defensive measures necessary for the struggle
against subversive activities of the Communist
International will be considered and discussed.

[signed] von Ribbentrop.

[signed] Mushakoji.

Secret Additional Agreement to the Agreement

against the Communist International[2]

The Government of the German Reich and the Imperial Japanese Government, recognizing that the Government of the Union of the Soviet Socialist Republics is working toward a realization of the aims of the Communist International and intends to employ its army for this purpose; convinced that this fact threatens not only the existence of the High Contracting States, but endangers world peace most seriously; in order to safeguard their common interests have agreed as follows:

Article I

Should one of the High Contracting States become the object of an unprovoked attack or threat of attack by the Union of Soviet Socialist Republics, the other High Contracting State obligates itself to take no measures which would tend to ease the situation of the Union of Soviet Socialist Republics.

Should the case described in paragraph 1 occur, the High Contracting States will immediately consult on what measures to take to safeguard their common interests.

Article II

For the duration of the present Agreement, the High Contracting States will conclude no political treaties with the Union of Soviet Socialist Republics contrary to the spirit of this Agreement without mutual consent.

Article III

The German as well as the Japanese text of the present Agreement is to be deemed the original text. The Agreement comes into force simultaneously with the Agreement against the Communist International signed today and will remain in force for the same period.

In witness whereof the undersigned, being duly and properly authorized by their respective Governments, have signed the Agreement and affixed their seals.

---

2. DCFP,D, 1, p. 734, note 2a.

Appendix A

Done in duplicate at Berlin on November 25, 1936,
i.e., November 25 of the 11th year of the Showa period.

[signed] Joachim von Ribbentrop
Extraordinary and Plenipotentiary
Ambassador of the German Reich.

[signed] Viscount Kintomo Mushakoji
Imperial Japanese Extraordinary
and Plenipotentiary Ambassador.

Annex I[3]

(Translation)
Berlin, November 25, 11 Showa

Mr. Ambassador:

I have the honor to inform Your Excellency on the
occasion of the signing today of the Secret Supplementary
Agreement to the Agreement against the Communist International that the Japanese Government and the German Government are in complete agreement in the following point:

The "political treaties" referred to in Article II of
the aforementioned Secret Supplementary Agreement include
neither fishery treaties nor treaties concerning concessions, nor treaties concerning frontier questions between
Japan, Manchukuo, and the Union of Soviet Socialist
Republics, and the like, which may be concluded between
Japan and the Union of Soviet Socialist Republics.

---

3. An English version of the four Annexes and the Agreement on keeping the secrecy of the Secret Supplementary
Agreement appear in Vierteljahrshefte für Zeitgeschichte
2, no. 2 (April 1954): 198-200. It was made from the
original Japanese for the IMTFE. The author's translation
of these five pieces is from copies of the German documents.
They were graciously provided by the Honorable Miss
Margaret Lambert, British Foreign and Commonwealth Office
Library. The Japanese text for only Annexes III and IV
appear in Ōhata Tokushiro, "Nichi-Doku-bōkyo kyotei, dō
kyoka mondai (1935-1939)," pp. 31-36. The German text is
in Sommer, Deutschland und Japan, pp. 493-99.

I would be grateful to Your Excellency if agreement of the German Government to the above interpretation could be confirmed.

At the same time I take the opportunity to renew to Your Excellency the assurance of my highest esteem.

[Mushakoji]
Imperial Japanese Extraordinary
and Plenipotentiary Ambassador

To:
His Excellency,
The Extraordinary and
Plenipotentiary Ambassador
of the German Reich,
Joachim von Ribbentrop

Annex II

Berlin, November 25, 1936

Mr. Ambassador:

I have the honor to acknowledge receipt of Your Excellency's courteous note of today regarding the Secret Supplementary Agreement to the Agreement against the Communist International, in which the following was communicated to me:

[paragraphs 1 and 2 of Annex I]

I have the honor to inform Your Excellency of the concurrence of the German Government with the above interpretation.

At the same time I take the opportunity to renew to Your Excellency the assurance of my highest esteem.

[signed] Joachim von Ribbentrop
Extraordinary and Plenipotentiary
Ambassador of the German Reich

To:
His Excellency,
The Imperial Japanese Extraordinary
and Plenipotentiary Ambassador,
Viscount Kintomo Mushakoji

Appendix A

Berlin, November 25, 1936

Mr. Ambassador:

I have the honor to inform Your Excellency on the occasion of the signing today of the Secret Supplementary
Agreement to the Agreement against the Communist International that the German Government does not regard the
provisions of the existing political treaties between the
German Reich and the Union of Soviet Socialist Republics,
such as the Rapallo Treaty of 1922 and the Neutrality Treaty
of 1926, insofar as they have not become null and void under
the conditions existing at the time this Agreement comes
into force, as being contradictory with the spirit of this
Agreement and the obligations arising from it.

At the same time I take the opportunity to renew to
Your Excellency the assurance of my highest esteem.

[signed] Joachim von Ribbentrop
Extraordinary and Plenipotentiary
Ambassador of the German Reich

To:
His Excellency,
The Imperial Japanese Extraordinary
and Plenipotentiary Ambassador,
Viscount Kintomo Mushakoji

Annex IV

(Translation)
Berlin, November 25, 11 Showa.

Mr. Ambassador:

I have the honor to acknowledge receipt of Your Excellency's courteous note of today regarding the Secret
Supplementary Agreement to the Agreement against the Communist International signed today, in which the following
was communicated to me:

[paragraph 1 of Annex III]

I have the honor to confirm to Your Excellency that my
Government acknowledges this communication with sincere
satisfaction.

At the same time I take the opportunity to renew to Your Excellency the assurance of my highest esteem.

[Mushakoji]
Imperial Japanese Extraordinary
and Plenipotentiary Ambassador

To:
His Excellency,
The Extraordinary and
Plenipotentiary Ambassador
of the German Reich,
Joachim von Ribbentrop

Agreement about Keeping the Secrecy of the "Secret Supplementary Agreement to the Agreement against the Communist International" Including the Annexes.

There exists between the two High Contracting States agreement about keeping secret the Secret Supplementary Agreement to the Agreement against the Communist International as well as Annexes I to IV.

In the case it should at some time be in the interest of the two High Contracting States to communicate the content of the Secret Agreement to third states, then such a communication may take place only by mutual consent.

Berlin, November 25, 1936, that is,
November 25 of the 11th year of the Showa period.

[signed] Joachim von Ribbentrop
Extraordinary and Plenipotentiary
Ambassador of the German Reich

[signed] Viscount Kintomo Mushakoji
Imperial Japanese Extraordinary
and Plenipotentiary Ambassador

Appendix A

German-Japanese Exchange of Notes on the Occasion of the

Initialling of the Agreement against the

Communist International[4]

(i)

The Japanese Ambassador in Germany to

Ambassador von Ribbentrop

Berlin, October 23, 1936.

Mr. Ambassador: I have the honour to inform Your
Excellency that I have today, together with a telegram
informing him that the initialling was performed this day,
sent the enclosed telegram to the Minister for Foreign
Affairs, Mr. Arita.

At the same time, I take the opportunity to renew to
Your Excellency the assurances of my highest esteem.

[signed] Mushakoji

[Enclosure]

The Ambassador in Berlin Count Mushakoji to His Excellency

the Minister for Foreign Affairs, Mr. Arita

Berlin, October 23, 1936.

With reference to the Annexes III and IV of the Secret
Supplementary Agreement to the Agreement against the Communist International, I have, on the basis of my negotiations with Ambassador von Ribbentrop, the firm conviction
that the spirit of the above-mentioned Secret Agreement is
alone decisive for the future policy of Germany towards the
USSR.

---

4. DGFP,C, 5, No. 625, pp. 1140-41.

I have shown Ambassador von Ribbentrop this telegram and received his agreement.

[signed] Mushakoji

(ii)

Ambassador von Ribbentrop to the Japanese Ambassador in

Germany

[Berlin], October 23, 1936.

Mr. Ambassador: I have the honour to confirm to Your Excellency the receipt of your letter of October 23. I have taken note of it, as well as of the contents of the telegram to the Minister for Foreign Affairs, Mr. Arita, of which a copy was enclosed.

At the same time I take the opportunity to renew to Your Excellency the assurances of my highest esteem.

[signed] R[ibbentrop]

APPENDIX B

Memorandum of a Conversation between Hiroshi

Oshima and Heinrich Himmler,

January 31, 1939[1]

File Memorandum

I visited General Oshima today. The conversation ranged over the following subjects:

1.) The Führer's speech pleased him very much especially because it had been spiritually well founded in every feature.

2.) We discussed the conclusion of a treaty to consolidate the Germany-Italy-Japan triangle into an even firmer bloc. He also told me that, together with German counter-espionage [Abwehr], he was undertaking long-range projects aimed at the disintegration of Russia and emanating from the Caucasus and the Ukraine. However, this organization was to become effective only in the event of war.

3.) Furthermore, he had succeeded up to now in sending ten Russians with bombs across the Caucasian frontier. These Russians had the mission to kill Stalin. A number of additional Russians, whom he had also sent across, had been shot at the frontier.

---

1. A photographic copy of the original document is found in National Archives Microfilm Publication T-988, roll 12, frames A/088013-14, and a printed copy is in IMT, Trial of the Major Criminals, 29: 327-28. Different English translations appear in IMTFE, Proceedings, pp. 6,026-28; IMTFE, Exhibit 489; and U. S., Office of United States Chief of Counsel for Prosecution of Axis Criminality, Nazi Conspiracy and Aggression, 8 vols. (Washington, D.C.: United States Government Printing Office, 1948), 4: 852.

Appendix B

4.) We then discussed the Mohammedan movement. He said
that a Japanese officer had worked in Afghanistan, but he
had been expelled later because of suspicion that he had
attempted to overthrow the Afghan government. I told him
that I had a police officer there and that the two could
very well collaborate once he again had someone there.

5.) He told me confidentially that he had bought a piece of
real estate at Falkensee under the name of a middleman and
that six Russians were employed there writing and printing
leaflets. The leaflets were flown into Russia from Poland
in small balloons when the wind was favorable. He had
reports and proof from Russia that the leaflets had
arrived in good condition and that they were being diligently distributed among the people.

6.) Also he had bought a motorboat in order to take leaflets from Romania to the Crimea via the Black Sea. However, this operation had not succeeded in the autumn, but
he would repeat it once more in the summer.

Berlin, 31 January 1939

                              The Reichsführer--SS:

                        [signed] H. Himmler

APPENDIX C

Ōshima's Military and Court Ranks, Major
Assignments, and Decorations[1]

19 April 1886:	Born, Gifu Prefecture, Japan.		
Military Rank	Assignments	Decorations	Court Rank
June 1906: 2nd Lt.			
			Oct. 1907: Senior Grade, 8th.
June 1909: 1st Lt.			
			Oct. 1909: Junior Grade, 7th.
			Nov. 1910: Senior Grade, 7th.
		Nov. 1915: War Medal of 1914 & 1915.	
		Nov. 1915: Imperial Order of the Rising Sun (6th class) with the Single Rays (Yen 500).	
May 1916: Capt.			
		Dec. 1919: Imperial Order of the Sacred Treasure (5th class).	Dec. 1919: Junior Grade, 6th.

1. IMTFE, Exhibit 121.

Appendix C

Military Rank	Assignments	Decorations	Court Rank
		Nov. 1920: Imperial Order of the Rising Sun (4th class) with the Small Cordon (Yen 1100).	
	May 1921: Asst. Mil. Attaché, Germany		
Jan. 1922: Major.			
	Feb. 1923: Mil. Attaché, Austria and Hungary.		
			Jan. 1925: Senior Grade, 6th.
Aug. 1926: Lt. Col.			
		Nov. 1929: Imperial Order of the Sacred Treasure (3rd class).	
			Mar. 1930: Junior Grade, 5th.
Aug. 1930: Col.			
	Mar. 1934: Mil. Attaché, Germany.		
		Apr. 1934: Imperial Order of the Rising Sun (3rd class) with the Medium Cordon.	

Military Rank	Assignments	Decorations	Court Rank
Mar. 1935: Maj. Gen.			Mar. 1935: Senior Grade, 5th.
Mar. 1938: Lt. Gen.			
		Apr. 1938: Imperial Order of the Sacred Treasure (2nd class).	Apr. 1938: Junior Grade, 4th.
Oct. 1938: Inactive, Lt. Gen., Army 1st Reserve.	Oct. 1938: Ambassador, Germany.		
		Nov. 1938: Imperial Order of the Rising Sun (2nd class) with the Double Rays.	
	Dec. 1939: Resigned as Ambassador, Germany.		
Jan. 1940: Promoted one rank by Special Grace.			Jan. 1940: Senior Grade, 4th.
		Apr. 1940: Imperial Order of the ising Sun (1st class) with the Grand Cordon.	
	Dec. 1940: Ambassador, Germany.		
	Apr. 1941: Envoy-Minister, Slovakia.		Apr. 1941: 1st rank, higher civil service.

Appendix C

Military Rank	Assignments	Decorations	Court Rank
			Feb. 1944: Junior Grade, 3rd.
	Feb. 1945: Resigned as Envoy-Minister, Slovakia. Apr. 1945, Resigned as Ambassador, Germany.		

April 1945:	Left Berlin.
May 1945:	Surrendered to U. S. armed forces at Badgastein, south from Salzburg about 150 kilometers.
July 1945:	Arrived in New York City and interned at a resort hotel near Bedford, Pennsylvania.
November 1945:	Returned to Japan.
December 1945:	Arrested and placed in Sugamo Prison, Toshima-ku, Tokyo.
April 1946:	Indicted on several counts.
May 1946-- November 1948:	Tried by the International Military Tribunal for the Far East.
November 1948:	Found guilty on Count 1, over-all conspiracy, and sentenced to life imprisonment.
December 1955:	Released from Sugamo Prison on parole.
April 1958:	Granted clemency.
6 June 1975:	Died, Chigasaki, Japan.

APPENDIX D

The State Secretary to the Embassy in Japan[1]

Telegram

Berlin, May 15, 1939--11:00 p.m.

No. 159

For the Ambassador personally.

Herewith for your personal information are the papers referred to in telegram No. 158, namely:

1) The draft pact for joint consultation and mutual assistance agreed upon by the German, Japanese and Italian Governments consisting of:

    a) the actual pact,
    b) the protocol of signature
    and
    c) the secret additional protocol.

2) The draft of a new article on the relationship of the Three Power pact to the pact between Germany and Italy to be inserted before the final article.

3) The draft of a note to be submitted by the Japanese Ambassador before the signature, on possible statements by the Japanese Government in reply to diplomatic enquiries.

4) The draft of a formal statement to be made orally by the Japanese Ambassador likewise before the signature.

The assent of the Japanese Government to the papers Nos. 2, 3, and 4 has not yet been received.

The text of the documents referred to above is as follows:

Pact for Joint Consultation and Mutual Assistance between

Japan, Italy and Germany

---

1. DGFP, D, 6, No. 383, pp. 496-500.

Appendix D

The Imperial Japanese Government,
The Italian Government,
and the Government of the German Reich,

having regard to the fact that friendly relations between
Japan, Italy and Germany have deepened since the conclusion of the Pact against the Communist International on
November 25, 1936, being convinced that the international
activities of the Communist International are a threat to
peace in Europe and Asia, and being resolved, in the spirit
of the above-mentioned Agreement, to reinforce their
defence against communist disintegration in Europe and Asia
and also to safeguard the common interests of the three
Contracting Parties, have agreed upon the following
provisions:

Article I

In the event of one of the Contracting Parties becoming involved in difficulties owing to the conduct of a
Power not party to this Pact, or of more than one of such
Powers, the Contracting Parties will immediately consult
together as to the common measures to be adopted.

Article II

In the event of one of the Contracting Parties being
menaced without provocation by one or more Powers not
party to this Pact, the other Contracting Parties pledge
themselves to afford the menaced Power their political
and economic support to remove this menace.

Article III

In the event of one of the Contracting Parties becom-
ing the victim of unprovoked aggression by one or more
Powers not party to this Pact, the other Contracting
Parties pledge themselves to render aid and assistance.

The three Contracting Parties will, if the need should
arise, immediately consult on and decide the necessary
measures for carrying out the obligations laid down in
the preceding paragraph.

Article IV

The original text of the Pact is drawn up in Japanese,
Italian and German.

The Pact shall come into force on the day of signature and be valid for five years. The Contracting Parties will reach agreement on the further form of the cooperation between them in good time before the expiry of this period.

In witness whereof the duly accredited plenipotentiaries of their Governments have signed this Pact and affixed thereto their seals.

Done in triplicate, each copy being equally authentic, etc.

Protocol of Signature

On the occasion of the signature of the Pact concluded this day the plenipotentiaries have agreed on the following:

(A) Relative to Articles 2 and 3 of the Pact, a threat to or aggression against Manchukuo will, pursuant to the provisions of paragraph 2 of the Protocol concluded between Japan and Manchukuo on September 15, 1932, be regarded as a threat to or aggression against Japan.

(B) Relative to paragraph 2 of Article 4 of the Pact, if support or aid and assistance are still being rendered pursuant to Article 2 or 3 when its period expires, the Pact will remain in force until the end of the situation in which the support or aid and assistance is necessary.

Berlin, the.....................

Secret Additional Protocol

On the occasion of the signature of the Pact concluded this day the aforementioned plenipotentiaries have agreed upon the following:

(A) Relative to Articles 2 and 3 of the Pact the competent authorities of the three Contracting Parties will, as soon as possible after the Pact comes into force, examine in advance what separate possibilities of conflicts exist and in what manner and to what extent the Contracting Parties, each according to its geographical situation, shall render support or aid and assistance.

Appendix D

(B) In the event of a war jointly conducted by them, the Contracting Parties pledge themselves not to conclude a separate armistice or peace.

(C) In the event of there being any commitments under existing treaties with third Powers, which are at variance with the provisions of this Pact, the Contracting Parties will not be bound by such commitments.

(D) This Secret Additional Protocol will not be published or communicated to third Powers without the concurrence of the Contracting Parties.

(E) This Secret Additional Protocol is valid for the same period as the Pact and the Protocol of Signature. It forms an integral unit with these two.

Paper No. 2

In the draft Pact for Joint Consultation and Mutual Assistance between Japan, Italy and Germany at present being negotiated a new Article worded as follows should be inserted before the final Article IV:

"The German Government and the Italian Government confirm in agreement with the Japanese Government that the Pact of Friendship and Alliance between Germany and Italy signed on May 22, 1939, which is the consequence of these countries being neighbours and of their special position in Europe, is not affected by the present Pact, and that therefore the present Pact is only applicable to the relationship between Germany and Italy insofar as the Pact of May 22, 1939, does not contain more extensive commitments."

Paper No. 3

Note

The Japanese Government will, on the conclusion of the Pact between Germany, Italy and Japan now under negotiation, reply orally to any diplomatic enquiries from the third party regarding the Pact on the following lines:

1. The Pact is a purely defensive Pact. It pursues no aggressive aims, but its object is to ensure the maintenance of peace. The Pact therefore is not directed against any country whatsoever.

2.   Historically the Pact has developed from the fact
that the three Contracting Parties have joined together
in recent years for common defence against the subversive
activities of the Comintern.   In the present international
situation Japan, for her part, feels herself to be primarily
menaced by the aspirations of the Communist International.
The Japanese Government have therefore viewed these Communist aspirations emanating from Soviet Russia as the most
acute menace to peace.

3.   If one of the Powers party to the Pact should be
attacked without provocation, the consequences for the
signatory Powers are evident from the text of the Pact.
As long as third Powers do not threaten or attack the
Contracting Parties, the obligations for support and the
rendering of aid and assistance provided for in the Pact
do not come into operation.

Paper No. 4

On behalf of my Government I beg Your Excellency to
take note of the fact that, at the present time and in the
immediate future, Japan will, in the military sense, only
be able to a limited extent to implement the obligations
to render aid and assistance undertaken in Article III of
the Pact.   Further details regarding the military assistance to be given at any time in the future are reserved
for the further discussions which are provided for in the
Secret Additional Protocol.

[signed] Weizsäcker

APPENDIX E

Ambassador Oshima's Account of His Conversation

with Hitler on 27 May*

Hitler: It is on the Italian front that the fighting
is now most acute; England and America have thrown against
us an infinitude of weapons and materials. In my opinion,
the main object of this new drive is to lure German military strength to that theater, and we are therefore not
making too great an effort to prevent the loss of territory.
Instead, we are gradually retiring, meanwhile putting up
very stiff resistance and inflicting huge losses on the
enemy.[1]

Since the military situation in Italy depends much
on the enemy's superiority in the air, it would be an effective measure for Germany to send in aerial reinforcements.
However, the other theaters would suffer as a result, and

1. On 19 May German Under Secretary for Foreign Affairs
von Steengracht told Oshima that: "In the new offensive
on the Italian front, the Americans are using everything
they have in materiel; the attack has been terrible. If
the German Army pours in reinforcements, it might be possible to maintain the present line, but that would fit in
exactly with the American strategy of attracting the German forces to the Italian area in anticipation of establishing a second front elsewhere. Therefore, we have
retreated in certain sections" (M.S. 22 May 44).

*"Magic," SRS 1320, 1 June 1944, RG 457. This "Magic"
document was in the War Department, Office of the Army
Chief of Staff, G-2, nearly four days before the fall of
Rome and six days before D-Day landings at Normandy--the
only changes I have made are in spacing and the use of
arabic numerals for footnote reference marks in lieu of
asterisks. I have neither deleted nor added material;
information in brackets was supplied by American intercept
personnel.

179

accordingly we are refraining from sending any more planes
to Italy.

For some time we Germans had been using the Apennine
range and had established a powerful position, but from the
point of view of expediency, it was decided that it was
best to defend Rome on a line running from the Alban Hills
on the West Coast to a point south of the Gransasso Moun-
tains and finally to a point north of Pescara on the East
Coast. Therefore, while inflicting as much damage as possible on the enemy, we will retire to that line, which we
call "Position C."

The lull on the Russian front continues, but I believe
that the Soviets will attack before long. For the time
being, Germany has taken the steps necessary to stave off
such a drive. The Hungarian Army has already sent 17 divisions to the front, and Rumania practically the same
number.[2] In view of past experience, we Germans have seen
fit to place some of our finest divisions, particularly
armored divisions, among those foreign troops.

We Germans have known all along that the Axis should
have defended along the Don, but Hungary and Rumania never
could grasp that fact. Now, however, the flames are close
to their own borders, and the Hungarian and Rumanian forces
are more aware of the peril. So far, they have stood up
rather well.

Oshima: What course do you expect the Soviet drive
to take?

Hitler: I think that it will be two-pronged; in my
opinion they will head northwest from the Lwow area and
penetrate into central Poland, and they will also invade
Rumania. I think that the drive from Lwow will come first,
and the attempted invasion of Rumania afterwards. As for
me, I am not satisfied to stay on the defensive forever
and, as I told you the last time we talked, when I see my
chance I intend to turn to the offensive again.

Oshima: What is your feeling about the second front?

---

2. Collateral information indicates that the figure for
Rumanian divisions is substantially correct, but that the
total Hungarian strength on the southeastern front is
probably no more than 11 divisions.

Hitler: I believe that sooner or later an invasion
of Europe will be attempted. I understand that the enemy
has already assembled about 80 divisions in the British
Isles. Of that force, a mere 8 divisions are composed of
first-class fighting men with experience in actual warfare.

Oshima: Does Your Excellency believe that those Anglo-
American forces are fully prepared to invade?

Hitler: Yes.

Oshima: I wonder what ideas you have as to how the
second front will be carried out.

Hitler: Well, judging from relatively clear portents,
I think that diversionary actions will take place in a number of places--against Norway, Denmark, the southern part
of western France, and the French Mediterranean coast.
After that--when they have established bridgeheads in
Normandy and Brittany and have sized up their prospects--
they will then come forward with an all-out second front
across the Straits of Dover. We ourselves would like nothing better to strike one great blow as soon as possible.
But that will not be feasible if the enemy does what I
anticipate; their men will be dispersed. In that event, we
intend to finish off the enemy's troops at the several
bridgeheads. The number of German troops in the west still
amounts to about 60 divisions.[3]

Oshima: I, too, figure that the signs point toward an
invasion sooner or later by the Anglo-Americans. Since the
enemy apparently intends to take that step--or even if perchance he does not--there is much to think about. During
our last conversation, you told me that, in case they did
not come, you thought you might blast southern England with
rocket guns and then find an opportunity to take the initiative again on the Eastern Front. Well, since then, the
Anglo-Americans have been bombing the channel area more
heavily than ever. I wonder if those weapons you were
going to use against England have not been destroyed.

Hitler: No, those guns are in an arsenal made of
impermeable concrete. They are in no danger.

Oshima: If the Anglo-Americans do not stage an inva-

---

3. Hitler's figure is in substantial accord with other
estimates.

sion, don't you think it would be a little dangerous to
return your troops to the Eastern Front?

Hitler: Well, I have no intention of waiting forever
for them to come. I will give them two or three more
months; if they don't come then, Germany will take the
offensive. By that time, we will have finished organizing
and equipping additional forces and will have between 60
and 70 [new] divisions, including 45 armored divisions
[Oshima interpolates that he is not sure his memory is
correct on the figure 45]; we will then be in a position to
attack. I have already exceeded my goal for S.S. divisions;
25 of them are now practically organized and equipped.[4]

Oshima: The line where both the German and Soviet
armies now face each other, leaving out the three Baltic
nations, is just about what it was when the war started.
For you to go ahead and repeat a drive with the same idea
in mind that you have always had could not--would not--
finally decide the conflict. I think that you ought to
adopt another view and wage an action like that at Cannae
long ago.[5] What does Your Excellency think of that?

Hitler: To tell you the truth, the Soviet striking
power has more or less weakened. Roughly speaking, the
Russians now have about 700 divisions on the front line,
and about 200 in reserve. But those figures are misleading.
For instance, a great many of the divisions are not even up
to regimental strength. Their materiel is also insuffi-
cient, and the quality of the Russian infantry has deteri-
orated extremely.

The cavalry and tanks, however, are still excellent.
As a result of their experience in actual warfare, the
Russians' ability to use great groups of cavalry has in-
creased tremendously. As to the Soviet shells, although

---

4. Hitler's figure for S.S. divisions tallies approximately with collateral estimates.

5. Hannibal decisively defeated the Romans at Cannae by
means of a famous double envelopment operation. The Roman
Army achieved a break-through in the center but was then
caught between the powerful Carthagenian flanks, which had
remained to the rear of the center. Additional flanking
troops then came around the Roman rear, and achieved a
complete encirclement. Only about one fourth of the Roman
troops escaped.

they are in no way technically superior to ours, they are
qualitatively better, since they use large amounts of tung-
sten and molybdenum. Moreover, considering the terrain on
the Eastern Front, their tanks, particularly the T-34's,
are better than Germany's. Our Tigers are too heavy, and
in time of mud, they cannot be used; our Panthers are still
in the experimental stage, and have had any number of minor
defects. Recently, however, we have succeeded in improving
them.

On the Russian front highly mobile assault guns are
absolutely necessary. Before long, we are going to attach
a considerable number of assault guns to every regiment.
We will also set up 45 [the figure is somewhat doubtful]
assault gun brigades as reserves. We are gradually making
progress. We have just ordered Speer to carry out plans
for increasing assault guns and tanks, principally for use
in our war with Russia. By January of next year, it appears
that we are likely to have a monthly output of 1,800 assault
guns and 1,500 tanks.[6] As for the Luftwaffe, we have been
found numerically wanting since America entered the war.
However, we have been concentrating on increasing fighter
planes, and by September our monthly amount is scheduled to
reach 6,000 and by January of 1945, 8,000. [Oshima interpolates that, although Hitler used the word "fighters,"
he probably meant to include other types.][7]

In the past, damage wrought by English and American
air raids has indeed not been small, but, as you know, most
of it has been to dwellings. Innocent people have been
killed and wounded and there has been great destruction of
property, but the damage to factories and other production
equipment has been relatively very light.

Important plane production has, for the most part,
gone underground, and in two months the job will be about
finished, thus enabling us further to reduce the effect of
air raids. Militarily, we Germans still have a hard time
ahead, but I am confident that before the end of the year

---

6. British and American estimates agree that at the end of
1943 Germany was producing approximately 300 tanks and 50
"assault guns" (mounted on tank chassis) per month.

7. The British Air Ministry estimates that, in the month
of March 1944, Germany's total production of combat aircraft
was 900.

we will begin to regain the initiative.

* * *

In a separate report, Ambassador Oshima states that,
in the course of the conversation, Hitler "spoke of a new
submarine war, saying that in several months he thought he
would be able to begin to get effective results." According
to the Ambassador, he himself took the opportunity to
"speak frankly about the items we want from the German
Navy."[8] Oshima's report continues:

> "The Chancellor congratulated me deeply on the
> glorious victories of the Imperial Navy and went on
> to say that in this great war, in order to win the
> victory, the armies of both Japan and Germany must,
> of extreme necessity, always be provided with the
> most modern materiel and that Germany would not keep
> anything secret but would let Japan have any and
> every thing. That was how he spoke."

---

8. It is not known just what items Oshima was referring
to. Recently the Japanese have been particularly interested in obtaining from the Germans (a) plans and samples
of the newest radar equipment and jamming devices, particularly equipment designed to protect submarines against
air attacks, and (b) details of the latest German plans
concerning submarines capable of traveling at high speeds
when submerged.

APPENDIX F

Excerpts from Ōshima's Reports of His Last

Conference with Hitler, 4 September 1944*

Hitler: The course of the war in the West has been a great disappointment. The reason for all our reverses on that front is that some of the conspirators in the incident of 20 July were also located in the West and carried on sabotage.[1]

---

1. In a short separate message, Oshima stated that Ribbentrop had deliberately left the discussion of the military situation to Hitler, but that he did say:

"The fact that Germany's military situation is very disadvantageous on both the Eastern and Western Fronts is largely due to sabotage on the part of those implicated in the affair of 20 July. For example, the collapse of Army Group Center on the Eastern Front was the result of an order to retreat issued without permission by Genmaj. von Tresckow, who was subsequently so conscience-stricken that he went to the front lines and committed suicide. Von Tresckow was Chief of Staff of the 4th Panzer Army" [then in Army Group South; Oshima may have meant the 4th Army, which was in Army Group Center; in previous reports he has identified von Tresckow as "Chief of Staff of an army in Army Group Center" and one of the ringleaders of the conspiracy against Hitler (DS 19 Aug; 1 Sept 44)].

---

*"Magic," SRS 1419, 8 September 1944, and SRS 1420, 9 September 1944, RG 457. Asterisk footnote reference marks in copy number MI-3 have been replaced with arabic numerals.

Appendix F

Throughout the reign of Wilhelm I [1861-1888] the German Officer Corps was really excellent, but beginning with the reign of Wilhelm II [1888-1918] members of the Army were treated too well and as a result became a special caste; as their life became more showy, their spirit degenerated. Although the old traditions survived through the last war and excellent officers were produced, after the revolution of 1918 the officers lost their sense of loyalty and of unity. [Sentence missing.] I strove to build a true 'peoples army,' but time was short and the present war broke out before I had been able completely to achieve my purpose.

Naturally, I consider that the recent incident was a misfortune; but, if it had to happen, it is fortunate that it came when it did, for if such a situation had arisen in the midst of a really decisive struggle Germany might have completely collapsed.

Oshima: The conspirators involved in the 20 July plot seem to have been widely scattered. I wonder whether it will be possible to liquidate every single one of them.

Hitler: Their number all told was not large, and I assure you that we are now carrying out a thorough purge which will extend even to the lowliest of those involved.

To return: As a result of all this, the situation of the German forces in the West became extremely critical and grave difficulties were encountered even in waging a retreating battle. However, the fighting spirit of the troops was excellent and they somehow or other fought through the crisis.

Nevertheless, in an area such as France, where there are many good roads, etc., once the German lines had been breached by a large tank force it was necessary to fall back to new positions. Accordingly, it was determined to withdraw most of the forces to the West Wall, even from the Antwerp area, leaving behind garrison troops in the most important coastal fortifications, such as Bordeaux, Le Havre and the Brittany ports.

From the beginning we have realized that in order to stabilize the lines it would be necessary to launch a German counterattack. Accordingly, troops are now being massed southeast of Nancy with the intention of striking from the flank at the American forces on the southeast wing, which have been pursuing us in five or six columns, each composed of three to four divisions. [Oshima interpolates at this point that Hitler calculated the present Allied strength in northern France at "about 50 divisions all told."]

In that attack it is planned to employ Army Group ["G"] commanded by Genobst. Blaskowitz and also troops moved up from Germany itself. Except for small security detachments operating on the banks of the Loire and rear guard units in the area of the Rhone River, the main strength of Blaskowitz's Army Group is falling back to a planned line without suffering serious losses.

The offensive which I have just mentioned will be only for the purpose of stabilizing the present front. However, when the current replenishment of the air forces is completed and when the new army of more than a million men, which is now being organized, is ready, I intend to combine the new units with units to be withdrawn from all possible areas and to open a large-scale offensive in the West.

Oshima: When do you plan to launch such an offensive?

Hitler: After the beginning of November. We will be aided in holding off the enemy during September and October by the comparatively rainy weather which will restrict the enemy's employment of their superior air power.

Oshima: The present struggle has developed more and more into a real two-front war and Germany must, therefore, strike a deadly blow at the enemy on one front or the other. However, in view of the present situation in the West, I am apprehensive about Germany's ability to maintain her battle lines there until she is in a position to launch a real offensive. Furthermore, I am concerned about the possibility that the offensive may be delayed because of the difficulties of organizing and equipping the new troops.

Hitler: I have complete confidence in the West Wall. Furthermore, even though ----- [word missing] line may require some withdrawal, I expect that we shall for the most part be able to maintain it. As for our ability to organize and equip new troops, I do not believe that there will be any difficulty, in view of the efforts of Speer [Minister for Armaments and War Production].

Appendix F

Oshima: When you speak of withdrawing German troops from every area in order to launch a large-scale offensive in the West, what areas do you have in mind?

Hitler: My plan is to withdraw the maximum number of troops wherever possible. I am thinking of evacuating Greece and the Balkans and defending either a line stretching southwest from the southern Carpathians in Transylvania to Yugoslavia or a line stretching west from the old Hungarian border.

On the Italian Front work was begun on the present line of defense about a year ago and there is no reason why we could not hold it if we chose to do so. However, the position which can be best defended by a small force is in the Alps, and our intention is to retreat that far in order to be able to divert troops to critical areas. I have also given some thought to withdrawing the units along the Baltic, now that Finland need no longer be considered, but it would be too great a loss to have the Baltic entirely under enemy control and we have gone no further with the idea of such a withdrawal. The loss of our submarine bases in western France has given added importance to such bases in Norway and I have been forced to abandon any idea of evacuating Norway.

Oshima: If too many areas are evacuated, won't Germany's war production be hampered by a shortage of raw material?

Hitler: That factor has naturally been considered. Generally speaking, we have a supply of important raw materials sufficient to last for two years and therefore our war production will not be interfered with by the contemplated withdrawals.

Oshima: If the enemy complete their encirclement of Germany, they will naturally carry out indiscriminate round-the-clock bombings in an effort to cripple military production and obstruct the organization of new forces.

Hitler: It is to be expected that the enemy will take such steps, but our anti-aircraft units are constantly increasing in strength. In addition, we intend to call back to Germany the fighter plane and air defense units which up to now have been scattered in many areas beyond the German borders.

As for the war in the East, a difficult situation arose on the Rumanian front in view of that country's treachery. Part of the German forces there have already reached Transylvania and part are still continuing to fight, but unhappily some divisions have been destroyed. Elsewhere on the Eastern Front, however, the battle lines have been fairly well stabilized and, although Russia is expected to take the offensive in the future, Germany has been able to post a great many units even on the second line of defense, and I believe there will be no great difficulty in maintaining our position and carrying on a defensive fight.

Oshima: Assuming that it is impossible to negotiate a peace at the present moment, would it not be possible to do so later on, at a time when the war situation in the West is going more favorably for Germany?

Hitler: I have made it a point to study carefully the policy and plans of my enemy Stalin. He, like myself, is a leader of a dictatorial state and therefore I believe that I fully comprehend his way of thinking. It is my opinion that, as long as Russia retains her strength, Stalin will not accept any peace offer.

Oshima: According to what you told me in the fall of 1935,[2] it was Germany's intention to split up the Soviet Union into several small states and it is my understanding that that was still Germany's objective at the outbreak of the Russo-German war. However, at present don't you think that such a scheme is utterly impossible?

Hitler: Such a goal seemed possible during 1941 and 1942 when the German Army was advancing on a line from Moscow to Stalingrad. However, as was not unnatural, we suffered some setbacks on the Eastern Front.

Hitler hinted that the aims of his war with Russia were not the same as they had been. I went on to ask him about his plans for the Eastern Front, and he replied:

"Although the critical war situation on the Western Front makes a definite statement impossible, it is my opinion that we will once again have to strike at the

---

2. This date appears clearly in the message. Oshima was Military Attaché in Berlin from 1934 to 1938.

Appendix F

Russian Army in the East."

    At the end of my conversation with Chancellor Hitler, Ribbentrop stated in Hitler's presence that, if Japan should directly sound out Russian opinion on the question of peace, the enemy would think that it was done at Germany's request and would conclude that Germany was showing the white feather. Therefore, he requested that Japan avoid taking such a step.

APPENDIX G

8 March Report from Ambassador Oshima

Describing Living Conditions in

Berlin*

Transportation

Except immediately after large air attacks, the Stadtbahn [electric train service to the suburbs] has continued to maintain service on practically all lines. However, at quite a few places within the city the U-Bahn [subway system] operates only shuttle runs [between bombed-out sections] from which transfers can be made to lines running from the central section of the city to the suburbs. The streetcar system within the city is repaired very slowly and service is extremely irregular; for that reason, its use has been greatly reduced. With the exception of the rush hours in the early morning and in the evening, traffic facilities have been reduced by half so that there is very great confusion, and after 9:30 or 10:00 p.m. practically all service stops.

Supplies of gasoline for civilian use have been more and more restricted. Our office had been receiving no more than 200 liters [about 53 gallons] per month, but on 1 March even that allowance was cut off. As a result, gasoline for both official and private cars is now being purchased on the black market in exchange for coffee. However, it has gradually become more difficult to buy gasoline even on the black market and, besides, the restricted facilities for transportation to and from foreign countries have made it hard to obtain coffee.

Traffic in the city is also made difficult by the

---

*"Magic," SRS 1607, 15 March 1945, RG 457. No changes have been made in this document except in the "Food" section where the numeral 1 replaces an asterisk.

barricades which have been constructed in a number of sections of the city, chiefly in the area around the Wilhelmstrasse. The barricades are from two to three meters high and from one to two meters thick; they are made of debris, bricks, etc., and are built by prisoners of war, convicts, the Volkssturm, women, etc.

Public Services

Every household has had to use less and less gas and coal, and recently electric power has been frequently cut off as an economy measure. Often there is virtually no electric power from sundown to bedtime, which makes it difficult to ----- [words missing] in the homes and impossible to use the radio or to show movies. As a result, the people generally are deprived of recreation.

Furthermore, in the houses of the general public cardboard has been used to replace window panes broken by the constant air attacks, so that electric light is needed even in the daytime. When the electric power is cut off, some of the retail stores have to close, which frequently makes it difficult for citizens to purchase daily necessities.

This situation has caused a sharp increase in the demand for candles, but it is practically impossible to procure them.

When air raid signals are sounded, the electric current is always turned on so that people can hear the radio announcements. On Sundays the current is turned on all day and special efforts are made to provide facilities for recreation, laundering, etc., on those days.

As another measure to save electricity, the use of the telephone has been greatly restricted. Although up to now government offices, foreign diplomatic missions, hotels, etc., have not been affected, the privilege of making calls on home telephones has been suspended in many places and it is only possible to receive calls. Furthermore, the recent daily large-scale air attacks on the central part of Berlin have left many areas still without telephone service, thus considerably hindering the activities of our office. (Contact between members of my staff and the Germans has also been made more difficult by the restricted transportation facilities.)

Hotels, restaurants, etc., have also been greatly
damaged by the continuous air attacks. The authorities
have provided special facilities for their restoration,
but in general there is great confusion, and eating and
drinking at night is practically impossible because of the
air raids and the transportation restrictions.

Air Attacks

Recent air attacks over Berlin have not been as heavy
as those of 3 and 26 February, but air attacks on central
Saxony have been so extensive that they have frequently
caused air raid alarms to be sounded in Berlin as well.
Then, too, there are frequent so-called "nuisance attacks";
most of them come at about 10:00 p.m. and last an hour or
so, but sometimes they occur for an hour before dawn, beginning about 3:00 a.m. Although they are called "nuisance
attacks," recently at least 40-50 Mosquito planes have par-
ticipated--the usual number is 60-80--dropping two-ton
bombs and attempting to destroy residences by means of
aerial mines. A large number of bombs have fallen in the
neighborhood of my office [on Tiergartenstrasse], but
usually have broken only window panes. On the whole damage
from such attacks has not been particularly great, but
since they come every night it is difficult to overcome a
feeling of annoyance. Furthermore, subways, streetcar
lines, etc., are often damaged.

Communications with foreign countries

As for communications with the outside world, practically the only air route still open is the one to Sweden,
which has four flights weekly. Air connections with Spain
are irregular and unreliable; air mail service to Switzerland on the government line via Basel is often suspended.
Recently express and first-class trains [to Switzerland]
have been discontinued; one must go by ordinary trains and
make a number of transfers. Because of the danger of air
attacks, a circuitous route has to be followed and the trip
takes two or three days. When couriers make the trip, the
baggage which they can take with them is very limited, and
it is impossible for them to carry on their business as
they have in the past.

There are also many difficulties in making telephone
connections with other countries; frequently such contact

is impossible for days at a time.

Morale

There are a large number of foreign laborers in Berlin, but even Russian prisoners of war are continuing to do their work as in the past. It is difficult to discover any evidence of unrest. Thefts of food, liquor, tobacco, etc., are not on the same level as in the past [i.e., presumably have increased]; no particular rise in burglaries and major crimes has been noted. Recently posters in the streets announced that a number of deserters under a certain sub-lieutenant had been shot, but the story that a large number of deserters and foreign laborers, etc., have hidden in the ruins of Berlin is nothing more than empty propaganda.

Food

As a result of the present emergency, some items of food have become unobtainable and there are temporary shortages of others due to transportation difficulties; on the other hand, there are supplies of commodities such as vegetables and items which can be preserved for a long time, such as sausage and hard bread. Although there have been various restrictions on the use of food ration coupons,[1] the principle has been maintained in spite of all difficulties that the people shall be able to purchase necessary food articles at officially established prices by means of those coupons and, therefore, a minimum stability in living conditions has been attained.

Housing

The destruction of residences by the continuous air attacks, together with the influx of refugees from the East, has greatly aggravated the housing problem. Consequently, when a large-scale air attack at one blow produces a large

---

1. On 4 February the German Food Minister announced that ration coupons would have to last 9 weeks instead of the scheduled 8, and on 28 February specific cuts were announced, effective 1 March, in the rations for rye bread, processed food and fats.

number of homeless persons, the task of housing them is not
an easy one, as can well be imagined. Yet even of late,
the homeless who swarm the streets on the day of an air
attack disappear into the shadows the next day, which
proves that the leaders possess organizing efficiency and
that their administrative ability is functioning as usual.
Recently, there has been some relaxation of the ban on
travel and permission has been granted for women with
children under ten to leave Berlin, a move doubtless
designed to ease the housing problem.

APPENDIX H

Excerpts from Ōshima's Reports of His Conversations with

Ribbentrop, March and April 1945, Followed by the

"Magic" Diplomatic Summary of 16 April 1945*

On the evening of 17 March, at the request of Foreign
Minister von Ribbentrop, I called on him. For a period of
about three hours we had a friendly chat centering chiefly
on Russo-German problems. (Ribbentrop expressed the wish
that it be regarded as just an exchange of views between
friends.) We met again later, and by the 28th we had had
three more talks [on the 19th, the 27th and the 28th].

Needless to say, these conversations deal with secret
matters of very great importance to Germany, and if even
only a part of them should perchance leak out to outsiders
(and this includes Germans), it would of course put Germany
in a very difficult position both from a political and a
military standpoint. Ribbentrop's action involves also the
question of faith in me, and hence in our Imperial Government. I fear that any carelessness on our part might become a great impediment whenever in the future the necessity arises to undertake a thing of this kind. So I wish
that you would give this information to as small a number
of people as possible.

Our interview on the 17th proceeded about as follows:

Ribbentrop: Today I should like to talk to Your
Excellency, who has been my friend for many years, not in
my capacity as Foreign Minister but as a private individual. What I shall say I have not discussed with the

*"Magic," SRS 1626, 3 April 1945; SRS 1632, 9 April 1945;
and SRS 1639, 16 April 1945, RG 457. Arabic numerals replace asterisks as footnote reference marks.

Chancellor or, naturally, with any of my own subordinates.

There has been no change in my view that in the present situation it will be very difficult to split Russia off from America and England and make a separate peace with her ----- [words missing] some sort of military success ----- [words missing] but the Chancellor has held a deep-seated belief that he would be able to produce a complete change in the war situation on the Eastern Front. Recently, in studying closely statements of American and English army officer prisoners, I have found evidence of a rather deep-rooted antipathy toward Russia. There are not a few who say that, after forcing the collapse of Germany, they intend to beat up Russia. At first I thought this was only the personal view of two or three individuals, but looking at the matter from all sides I have been compelled to the view that this may perhaps indicate the basic idea of America and England.

After all, now that the democratic states like America and England have such a mighty military force, particularly in the air, they have an opportunity which, once lost, it would be difficult to recapture. The idea of annihilating Russia also at this time might well arise from ambition for world domination on the part of America, and from the desire to protect the British Empire against the Red peril on the part of England. And if America and England have such designs, Stalin will certainly be apprehensive about this. (For example, at the Yalta Conference Stalin interpreted the American and British plan to set up governments pleasing to them in Japan and Germany after the war as an intrigue directed against Russia.) Furthermore, if Russia could not succeed against the American and British sea and air forces today, how much worse off would she be if an anti-Russian crusade army were organized by America and England, taking advantage of the very deep-seated trend of opposition to Russia existing in all the countries of Europe (there would be not a few, even in Germany, who would participate as volunteers).

If all this is true, Stalin, in order to oppose America and England in the future, might possibly come around to the idea of making allies of Japan and Germany.

If by any chance Stalin harbors such an idea, it would be proper for us to seize any offer whatever, without making the question of terms a problem. To give my own private opinion, I think Germany would consider it all

right to offer Russia all the Balkans, northern Europe,
etc., retaining only old German territory, Hungary and
Croatia, and further, to support Russia if she wished to
penetrate to the Dardanelles, or even to Suez.

If it were possible even to make contact, I feel that
I would be willing to fly to Moscow myself and negotiate
directly with Stalin.

What does Your Excellency think?

Oshima: I, too, recognize that relations between
Russia and America and England are delicate, but before
giving my [final] views I should like to find out a little
more about whether relations are as strained as Your
Excellency has said. At the moment, my personal idea is
that it will not be easy to arrange a compromise peace,
since Germany is without military success, but--however
that may be--[in any such attempt] it would be vital to
ascertain Stalin's intentions and it would be proper for
Germany to sound out Russia's intentions through the
channels she possesses.

Ribbentrop: Germany will have to find some way of
getting in contact with the Soviet Union. If this were
done through citizens of some third power, there would be
considerable danger that the whole story might leak out.
On the other hand, if Germany should directly initiate such
a move herself, there would be great danger that the Soviet
Union might use it against us. I therefore cannot but feel
that it would be most desirable for Japan to act as intermediary.

Which approach does the Japanese Government consider
the most likely to succeed?

Oshima: As far as a likely place for arranging such
a move is concerned, I might suggest Moscow, Tokyo or
Stockholm. However, I do not know what Japanese-Soviet
relations are like in general, or what the specific relations are between the Japanese and Soviet authorities at
those three places, and so I cannot give you a positive
reply. However, it might be possible to sound out the
views of the Soviet Union by raising this question in connection with negotiations on some important issue now at
stake between Japan and the Soviet Union.

Ribbentrop: Personally, I feel that the time has not

yet come for bringing this matter up as a formal question.
I do think, however, that the matter might be broached informally to the Soviet officials in Stockholm through your
Military Attaché, some newspaperman, or some other appropriate person.

At this point Ribbentrop asked me various questions
about the situation in Stockholm, but I avoided a definite
reply, saying that I was not familiar with the present
state of affairs in that city. As for the idea of using a
newspaperman, I said that, from the point of view of security, that was absolutely out of the question. Ribbentrop
evinced some interest in the possibility of using Attaché
Onodera [Major General, Military Attaché in Stockholm].

We then both decided that the question was one which
merited deeper study, and decided to exchange views at
some later date.

We met again on the 19th, and I spoke as follows:

"Unfortunately I have no way of finding out the
actual state of affairs at the localities which we
discussed, so that anything I tell you is more or less
in the nature of a surmise. However, I must tell you
frankly that, no matter what approach you adopt, no
one can give you any absolute guarantee that the Soviet
Union will not misuse any move you make. No matter
what you do, there will be a certain risk involved,
and if you are afraid of risk you will simply not be
able to do anything.

"Japan for her part will do her best to find the
most suitable approach, as you have suggested."

I then once again urged him to consider the idea of
having the Japanese Government sound out the views of the
Soviet Union. Ribbentrop agreed to the idea, but still
showed some hesitancy about broaching the matter formally,
and said that before trying this approach he would still
like to investigate the possibility of having the thing
taken up informally with the Soviet Government by somebody
like Onodera, our Attaché in Stockholm.

I replied that, that being the case, I would on my own
responsibility either ask Attaché Onodera to come to Berlin,
after I had conferred with my own Military Attaché [Lt.
Gen. Komatsu], or else I would send someone to Stockholm in

order to investigate local conditions there. After this,
our next talk could be held. I then took my leave.

In accordance with the above, Attaché Komatsu made
inquiries of Onodera, who came to Berlin on the 27th. I
saw Ribbentrop again later that day and told him that
Attaché Onodera was apparently not especially familiar with
any of the members of the Soviet Legation, but was acquaint-[1]
ed with the Acting Minister [presumably Counselor Semenov].
In addition, I said, although there was no assurance that
it would be immediately ----- [word missing] because
Onodera ----- [words missing], Onodera was prepared to make
an initial investigation of the actual situation within the
Soviet Legation and of suitable methods of establishing
contact, in accordance with the wishes of the German authorities. I went on to say that, in the event contact was
established with the Russians at some time in the future,
I would proceed on the assumption that my Government would
approve.

Ribbentrop then said that, after our second talk [on
the 19th], he had exchanged views on the matter with
Chancellor Hitler. As in the past, the latter was of the
opinion that, since it was very unlikely that Stalin was at
present considering peace with Germany, it was necessary to
rely on military results to the bitter end ----- [words
missing[2]]. Ribbentrop added that it was necessary to have
complete trust in the words of the Fuehrer.

I insisted:

"Naturally it is fine that Germany possesses the
hope of military success; but in any event it would be
a timely step to find out Stalin's real intentions.
Also, if by any chance Germany could make peace with
Russia and could make use of the troops being held in
reserve on the Eastern Front to achieve a victory
against the American and British armies, nothing could

---

1. Russian Minister Kollontay left Stockholm for Russia in
mid-March. Semenov's name was mentioned last year in connection with a peace rumor.

2. From what follows it seems likely that Ribbentrop quoted
Hitler as expressing confidence in the outcome of forthcoming military operations.

be better. For my part, I hope that this [i.e., Hitler's decision] will be reconsidered, not only for Germany's sake but from the standpoint of the joint conduct of the war by Japan and Germany."

Ribbentrop said that he was in entire agreement with my views.

I went on:

"With regard to choosing a method which will cause Germany as little trouble as possible, I don't know whether they have any brilliant ideas in Tokyo. However, whether the proposal would be made in Moscow or in Stockholm, I should like to talk once more with Hitler about a proposal for sounding out Russia's views."

Ribbentrop agreed to this.

Our final interview, on the 28th, may be summarized as follows:

Ribbentrop: I talked with Chancellor Hitler again today, and he is still of the same opinion: he believes that under present circumstances it would react to Germany's disadvantage for a hand to be extended to Russia, whether by Germany or by Japan. It is much to be regretted that Your Excellency has been troubled on several occasions for hours at a time and that Attaché Onodera has come to Berlin, but I should like to drop the matter herewith for the time being.

Oshima: If that is the Chancellor's determination, there is nothing to be done. Is he opposed to peace with Russia as a matter of principle, or does he intend to follow the matter up if the situation should change?

Ribbentrop: If the Chancellor comes to feel that this [peace with Russia] is possible, he will take action. In 1939 also, the Chancellor did not readily agree to the German-Russian Non-Aggression Treaty, but finally I was able to bring him around. With that example, I intend to work unremittingly in the future also.

Oshima: As to the basis of the Chancellor's hesitation about making peace with Russia, is it not because he has hopes for peace with America and England?

Ribbentrop: There is absolutely no such consideration [in his mind].

Oshima: May I ask again whether his attitude is based on the thought that there is no possibility of this [i.e., peace with England and America] or on principle?

Ribbentrop: The Chancellor has categorically refused such a thing as a compromise peace with America and England.

Oshima: I fully understand Germany's views. Since we do not know when in the future this matter may become acute, however, it would be proper to seek contacts with agencies in touch with Russia in Stockholm so as to have the way clear at that time.

Ribbentrop: Naturally there is no objection to that, but it will be essential that the Americans and English do not become aware of it. Actually I should like such activity to go no further than neutral contacts.

Oshima: Such matters as this are outside my powers and I could do nothing about it.

At the end, Ribbentrop expressed his deep thanks for my cooperation and that of other Japanese agencies since the first conference, and particularly for the friendly action on the part of Attaché Onodera in leaving his business and coming immediately to Berlin. He asked for Japan's cooperation in the future also.

On 5 April I called on Ribbentrop at his request. Set forth below are the main points of our conversation.

Ribbentrop asked me various questions about the change in the Japanese Cabinet, but since I too was not aware of the details I gave an explanation, based on recent general reports, that the shift was designed further to strengthen the domestic administration of the nation and to carry out the aim of prosecuting the war.

The Foreign Minister discussed the general trend of the [German] war situation as follows:

"Chancellor Hitler, under a plan to mount a great offensive in the East after May or June, has been working diligently to build up a supply of all possible materiel, in spite of the damage to munitions production and transportation facilities caused by the incessant air raids.

"In the West, the Rhine line has collapsed and the fact that the enemy has been able to advance as far as Thuringia is a great blow. (That region at present is regarded as more important to Germany even than the Ruhr;[3] it is also said that the basic reason for the enemy advance is the inferiority of our air force.)

"Germany will not stop at stabilizing the front in that sector, but will go further and launch an offensive in the West, although this of necessity requires changing former plans to some extent. This is what the Chancellor has in mind, but under present conditions it is both difficult and dangerous to transfer large units from the East and, therefore, it will require some time [to prepare for an attack in the West]."

Continuing our recent conferences [of 17, 19, 27 and 28 March, on the subject of a German-Russian peace--DS 3 Apr 45], the following remarks were then exchanged:

Ribbentrop: I had Ambassador Hewel [member of the Foreign Office in charge of liaison with the OKW] approach Hitler once again today, but the Ambassador says that Hitler replied, 'I have already made by attitude on this matter clear to Ribbentrop,'[4] and scowled. I understand completely how the Chancellor's mind works.

Have the Japanese noticed any signs whatsoever which

----

3. As noted in item A-3 of today's Summary, Under Secretary for Foreign Affairs von Steengracht told Oshima on 4 April that "from the standpoint of ordnance production, the fact that Thuringia is in danger is more unfortunate [than the loss of the Ruhr]."

4. According to Oshima, Hitler told Ribbentrop shortly before 27 March that it was very unlikely that Stalin was considering peace with Germany and that it was necessary for Germany to rely on "military results to the bitter end" (DS 3 Apr 45).

would indicate that Russia has been considering peace with Germany?

Oshima: I don't know of any such signs. However, in view of the fact that Russia is an ally of the Anglo-Americans while Japan is an ally of Germany, the Soviet Union, from the standpoint of its relations with England and the United States, would not find it easy to reveal such an attitude to Japan [i.e., an attitude favorable to peace with Germany].

Ribbentrop: Have you received any reports whatsoever from Stockholm?[5]

Oshima: At present we have gone no further than attempting to make contact with Soviet agencies; there have not been any actual conversations so that no reports will be immediately forthcoming.

Ribbentrop: [Words missing] and I should like you at present to refrain from doing anything more than this.

Oshima: With the war situation now becoming worse and worse and with your fear that this [effort to sound out Russia on the question of peace] will secretly and mischievously be used against us by the Anglo-Americans, I am very much worried that in the end we will lose the opportunity.

Ribbentrop: Your views are sound, but since I do not yet have a clear perspective I cannot take a step which would appear irrational in the eyes of Germany. I must obey the Chancellor's orders. Regardless of my own views, I believe that, as far as the problem of taking active steps is concerned, there is nothing to do but await the repairing of the battle fronts.

I then asked whether Hitler had turned down peace with Russia as a matter of principle, and Ribbentrop emphatically answered, "the Chancellor is disposed to do this [i.e.,

---

5. In their interview of 28 March Ribbentrop agreed with Oshima's suggestion that it was advisable "to seek contacts with agencies in touch with Russia in Stockholm" in order to be prepared for any future developments (DS 3 Apr 45).

make peace with Russia] if he can."[6]

Ribbentrop also made the following statement:

"Since Minister Schmidt [head of the Press Section of the Foreign Office] told me that Japanese
newspapermen had given credence to the Hesse affair[7]
and said I ought to make a suitable explanation, I
did so yesterday [on 4 April Ribbentrop entertained
Japanese diplomats and newspapermen at a tea party].
Germany would not commit any act which would on its
face run counter to the [provision of the 1941] treaty
between Japan and Germany [prohibiting a separate
peace], and naturally we would not carry on peace
negotiations with the Anglo-Americans who seek the
annihilation of the German people. As you know, in
considering the various possibilities, as far as I am
concerned, it is the Soviet Union [with whom Germany
should make peace]. If by any chance the Anglo-
Americans were to extend the hand of peace (I do not
believe that such a thing is possible) we would
immediately get in touch with the Japanese. The same
thing also holds true for Russia [i.e., a Russian
peace offer].

* * *

"Magic" Diplomatic Summary of 16 April 1945

. . . Ambassador Oshima has left Berlin for the
Salzburg area, having been told that the German High
Command and Government plans to move "to the south after
developments have been studied a little longer."

---

6. When Oshima asked Ribbentrop the same question on 28
March, the latter replied: "If the Chancellor comes to
feel that this [peace with Russia] is possible, he will
take action" (DS 3 Apr 45).

7. In mid-March Allied and neutral newspapers reported
that Dr. Fritz Hesse, who at one time served as German
Press Attaché in London, had attempted to approach a
member of the British Legation in Stockholm in order to
open preliminary negotiations for an armistice.

As noted in the Summary for 9 April, on the 7th the Chief of the Protocol Section of the German Foreign Office had told Oshima that it might become necessary to move the Government to southern Germany and had asked that as many of the Japanese Embassy as possible should leave the next day for Badgastein (about 47 miles south of Salzburg, where a number of Japanese nationals had already been located).

On 13 April Oshima reported that he had just talked with Foreign Minister von Ribbentrop and had asked him whether there was any truth to the rumor that the German Government was about to leave Berlin. According to Oshima, Ribbentrop replied that, in view of the advance of the Anglo-American armies, preparations were being made for "the most remote contingencies" and that a decision to move the Government might be made by Hitler during the course of the day. Oshima reminded the Foreign Minister that he wished to maintain close contact with the German authorities to the very end, regardless of the danger involved.

About 10:00 p.m. that evening--according to a report from Oshima sent the next day--the Chief of the Protocol Section called him to say that diplomats remaining in Berlin were requested to leave immediately for Badgastein. Oshima's report proceeds as follows:

"I telephoned Foreign Minister Ribbentrop and asked him whether the German High Command and Government were also being moved, saying that I wished to maintain close contact with them to the very end.

"Ribbentrop replied that the withdrawal of the diplomatic corps had been decided upon that day by Chancellor Hitler and added, begging me to keep the fact very secret: 'It is planned to transfer the German High Command and Government to the south after developments have been studied a little longer.'"

Oshima's report adds that he and his Military and Naval Attachés accompanied by 13 other Japanese officers were leaving Berlin at 3:00 p.m. on the 14th, but that a group of 10, headed by Counselor Kawahara, were to remain in Berlin to handle communications, to guard the Imperial portraits stored in the air raid shelter of the Embassy, and to protect the local Japanese residents.

Note: Oshima's messages contain no indication of

207

where in "the south" the German Government will be located. However, it seems unlikely that Badgastein would have been picked for the diplomatic corps if the Government were not planning to settle in the same general area. . . .

Ambassador Oshima's report of his conversation with Ribbentrop during the day of the 13th also quoted the Foreign Minister as follows:

"Last evening [12 April] I had a chance to talk with Chancellor Hitler and he has still not abandoned hope that there will be a turn in the war situation. On the Eastern Front there are strong indications that the Russian Army will launch a large-scale offensive from the Oder front in the next few days, but we expect to be able to repulse it. The penetration of the Anglo-American armies is extremely deep and it is urgently necessary to stabilize that front, at the very least. Therefore, we will have to counter-attack at once. While one cannot prophesy today as to the success of the attack, I think that it will be carried out soon." . . .

BIBLIOGRAPHY

1. Unpublished Documents (including microfilm)

International Military Tribunal for the Far East (1946-
1948). Proceedings, 113 vols.; Exhibits, 131 vols.;
Narrative Summary, 14 vols.; Prosecution Summation, 7
vols.; Defense Summation, 17 vols.; Analyses of Documentary Evidence, 29 vols. University of California
Library, Berkeley.

Exhibit 121   Military Record of Hiroshi Ōshima,
April 13, 1946.

487   Excerpts from the Interrogation of
Hiroshi Ōshima, February 4, 1946.

488   Interrogation of Hiroshi Ōshima of
March 5, 1946.

491   Minutes of the Privy Council Meeting,
February 22, 1939.

492   Record of the Proceedings of the Privy
Council Session, November 12, 1937.

497   Excerpts of Interrogations of Hiroshi
Ōshima of February 4, 6, and 7, 1946.

498   Ott to Weizsäcker, September 8, 1939.

502   Ribbentrop to Ott, April 26, 1939.

506   Memorandum by Weizsäcker on a Conversation with Ōshima, September 18,
1939.

507   Ribbentrop to Ott, September 9, 1939.

508   Woermann to Ott, October 27, 1939.

Bibliography

509   Memorandum on the Conversations among Hitler, Ribbentrop, Keitel, Stahmer, Terauchi, Ōshima, and Kawabe, September 25, 1939.

527   Minutes of the Joint Conference of the War, Navy, and Foreign Ministry Representatives on Strengthening Relations between Japan, Germany, and Italy, July 12, 1940.

528   Minutes of the Joint Conference of the War, Navy, and Foreign Ministry Representatives on Strengthening Relations between Japan, Germany, and Italy, July 16, 1940.

560   Ott to Ribbentrop, December 13, 1940.

596   Extract from a Letter of Ambassador Ott, Tokyo, of March 15, 1939 to Ministerial Director Wiehl.

604   Excerpts from the Interrogation of Hiroshi Ōshima, February 26, 1946.

609   Summary of the Reception of Ōshima by Hitler, December 14, 1941.

776-A   Minutes of Interrogation of Hiroshi Ōshima of April 22, 1946.

811   Affidavit of Examination of Komakichi Nohara, Assistant Press Agent of the Japanese Embassy in Berlin, February 15, 1946.

2198   Ott to Ribbentrop, August 11, 1939.

2230   Ribbentrop to Ott, May 28, 1939.

2232   Mackensen to Ribbentrop, September 2, 1939.

2614   Arita to Mushakōji, May 8, 1936.

2744-A Interrogatories of Ambassador Stahmer, 1947.

2762   Affidavit of Joachim von Ribbentrop,
        October 15, 1946.

3146   Affidavit of Eugen Ott, August 30,
        1947.

3488   Affidavit of Michinori Yoshii Con-
        cerning the Destruction of Certain
        Japanese Records, November 8, 1947.

3489   Affidavit of Hidehiko Makata Concern-
        ing the Destruction of Certain Japa-
        nese Records, November 5, 1947.

3490   Affidavit of Hisashi Nishi Concerning
        the Destruction of Certain Japanese
        Records, November 4, 1947.

3491   Affidavit of Yasumaro Taniguchi Con-
        cerning the Destruction of Certain
        Japanese Records, November 10, 1947.

3492   Affidavit of Tadaichi Wakamatsu,
        special emissary to Berlin in 1935,
        November 1, 1947.

3493   Affidavit of Yukio Kasahara, Assistant
        Military Attaché of the Japanese
        Embassy in Berlin, September 20, 1947.

3494   Affidavit of Uzuhiko Usami, Councilor
        of the Japanese Embassy in Berlin,
        September 10, 1947.

3495   Affidavit of Torashiro Kawabe, Mili-
        tary Attaché of the Japanese Embassy
        in Berlin, September 9, 1947.

3496   Affidavit of Torashiro Kawabe, Mili-
        tary Attaché of the Japanese Embassy
        in Berlin, October 27, 1947.

3501   Affidavit of Michitoshi Takahashi,
        Secretary of Protocol of the Japanese
        Embassy in Berlin, January 14, 1947.

3502   Affidavit of Hiroshi Sugiura, Secre-
        tary of Protocol of the Japanese
        Embassy in Berlin, January 14, 1947.

Bibliography

3503   Interrogatory and Cross-Interrogatory
        of Eugen Ott, August 15, 1947.

3503-B Re-direct Interrogatory of Eugen Ott,
        August 1947, and Ott to Ribbentrop,
        December 31, 1939; January 23, 26,
        1940.

3505   Affidavit of Mitsuhiko Komatsu,
        Assistant Military Attaché of the
        Japanese Embassy in Berlin, March
        31, 1947.

3506   Affidavit of Eiichi Tatsumi, Military
        Attaché of the Japanese Embassy in
        London, September 29, 1947.

3508   Affidavit of Hiroshi Ōshima,
        November 12, 1947.

3512   Excerpts from the Interrogation of
        Hiroshi Ōshima, February 27, 1946.

3513   Summary of Recollections by Hiroshi
        Ōshima, February 19, 1946.

3516-A "Doitsu gaikō no rinen [The idea of
        German diplomacy] by Hiroshi Ōshima,
        January 1940.

3523   Ugaki to Konoye, September 16, 1938.

3523-A Konoye to Ugaki, September 22, 1938.

3523-B Konoye to Itagaki, October 6, 1938.

3523-C Itagaki to Konoye, October 7, 1938.

3579   Interrogation and Affidavit of Eugen
        Ott, May 18, 1947.

3595   Affidavit of Toshio Shiratori,
        November 20, 1947.

3614   Affidavit of Katsushirō Narita, Third
        Secretary of the Japanese Embassy in
        Berlin.

3614-A Narita to Tōgō, December 6, 1938.

212

3618 Affidavit of Yukio Kasahara, Assistant Military Attaché of the Japanese Embassy in Berlin, October 23, 1947.

3619 Affidavit of Yasuto Shudō, Commercial Attaché of the Japanese Embassy in Berlin, March 4, 1947.

3620 Affidavit of Tadashi Sakaya, First Secretary of the Japanese Embassy in Berlin.

3622 Affidavit of Kurt Meissner, President of the German Society for East Asiatic Natural History and Ethnography, 1920-1946, July 9, 1947.

3646 Affidavit of Shigenori Tōgō, December 12, 1947.

National Archives, Washington, D.C.

Record Group 38, Office of the Chief of Naval Operations. Office of Naval Intelligence Reports, 1880-1939 (ONI).

Record Group 226, Records of the Office of Strategic Services (OSS).
Name Indices, including "L" and "XL" documents.

Record Group 242, National Archives Collection of Foreign Records Seized, 1941- (Still Pictures Branch).
Hoffmann--Leica--Berlin (HLB).

Record Group 331, Records of Allied Operational and Occupation Headquarters, World War II. International Prosecution Section (IPS), Supreme Commander for the Allied Powers (SCAP).
 IPS 18: Terauchi, Juichi (Hisaichi).
 IPS 100: Japanese Army High Command, 2 December 1942.
 IPS 101: Japanese Navy High Command, 2 December 1942.
 IPS 247: Oshima, Hiroshi.
 IPS 302: February 26, 1936 Incident.
 IPS 324: Ott, Eugen.
 IPS 448: Relations with Germany, Italy, France, and Thailand.
 IPS 453: Wakamatsu, Tadakazu (Tadaichi).

Bibliography

Record Group 457, Records of the National Security
   Agency.
      Friedman, William F., "Six Lectures on Cryptology,"
      April 1963.
      Japanese Army Attaché Messages Translations, 1943-
      1945.
      "Magic" Summaries and "Magic" Diplomatic
      Summaries, 1938-1945.

National Archives (Washington, D.C.) Microfilm Publications

   Microfilm Publication No. M-679, Records of the Department of State Special Interrogation Mission to
   Germany, 1945-46.

   Microfilm Publication No. M-975, Selected Naval Attaché
   Reports Relating to the World Crisis, 1937-1943.

   Microfilm Publication No. T-81, Records of the National
   Socialist German Labor Party.

   Microfilm Publication No. T-82, Records of Nazi Cultural
   and Research Institutions and Records Pertaining to
   Axis Relations and Interest in the Far East.

   Microfilm Publication No. T-179, Records of German and
   Japanese Embassies and Consulates, 1890-1945.

   Microfilm Publication No. T-314, Records of German Field
   Commands: Corps.

   Microfilm Publication No. T-988, Prosecution Exhibits
   Submitted to the International Military Tribunal.

Naval Historical Center, Operational Archives Branch,
   Washington, D.C.

   Records of the Imperial Japanese Navy, Related
   Translations, and Studies, 1939-1945.

   Translated Records of the German Navy, Essays by
   German Officers, and Related Studies, 1922-1945.

              2. Published Documents

Carnegie Endowment for International Peace, "Developments
   in the European Situation." International Conciliation,
   no. 351 (1939), pp. 293-365.

Documents on German Foreign Policy, 1918-1945. 5- vols.
series C (1933-1937). Washington, D.C.: United States
Government Printing Office, 1957- .

  DGFP,C,5

    Doc. No. 197   Ambassador Dirksen to State
                        Secretary Bülow, March 23, 1936.

            362   Memorandum by the State Secre-
                        tary and Head of the Presiden-
                        tial Chancellery, June 9, 1936.

            509   Note by Ambassador Ribbentrop,
                        August 16, 1936.

            625   German-Japanese Exchange of
                        Notes on the occasion of the
                        Initialling of the Agreement
                        against the Communist Inter-
                        national.

Documents on German Foreign Policy, 1918-1945. 13 vols.
series D (1937-1941). Washington, D.C.: United States
Government Printing Office, 1949-1964.

  DGFP,D,1

    Doc. No. 19   Memorandum: "Minutes of the
                        Conference in the Reich Chan-
                        cellery, Berlin, November 5,
                        1937, from 4:15 to 8:30 p.m."

    No Doc. No.   Secret Additional Agreement to
    (p. 734)   the Agreement against the Com-
                        munist International.

    Doc. Nos. 564-86   "Concessions to Japan, January-
                        May 1938."

            587-601   "The Search for a Preferential
                        Position in North China, May-
                        June 1938."

    Doc. No. 603   Memorandum by the Foreign
                        Minister, July 5, 1938.

Bibliography

| | 628 | The German Ambassador in the Soviet Union (Schulenburg) to the German Foreign Ministry, July 4, 1938. |

DGFP,D,4

Doc. No. 421   Foreign Minister Ciano to Foreign Minister Ribbentrop, January 2, 1939.

426   Foreign Minister Ribbentrop to Foreign Minister Ciano, January 9, 1939.

542   Memorandum by the State Secretary, January 13, 1939.

543   The Ambassador in Japan to the Foreign Ministry, January 28, 1939.

547   The Ambassador in Japan to the Foreign Ministry, February 18, 1939.

DGFP,D,6

Doc. No. 185   Directive by the Führer, April 11, 1939.

200   President Roosevelt to the Führer and Chancellor, April 15, 1939.

211   Record of the Conversation between Field Marshal Göring and the Duce, in the Presence of Count Ciano in Rome on April 16, 1939.

224   The State Secretary to the Legation in Portugal, April 18, 1939.

270   The Foreign Minister to the Embassy in Japan, April 26, 1939.

304   The Foreign Minister to the Embassy in Japan, May 1, 1939.

216

325 The Chargé d'Affaires in the Soviet Union to the Foreign Ministry, May 4, 1939.

326 The Ambassador in Japan to the Foreign Ministry, May 4, 1939.

339 The Ambassador in Japan to the Foreign Ministry, May 6, 1939.

No Doc. No. (pp. 444-45) Subjects for discussion at the meeting between the Reich Foreign Minister and Count Ciano, May 4, 1939.

345 Memorandum by the State Secretary, May 8, 1939.

382 The Foreign Minister to the Embassy in Japan, May 15, 1939.

383 The State Secretary to the Embassy in Japan, May 15, 1939.

400 The Ambassador in Japan to the Foreign Ministry, May 17, 1939.

426 Pact of Friendship and Alliance between Germany and Italy, May 22, 1939.

433 Minutes of a Conference on May 23, 1939.

536 Ambassador Mackensen to State Secretary Weizsäcker, June 16, 1939.

538 The Foreign Minister to the Embassy in Japan, June 17, 1939.

619 Ambassador Ott to State Secretary Weizsäcker, July 5, 1939.

688 Memorandum by the Director of the Political Department, July 19, 1939.

Bibliography

713 Memorandum by the State Secretary, July 24, 1939.

735 The Ambassador in Japan to the Foreign Ministry, July 29, 1939.

757 Senior Counselor Schnurre to Ambassador Schulenburg, August 2, 1939.

766 The Ambassador in the Soviet Union to the Foreign Ministry, August 4, 1939.

772 Memorandum by an Official of the Economic Policy Department, August 5, 1939.

DGFP,D,7

Doc. No. 7 The Ambassador in Japan to the Foreign Ministry, August 10, 1939.

25 The Ambassador in Japan to the Foreign Ministry, August 11, 1939.

110 The Ambassador in Japan to the Foreign Ministry, August 18, 1939.

183 The State Secretary to the Embassy in Japan, August 22, 1939.

186 Memorandum by the State Secretary, August 22, 1939.

262 The Ambassador in Japan to the Foreign Ministry, August 25, 1939.

329 Memorandum by the State Secretary, August 26, 1939.

403 Note by an Official of the Dienststelle Ribbentrop, August 28, 1939.

218

DGFP,D,8

    Doc. No. 11   Ambassador Mackensen to State
                      Secretary Weizsäcker, September
                      5, 1939.

International Military Tribunal. Trial of the Major War
    Criminals. 42 vols. Nuremberg: The Secretariat of the
    Tribunal, 1947-1949.

Maier-Hartmann, Fritz. Dokumente des Dritten Reiches. Vol.
    2 of Die Sammlung Rehse. Edited by Adolf Dresler. 2
    vols. 2nd ed. Munich: Zentralverlag der NSDAP, Franz
    Eher Nachfolger, 1940.

Menzel, Johanna M. "Der geheime deutsch-japanische
    Notenaustausch zum Dreimächtepakt." Vierteljahrshefte
    für Zeitgeschichte 5, no. 2 (1957): 182-93.

Nit-Chū sensō III [The Sino-Japanese war, III]. Vol. 10 of
    Gendaishi shiryo [Documents on contemporary history]. 7
    vols. Tokyo: Misuzu Shobo, 1964-1966.

Royal Institute of International Affairs. Documents on
    International Affairs, 1936. Edited by Stephen Heald.
    London: Oxford University Press, 1937.

Shapiro, Leonard, ed. Soviet Treaty Series, 1917-1939. 2
    vols. Washington, D.C.: Georgetown University Press,
    1950-1955.

Slusser, Robert M., and Triska, Jan F. A Calendar of
    Soviet Treaties, 1917-1957. Stanford: Stanford Univer-
    sity Press, 1959.

Trevor-Roper, H. R., ed. Blitzkrieg to Defeat: Hitler's
    War Directives, 1939-1945. New York: Holt, Rinehart
    and Winston, 1965.

U.S., Department of Defense. The "Magic" Background of
    Pearl Harbor. 8 vols. in 5. Washington, D.C.: United
    States Government Printing Office, 1978.

U.S., Office of United States Chief of Counsel for Prosecu-
    tion of Axis Criminality. Nazi Conspiracy and Aggres-
    sion. 8 vols. Washington, D.C.: United States Govern-
    ment Printing Office, 1948.

Bibliography

Weinberg, Gerhard L. "Die geheimen Abkommen zum Antikominternpakt." Vierteljahrshefte für Zeitgeschichte 2, no. 2 (1954): 193-201.

3. Reference Works and Research Aids

Brown, Delmer M. "Recent Japanese Political and Historical Materials." American Political Science Review 43, no. 5 (1949): 1010-17.

Clyde, Paul H. "Japan's March to Empire: Some Bibliographical Evaluations." Journal of Modern History 31, no. 4 (1949): 333-43.

Dull, Paul S., and Umemura, Michael Takaaki. The Tokyo Trials: A Functional Index to the Proceedings of the International Military Tribunal for the Far East. Ann Arbor: University of Michigan Press, 1962.

Goedertier, Joseph M. A Dictionary of Japanese History. New York: Walker/Weatherhill, 1968.

Hayashi, Kentarō. "Japanische Quellen zur Vorgeschichte des Pazifischen Krieges." Vierteljahrshefte für Zeitgeschichte 5, no. 1 (1957): 199-207.

"Index and Catalog of Serials 77-320." (Covers a part of Record Group 1036 of Records of Nazi Cultural and Research Institutions and Records Pertaining to Axis Relations and Interests in the Far East.) National Archives, Washington, D.C. Microfilm Publication No. T-82, Roll 63.

Iriye, Akira. "Japanese Imperialism and Aggression: Reconsiderations. II." Journal of Asian Studies 23, no. 1 (1963): 103-13.

_____. "Japan's Foreign Policies between World Wars: Sources and Interpretations." Journal of Asian Studies 26, no. 4 (1967): 677-82.

The Japan Biographical Encyclopedia and Who's Who. 2nd ed. Tokyo: Rengo Press, 1961.

Japan Illustrated, 1934. Edited by Nippon Dempo News Agency. Tokyo: Nippon Dempo News Agency, 1934.

The Japan Year Book, 1939-40. Tokyo: Kenkyusha Press, 1939.

The Japan Year Book, 1940-41. Tokyo: Foreign Affairs Association of Japan, 1940.

Liu, James T. C. "The Tokyo Trial: Source Materials." Far Eastern Survey 17, no. 14 (1948): 168-70.

Morley, James William. "Check List of Seized Japanese Records in the National Archives." Far Eastern Quarterly 9, no. 3 (1950): 306-33.

_____, ed. Japan's Foreign Policy, 1868-1941: A Research Guide. New York: Columbia University Press, 1974.

[Nachod, Oskar, and Praesent, Hans]. Bibliographie von Japan, 1906-1937. 6 vols. Leipzig: Verlag Karl W. Hiersemann, 1928-1940. Microfilm of the manuscript of vol. 7 is in the Library of Congress.

Nihon kindaishi jiten [Dictionary of modern Japanese history]. Edited by Kyōto Daigaku, Bungakubu, Kokushi Kenkyūshitsu [Kyōto University, Department of Literature, Japanese History Research Office]. Tokyo: Tōyō Keizai Shimbun Sha, 1958.

Ramming, Martin, ed. Japan-Handbuch: Nachschlagewerk der Japankunde. Berlin: Steiniger Verlage, 1941.

Rangliste der Deutschen Kriegsmarine: Nach dem Stande vom 1. November 1935. Berlin: E. S. Mittler und Sohn, 1935.

"Records of Former German and Japanese Embassies and Consulates, 1890-1945, No. 15, T-179." Guides to German Records Microfilmed at Alexandria, Va. Washington, D.C.: General Services Administration, 1960.

Uyehara, Cecil H., comp. Checklist of Archives in the Japanese Ministry of Foreign Affairs, Tokyo, Japan, 1868-1945 Microfilmed for the Library of Congress, 1949-1951. Washington, D.C.: United States Government Printing Office, 1954.

Young, John, comp. Checklist of Microfilm Reproductions of Selected Archives of the Japanese Army, Navy, and Other Government Agencies, 1868-1945. Washington, D.C.: Georgetown University Press, 1959.

221

Bibliography

4. Biographies, Diaries, Interviews, Letters, Memoirs

Abshagen, Karl Heinz. Canaris: Patriot und Weltbürger.
Stuttgart: Union Deutsche Verlagsgesellschaft, 1950.

Buckle, George Earle, ed. The Letters of Queen Victoria.
3 vols. 3rd ser. London: John Murray, 1930-1932.

Butow, Robert J. C. Tojo and the Coming of the War. 1961.
Reissued. Stanford: Stanford University Press, 1969.

Chaney, Otto Preston, Jr. Zhukov. Newton Abbot: David
and Charles, 1972.

Ciano, Galeazzo. The Ciano Diaries, 1939-1943: The Complete, Unabridged Diaries of Count Galeazzo Ciano,
Italian Minister for Foreign Affairs, 1936-1943.
Edited by Hugh Gibson. Garden City, N.Y.: Doubleday,
1946.

_____. Ciano's Diplomatic Papers. Edited by Malcolm
Muggeridge. Translated by Stuart Hood. London: Odhams,
1948.

_____. Ciano's Hidden Diary, 1937-1938. Translated by
Andreas Mayor. New York: E. P. Dutton, 1953.

Craigie, Robert. Behind the Japanese Mask. London:
Hutchinson, [1946].

François-Poncet, André. The Fateful Years: Memoirs of a
French Ambassador in Berlin, 1931-1938. Translated by
Jacques LeClereq. New York: Harcourt, Brace, 1949.

Fromm, Bella. Blood and Banquets: A Berlin Social Diary.
New York: Harper, 1942.

Dallek, Robert. Democrat and Diplomat: The Life of
William E. Dodd. New York: Oxford University Press,
1968.

Dirksen, Herbert von. Moscow, Tokyo, London: Twenty Years
of German Foreign Policy. Norman: University of
Oklahoma Press, 1952.

Dodd, William E., Jr., and Dodd, Martha, eds. Ambassador Dodd's Diary, 1933-1938. New York: Harcourt, Brace, 1941.

Futara Yoshinori, and Sawada Setsuzo. The Crown Prince's European Tour. Osaka: Osaka Mainichi, 1926.

Grew, Joseph C. Ten Years in Japan: A Contemporary Record Drawn from the Diaries and Official Papers of Joseph C. Grew, United States Ambassador to Japan, 1932-1942. New York: Simon and Schuster, 1944.

Hayashi, Saburo, and Coox, Alvin D. Kogun: The Japanese Army in the Pacific War. Quantico, Va.: Marine Corps Association, 1959.

Hilger, Gustav, and Meyer, Alfred G. The Incompatible Allies: A Memoir-History of German-Soviet Relations, 1918-1941. New York: Macmillan, 1953.

Hitler, Adolf. Mein Kampf. Edited by John Chamberlain et al. New York: Reynal and Hitchcock, 1941.

Hossbach, Friedrich. Zwischen Wehrmacht und Hitler, 1934-1938. Wolfenbüttel and Hannover: Wolfenbütteler Verlagsanstalt, 1949.

Hull, Cordell. The Memoirs of Cordell Hull. 2 vols. New York: Macmillan, 1948.

Interviews with Hiroshi Oshima conducted by John Toland, Chigasaki, Japan, 9 October 1962, 17 January 1967, and 24 March 1971.

Kato, Masuo. The Lost War: A Japanese Reporter's Inside Story. New York: Alfred A. Knopf, 1946.

Keitel, Wilhelm. Generalfeldmarschall Keitel: Verbrecher oder Offizier? Edited by Walter Görlitz. Göttingen: Musterschmidt-Verlag, 1961.

Kordt, Erich. "German Political History in the Far East during the Hitler Regime." Edited and translated by E. A. Bayne. Washington, D.C.: Library of Congress, Manuscript Division, Box 809, Folder D.

_____. Nicht aus den Akten. Stuttgart: Union Deutsche Verlagsgesellschaft, 1950.

Bibliography

_____. Wahn und Wirklichkeit. Stuttgart: Union Deutsche
Verlagsgesellschaft, 1948.

Krausnick, Helmut. "Aus den Personalakten von Canaris."
Vierteljahrshefte für Zeitgeschichte 10 (1962): 280-310.

Leverkuehn, Paul. Der geheime Nachrichtendienst der
deutschen Wehrmacht im Kriege. 3rd ed. Frankfurt am
Main: Verlag für Wehrwesen Bernard und Graefe, 1960.

Oki Shūji. Ningen Yamashita Tomoyuki, higeki no shōgun
[The life of Tomoyuki Yamashita: the tragedy of a
general]. Tokyo: Nihon Shūhō Sha, 1959.

Piggott, F.S.G. Broken Thread. Aldershot: Gale and
Polden, 1950.

Potter, John Deane. A Soldier Must Hang: The Biography of
an Oriental General. London: Frederick Muller, 1963.

Ribbentrop, Joachim von. The Ribbentrop Memoirs. Translated by Oliver Watson. London: Weidenfeld and
Nicolson, 1954.

The Saionji-Harada Memoirs, 1931-1940: Complete Translation into English. Washington, D.C.: University
Publications of America, [1978].

Schmidt, Paul. Hitler's Interpreter. Edited by R. H. C.
Steed. London: William Heinemann, 1951.

Schwarz, Paul. This Man Ribbentrop: His Life and Times.
New York: Julian Messner, 1943.

Shigemitsu, Mamoru. Japan and Her Destiny: My Struggle
for Peace. Edited by F.S.G. Piggott. Translated by
Oswald White. New York: E. P. Dutton, 1958.

Shirer, William L. Berlin Diary: The Journal of a
Foreign Correspondent, 1934-1941. New York: Alfred A.
Knopf, 1941.

Thomas, Georg. Geschichte der Deutschen Wehr- und
Rüstungswirtschaft (1918-1943/45). Boppard am Rhein:
Harald Boldt Verlag, 1966.

Tōgō, Shigenori. The Cause of Japan. Translated and
edited by Fumihiko Tōgō and Ben Bruce Blakeney. New
York: Simon and Schuster, 1956.

Trevor-Roper, H. R., ed. Hitler's Secret Conversations, 1941-1944. Translated by Norman Cameron and R. H. Stevens. New York: Farrar, Straus and Young, 1953.

United States Strategic Bombing Survey (Pacific). Interrogations of Japanese Officials. 2 vols. Washington, D. C.: United States Government Printing Office, 1946.

Weizsäcker, Ernst von. Memoirs of Ernst von Weizsäcker. Translated by John Andrews. Chicago: Henry Regnery, 1951.

5. Works by Hiroshi Ōshima
and
Contemporary Works about Him

"Abschiedsempfang für Botschafter Oshima im Hause Ribbentrop/Ricevimento di congedo per l'ambasciatore Oshima in casa Ribbentrop." Berlin--Rom--Tokio 1, no. 7 (1939): 10.

Baumann, Paula. "Besuch in der kaiserlich japanischen Botschaft." Elegante Welt no. 19 (1939): 34-35, 56.

"Besuch des japanischen Botschafters Graf Mushakoji in Hamburg, 12.-14. Juni 1935." Ostasiatische Rundschau 16, no. 12 (1935): 328-31.

"Besuch des japanischen Botschafters in Hamburg." Ostasiatische Rundschau 20, no. 5 (1939): 128-30.

"Botschafter Oshima Besuch in Hamburg." Ostasiatische Rundschau 23, no. 1 (1942): 20-24.

"Botschafter Oshima beim Führer/L'ambasciatore Oshima ricevulo dal Führer." Berlin--Rom--Tokio 3, no. 3 (1941): 13.

"Botschafter Oshimas Ankunft in Berlin." Ostasiatische Rundschau 22, no. 2 (1941): 43-44.

"Der Führer empfing den kaiserlich-japanischen Botschafter Oshima." Berlin--Rom--Tokio 6, no. 5 (1944): 2.

"Gründung der Zweiggesellschaft Hamburg der deutsch-japanischen Gesellschaft." Ostasiatische Rundschau 23, no. 12 (1942): 256-58.

Bibliography

Ōshima, Hiroshi. "Botschafter Oshima an Berlin--Rom--Tokio." Berlin--Rom--Tokio 3, no. 2 (1941): 11-12.

_____. "Doitsu gaikō no rinen" [The idea of German diplomacy]. Bungei Shunjū (January 1940). Washington, D.C.: Library of Congress, Reel WT (War Trials) 82, IMT (International Military Tribunal) 623, IPS (International Prosecution Section) Document No. 3268. Also IMTFE, Exhibit 3516-A.

_____. "Japan, Deutschland und Italien." Berlin--Rom--Tokio 4, no. 1 (1942): 9.

_____. "Japan und der Dreimächtepakt." Volk und Reich 17, no. 5 (1941): 293-94.

_____. "Japan in der Front der Antikominternmächte." Volk und Reich 15, no. 5 (1939): 310-12.

_____. "Die Japanerin und die Kunst." Elegante Welt, no. 19 (1939), pp. 33, 56.

_____. "Katte kabuto no o wo shimeyo" [After winning, keep the string tight on your helmet]. Bungei Shunjū (April 1940). Washington, D.C., Library of Congress, Reel WT 21, IMT 89, IPS Doc. No. 756.

_____. Das neue Deutschland im Spiegel der japanischen Freundschaft/La nuova Germania nello speechio dell'amicizia qiapponese." Berlin--Rom--Tokio 1, no. 3 (1939): 12-14.

_____. "Das neue Gebäude der japanischen Botschaft." Die Kunst im deutschen Reich 7, no. 2 (1943): 22-24.

_____. "Neuordnung des Fernen Ostens, Neuordnung Europas." Die Aktion: Kampfblatt für das Neue Europa 2 (1941), 341-42.

_____, and Voss, Erich. "Der Neubau der Kaiserlich japanischen Botschaft in Berlin." Die Kunst im deutschen Reich 7, no. 1 (1943): 24-40.

Ostasiatische Rundschau 24, no. 3 (1943): 57-58.

"Unterstaatssekretär Dr. Woermann vom Auswärtigen Amt überreicht Exzellenz Oshima den Schlüssel zum Botschaftsgebäude." Ostasiatische Rundschau 24, no. 3 (1943): 57.

Voigt, Walter. "Begegnung mit Hauptmann Oshima." Das Deutsche Rote Kreuz 7 (1943): 32-33.

6. Other Contemporary Works

Albrecht, von, Fürst von Urach. Das Geheimnis japanischer Kraft. Berlin: Zentralverlag der NSDAP, 1944.

"Antikominternpakt-Dreimächtepakt-Antikominternpakt." Berlin--Rom--Tokio 4, no. 1 (1942): 16-17.

"Aus der japanischen Botschaft in Berlin/L'Ambasciata giapponese in Berlino." Berlin--Rom--Tokio 2, no. 3 (1940): 27.

Berber, Fritz. "Der Bündnispakt Berlin-Rom-Tokio." Monatshefte für Auswärtige Politik 7, no. 10 (1940): 743-48.

"Der Besuch des japanischen Botschafters Dr. M. Nagai in Hamburg." Ostasiatische Rundschau 14, no. 18 (1933): 404-5.

Bloch, Kurt. German Interests and Policies in the Far East. New York: Institute of Pacific Relations, 1940.

Boxer, C. R. "Notes on Early European Military Influence in Japan (1543-1853)." Transactions of the Asiatic Society of Japan (Tokyo) 2nd ser., 8 (1931): 67-93.

Buell, Raymond Leslie. "German-Japanese Pact Arouses Democracies." Foreign Policy Bulletin (New York) 16, no. 6 (1936): 1-2.

Colegrove, Kenneth. "The Japanese Cabinet." American Political Science Review 30, no. 5 (1936): 903-23.

_____. "The Japanese Constitution." American Political Science Review 31, no. 6 (1937): 1027-49.

_____. "The Japanese Foreign Office." American Journal of International Law 30, no. 4 (1936): 585-613.

_____. "Military Propaganda in Japan." Amerasia: A Review of America and the Far East 1, no. 2 (1937): 63-67.

Bibliography

_____. Militarism in Japan. Boston: World Peace Foundation, 1936.

Das, Taraknath. "The German-Japanese Alliance: Will It Precipitate a World War?" Modern Review: A Monthly Review and Miscellany (Calcutta) 61, no. 2 (1937): 137-44.

Dirksen, [Herbert] von. "Geistige Brücken zwischen Deutschland und Japan." Blätter des Deutschen Roten Kreuzes 13, no. 8 (1934): 348-50.

"The Foreign Office Statement Regarding the Above [Text of the Pact], November 25, 1936." Contemporary Japan: A Review of Japanese Affairs (Tokyo) 5, no. 3 (1936): 515-17.

Gadow, [Reinhold]. "Die fremden Kriegsmarinen." Nauticus: Jahrbuch für Seeinteressen und Weltwirtschaft 20 (1936): 33-76.

Haushofer, Karl. "Ähnlichkeiten der Entwicklung von Staat und Kultur in Italien, Deutschland und Japan." Nippon: Zeitschrift für Japanologie (Berlin) 3, no. 2 (1937): 65-78.

_____. "Eine geopolitische Dreiecks-Vollendung zum 27. September 1940." Zeitschrift für Geopolitik 17, no. 10 (1940): 455-56.

_____. Japan baut sein Reich. Berlin: Zeitgeschichte-Verlag, 1941.

_____. "Militärische und seelische Kräfte im Fernen Osten." Zeitschrift für Geopolitik 15, no. 12 (1938): 937-42.

Ida, Iwakusu. "The Meaning of the Japan-German Pact." Contemporary Japan: A Review of Japanese Affairs (Tokyo) 5, no. 4 (1937): 519-27.

"Interview mit dem japanischen Botschafter Dr. M. Nagai." Ostasiatische Rundschau 14, no. 18 (1933): 387.

Italiaander, Rolf. Banzai! Japanische Heldengeschichten aus alter und neuer Zeit. Berlin: Verlag Die Wehrmacht, 1942.

Jaffe, Philip J. "America and the German-Japanese Pact." Amerasia: A Review of America and the Far East 1, no. 1 (1937): 20-23.

"Japan's Foreign Relations: The Berlin-Tokyo Pact." Oriental Affairs: A Monthly Review (Shanghai) 6, no. 6 (1936): 267-69.

"Japan's Military Strength: An Army Pamphlet." Oriental Affairs: A Monthly Review (Shanghai) 6, no. 6 (1936): 280-82.

"Die japanische Botschaft in Berlin." Sport im Bild 36, no. 11 (1930): 817-18.

"Der japanische Botschafter, Exz. Togo, in Hamburg." Ostasiatische Rundschau 19, no. 7 (1938): 160-62.

Kawabe, [Torashirō]. "Das japanische Heer: Die Entwicklung des japanischen Heeres zur modernen Armee, ihre Grundlage und ihr Geist." Yamato: Zeitschrift der Deutsch-Japanischen Gesellschaft, no. 4 (1930), pp. 176-84.

Lory, Hillis. Japan's Military Masters: The Army in Japanese Life. New York: Viking Press, 1943.

Meissner, Kurt. Deutsche in Japan, 1639-1939: Dreihundert Jahre Arbeit für Wirtsland und Vaterland. Stuttgart: Deutsche Verlags-Anstalt, 1940.

_____. "Die Deutschen in Japan einst und heute." China-Dienst 3, no. 24 (1934): 978-90.

"Navies and the Pacific." Round Table (London) 24, no. 96 (1934): 693-716.

Obata, Y[ukichi]. "Deutsch-japanische Beziehungen: Dr. Wilhelm Solf zum 5. Oktober 1932." Europäische Revue (Berlin) 8, no. 10 (1932): 628-31.

Parry, Albert. "Japan and Germany Joins Hands." Asia and the Americas 37, no. 1 (1937): 43-46.

Penzel, Hans. "Konferenz der japanischen Botschafter vom 28. Mai." Die Tat 26, no. 3 (1934): 234-35.

Phayre, Ignatius. "Germany and Japan: The Inner Story." Saturday Review (London), 12 December 1936, pp. 750-51.

Bibliography

"Protocol Agreed upon by Japan and Russia, December 28,
    1936." Contemporary Japan: A Review of Japanese Affairs
    (Tokyo) 5, no. 4 (1937): 704.

Püllmann, Alfred. "Japan-nach dem Berliner Pakt."
    Deutsches Wollen (Nationalsozialistische deutsche
    Arbeiterpartei, Auslands-Organisation) 2, no. 11 (1940):
    17-19, 30.

Rieder, Charlotte. "Die Japaner in Europa." Reichswart:
    Wochenschrift für nationale Unabhängigkeit und Deutschen
    Sozialismus 22, no. 38 (1941): 1-2.

Rosinger, Lawrence K. "The Far East and the New Order in
    Europe." Pacific Affairs 12, no. 4 (1939): 357-69.

_____. "The Far East as Reflected in the German Press."
    Amerasia: A Review of America and the Far East 1, no. 6
    (1937): 270-75.

"Die Sendung der jungen Völker/La missione dei popoli
    giovani." Berlin--Rom--Tokio 1, no. 1 (1939): 8-11.

Shiratori, Toshio. "The Reawakening of Japan." Contem-
    porary Japan: A Review of Japanese Affairs (Tokyo) 3
    (1934): 8-13.

S[orge], R[ichard]. "Die japanische Expansion."
    Zeitschrift für Geopolitik 16, nos. 8-9 (1939): 617-22.

Stoye, Johannes. "Der Geist des japanischen Heeres."
    Deutsche Rundschau 62 (1936): 76-78.

Toynbee, Arnold, ed. Survey of International Affairs,
    1926. London: Oxford University Press, 1928.

_____. Survey of International Affairs, 1934. London:
    Oxford University Press, 1935.

_____. Survey of International Affairs, 1936. London:
    Oxford University Press, 1937.

"Überreichung des Beglaubigungsschreibens des neuen
    japanischen Botschafters in Berlin." Ostasiatische
    Rundschau 16, no. 4 (1935): 88.

Weigert, Hans W. "Haushofer and the Pacific." Foreign
    Affairs 20, no. 4 (1942): 732-42.

Zischka, Anton. Japan in der Welt: Die japanische Expansion seit 1854. Leipzig: Wilhelm Goldmann Verlag, 1937.

7. Later Secondary Works

Allen, Louis. "Diplomacy." In vol. 8, no. 4 of History of
the Second World War, edited by Basil Liddell Hart and
Barrie Pitt, pp. 3221-30. 8 vols. London: Purnell,
1966-1969.

_____. Singapore, 1941-1942. London: Davis-Poynter,
1977.

Broszat, Martin. "Zeitgeschichte in Japan."
Vierteljahrshefte für Zeitgeschichte 22, no. 3 (1974):
287-98.

Bullock, Alan. Hitler: A Study in Tyranny. 2nd ed., rev.
New York: Harper and Row, 1962.

Burden, Hamilton T. The Nuremberg Party Rallies: 1923-39.
New York: Frederick A. Praeger, 1967.

Butow, Robert J. C. Japan's Decision to Surrender.
Stanford: Stanford University Press, 1954.

Compton, James V. The Swastika and the Eagle: Hitler, the
United States, and the Origins of World War II. Boston:
Houghton Mifflin, 1967.

Coox, Alvin D. "High Command, Field Army, and Government:
The Kwantung Army, 1939." Paper read at the meeting of
the Pacific Coast Branch, American Historical Association,
29 August 1968, at University of Santa Clara. Mimeographed.

Craig, Gordon A. "The German Foreign Office from Neurath
to Ribbentrop." In vol. 2 of The Diplomats, 1919-1939,
edited by Gordon A. Craig and Felix Gilbert, pp. 406-36.
2 vols. New York: Atheneum, 1963.

_____. The Politics of the Prussian Army, 1640-1945.
New York: Oxford University Press, Galaxy Book, 1964.

_____. "Totalitarian Diplomacy." In Diplomacy in Modern
European History, edited by Laurence W. Martin, pp. 74-92.
New York: Macmillan, 1966.

Bibliography

Craig, William. The Fall of Japan. New York: Dial Press, 1967.

Crowley, James B. Japan's Quest for Autonomy: National Security and Foreign Policy, 1930-1938. Princeton: Princeton University Press, 1966.

Deakin, F. W., and Storry, G. R. The Case of Richard Sorge. New York: Harper and Row, 1966.

Deborin, G. Secrets of the Second World War. Translated by Vic Schneierson. Moscow: Progress Publishers, 1971.

Falin, V. M. et al., eds. Soviet Peace Efforts on the Eve of World War II (September 1938--August 1939): Documents and Records. 2 pts. Moscow: Novosti Press, 1973.

Feis, Herbert. The Road to Pearl Harbor: The Coming of the War between the United States and Japan. Princeton: Princeton University Press, 1950.

Haruki, Takeshi. "Matsuoka and the Japanese-American Nego-tiations, 1941." Aoyama keizai ronshu [Aoyama journal of economics] 10, no. 4 (1959): 1-31.

_____. "The Tripartite Pact and Soviet Russia: An Attempt at a Quadripartite Pact." In Hogaku ronbun shu [A collection of law treatises], pp. 1-27. Tokyo: Aoyama Gakuin University, 1964.

Havas, Laslo. Hitler's Plot to Kill the Big Three. Trans-lated by Kathleen Szasz. New York: Cowles Book, 1967.

Hayashi, Kentarō. "Japan and Germany in the Interwar Period." In Dilemmas of Growth in Prewar Japan, edited by James William Morley, pp. 461-88. Princeton: Princeton University Press, 1971.

Hildebrand, Klaus. The Foreign Policy of the Third Reich. Translated by Anthony Fothergill. Berkeley: University of California Press, 1973.

Hillgruber, Andreas. Hitlers Strategie: Politik und Kriegführung, 1940-1941. Frankfurt am Main: Bernard und Graefe Verlag für Wehrwesen, 1965.

232

_____. "Japan und der Fall'Barbarossa': Japanische
Dokumente zu den Gesprächen Hitlers und Ribbentrops mit
Botschafter Oshima von Februar bis Juni 1941."
Wehrwissenschaftliche Rundschau: Zeitschrift für die
Europäische Sicherheit 18, no. 6 (1968): 312-36.

Horwitz, Solis. "The Tokyo Trial." Carnegie Endowment for
International Peace, International Conciliation, no. 465
(1950), pp. 475-584.

Hosoya Chihiro. "Retrogression in Japan's Foreign Policy
Decision-Making Process." In Dilemmas of Growth in
Prewar Japan, edited by James William Morley, pp. 81-105.
Princeton: Princeton University Press, 1971.

_____. "The Role of Japan's Foreign Ministry and Its
Embassy in Washington, 1940-1941." In Pearl Harbor as
History: Japanese-American Relations, 1931-1941, edited
by Dorothy Borg and Shumpei Okamoto with the assistance
of Dale K. A. Finlayson, pp. 149-64. New York: Columbia
University Press, 1973.

_____. "The Tripartite Pact, 1939-1940." Translated by
James William Morley. In Deterrent Diplomacy: Japan,
Germany, and the USSR, 1935-1940, edited by James William
Morley, pp. 191-336. New York: Columbia University
Press, 1976.

Huizenga, John. "Yosuke Matsuoka and the Japanese-German
Alliance." In vol. 2 of The Diplomats, 1919-1939,
edited by Gordon A. Craig and Felix Gilbert, pp. 615-48.
2 vols. New York: Atheneum, 1963.

Ienaga, Saburo. The Pacific War: World War II and the
Japanese, 1931-1945. New York: Pantheon Books, 1978.

Iklé, Frank William. German-Japanese Relations, 1936-1940.
New York: Bookman Associates, 1956.

_____. "Japanese-German Peace Negotiations during World
War I." American Historical Review 71, no. 1 (1965):
62-76.

Issraeljan, V., and Kutakov, L. Diplomacy of Aggression:
Berlin-Rome-Tokyo Axis, Its Rise and Fall. Translated
by David Skvirsky. Moscow: Progress Publishers, 1970.

Bibliography

Jones, F. C. Japan's New Order in East Asia: Its Rise and
Fall, 1937-45. London: Oxford University Press, 1954.

Kase, Toshikazu. Journey to the Missouri. Edited by David
Nelson Rowe. New Haven: Yale University Press, 1950.

Kutakov, Leonid N. Japanese Foreign Policy on the Eve of
the Pacific War: A Soviet View. Edited by George
Alexander Lensen. Tallahassee: Diplomatic Press, 1972.

Langer, William L., and Gleason, S. Everett. The Challenge
to Isolation: The World Crisis of 1937-1940 and American
Foreign Policy. New York: Harper and Row, 1952.

Lewin, Ronald. Ultra Goes to War: The Secret Story.
London: Hutchinson, 1978.

Liddell Hart, B. H. History of the Second World War.
London: Cassell, 1970.

Liu, F. F. A Military History of Modern China, 1924-1949.
Princeton: Princeton University Press, 1956.

Lu, David J. From the Marco Polo Bridge to Pearl Harbor:
Japan's Entry into World War II. Washington, D.C.:
Public Affairs Press, 1961.

Mackintosh, Malcolm. "The Development of Soviet Military
Doctrine since 1918." In The Theory and Practice of War,
edited by Michael Howard, pp. 247-69. London: Cassell,
1965.

McSherry, James E. Stalin, Hitler, and Europe. 2 vols.
Cleveland: World Publishing, 1968-1970.

Martin, Bernd. "Die deutsch-japanischen Beziehungen während
des Dritten Reiches." In Hitler, Deutschland und die
Mächte: Materialien zur Assenpolitik des Dritten Reiches,
edited by Manfred Funke, pp. 454-70. Düsseldorf: Droste,
1977.

_____. Deutschland und Japan im Zweiten Weltkrieg: Vom
Angriff auf Pearl Harbor bis zur deutschen Kapitulation.
Göttingen: Musterschmidt-Verlag, 1969.

_____. "Zur Vorgeschichte des deutsch-japanischen
Kriegsbündnisses." Geschichte in Wissenschaft und
Unterricht 21, no. 10 (1970): 606-15.

234

Maruyama, Masao. "Japan's Wartime Leaders, Part I."
Orient/West 7, no. 3 (1962): 33-45.

_____. "Japan's Wartime Leaders, Part II." Orient/West
7, no. 7 (1962): 37-53.

_____. Thought and Behaviour in Modern Japanese Politics.
Expanded ed. London: Oxford University Press, 1969.

Matloff, Maurice. "Comments" on the paper read by Alvin D.
Coox at the meeting of the Pacific Coast Branch, American
Historical Association, 29 August 1968. University of
Santa Clara. Mimeographed.

Maxon, Yale Candee. Control of Japanese Foreign Policy: A
Study of Civil-Military Rivalry, 1930-1945. Berkeley:
University of California Press, 1957.

Meissner, Kurt. Deutsche in Japan, 1639-1960. Tokyo:
Deutsche Gesellschaft für Natur- und Völkerkunde
Ostasiens, 1961.

Meskill, Johanna Menzel. Hitler and Japan: The Hollow
Alliance. New York: Atherton Press, 1966.

Minear, Richard H. Victors' Justice: The Tokyo War Crimes
Trial. Princeton: Princeton University Press, 1971.

Miyake, Masaki. "Die Achse Berlin-Rom-Tokio im Spiegel der
japanischen Quellen." Mitteilungen des Österreichischen
Staatsarchivs 21 (1968), pp. 408-45.

_____. Nichi-Doku-I sangoku dōmei no kenkyū [A study on
the tripartite alliance Berlin-Rome-Tokyo]. Tokyo:
Nansō-sha, 1975.

Morley, James William. The Japanese Thrust into Siberia,
1918. New York: Columbia University Press, 1957.

Moses, Larry W. "Soviet-Japanese Confrontation in Outer
Mongolia: The Battle of Nomonhan-Khalkin Gol." Journal
of Asian History 1, no. 1 (1967): 64-85.

Nish, Ian. Japanese Foreign Policy, 1869-1942:
Kasumigaseki to Miyakezaka. London: Routledge and
Kegan Paul, 1977.

235

Bibliography

Norton, Donald H. "Karl Haushofer and the German Academy, 1925-1945." Central European History 1, no. 1 (1968): 80-99.

Ōhata Tokushiro. "The Anti-Comintern Pact, 1935-1939." Translated by Hans H. Baerwald. In Deterrent Diplomacy: Japan, Germany, and the USSR, 1935-1940, edited by James William Morley, pp. 9-111. New York: Columbia University Press, 1976.

———. "Nichi-Doku bōkyō kyōtei, dō kyōka mondai (1935-1939)" [The question of strengthening the Japanese-German anti-Comintern pact, 1935-1939]. Part 1 of Sangoku dōmei, Nis-So chūritsu jōyaku cited below, pp. 3-155.

Picker, Henry, and Hoffmann, Heinrich. Hitlers Tischgespräche im Bild. Oldenburg: Gerhard Stalling Verlag, 1969.

Plehwe, Friedrich-Karl von. The End of an Alliance: Rome's Defection from the Axis in 1943. Translated by Eric Mosbacher. London: Oxford University Press, 1971.

Presseisen, Ernst L. Before Aggression: Europeans Prepare the Japanese Army. Tucson: University of Arizona Press, 1965.

———. Germany and Japan: A Study in Totalitarian Diplomacy, 1933-1941. The Hague: Martinus Nijhoff, 1958.

Robertson, E. M. Hitler's Pre-War Policy and Military Plans, 1933-1939. New York: Citadel Press, 1967.

Sangoku dōmei, Nis-So chūritsu jōyaku [The triple alliance and the Japanese-Soviet neutrality treaty]. Vol. 5 of Taiheiyō sensō e no michi, kaisen gaikō-shi [The road to the Pacific war: a diplomatic history before the war]. Edited by Nihon Kokusai Seiji Gakkai Taiheiyō Sensō Gen'in Kenkyubu [The Japan Association of International Relations, Committee to Study the Origins of the Pacific War]. 8 in 7 vols. Tokyo: Asahi Shimbun Sha, 1962-1963.

Sheldon, Charles D. "Japanese Aggression and the Emperor, 1931-1941, from Contemporary Diaries." Modern Asian Studies 10, no. 1 (1976): 1-40.

Shirer, William L. The Rise and Fall of the Third Reich:
A History of Nazi Germany. New York: Simon and Schuster,
1960.

Sommer, Theo. Deutschland und Japan zwischen den Mächten,
1935-1940: Vom Antikominternpakt zum Dreimächtepakt:
Eine Studie zum diplomatischen Vorgeschichte des
Zweiten Weltkriegs. Tübingen: J. C. B. Mohr, 1962.

Tinch, Clark W. "Quasi-War between Japan and the U.S.S.R.,
1937-1939." World Politics 3, no. 2 (1951): 174-99.

Toscano, Mario. Designs in Diplomacy: Pages from European
Diplomatic History in the Twentieth Century. Trans-
lated and edited by George A. Carbone. Baltimore:
Johns Hopkins Press, 1970.

_____. The Origins of the Pact of Steel. 2nd ed., rev.
Baltimore: Johns Hopkins Press, 1967.

Trevor-Roper, H. R. The Last Days of Hitler. New York:
Macmillan, 1947.

U.S., Department of the Army. Headquarters, Army Forces
Far East, Military History Section, Japanese Research
Division. Japanese Preparations for Operations in
Manchuria Prior to 1943. Japanese Monograph No. 77.
[Tokyo and Washington, D.C.]: 1954.

_____. Political Strategy Prior to Outbreak of War, pt.
1. Japanese Monograph No. 146. [Tokyo and Washington,
D.C.]: 1953.

Usui Katsumi. "The Role of the Foreign Ministry." In
Pearl Harbor as History: Japanese-American Relations,
1931-1941, edited by Dorothy Borg and Shumpei Okamoto
pp. 127-48. New York: Columbia University Press, 1973.

Vagts, Alfred. The Military Attaché. Princeton: Princeton
University Press, 1967.

Weinberg, Gerhard L. The Foreign Policy of Hitler's Germany: Diplomatic Revolution in Europe, 1933-36.
Chicago: University of Chicago Press, 1970.

Wheeler-Bennett, John W. The Nemesis of Power: The German
Army in Politics, 1918-1945. 2nd ed. London: Macmillan,
1964.

237

Bibliography

Willoughby, Charles A. Shanghai Conspiracy: The Sorge Spy Ring. New York: E. P. Dutton, 1952.

Young, Katsu H. "The Nomonhan Incident: Imperial Japan and the Soviet Union," Monumenta Nipponica: Studies in Japanese Culture 22, nos. 1-2 (1967): 82-102.

8. Newspapers

New York Times.

News Chronicle (London).

Times (London).

9. Dissertations

Dolman, Arthur. "The Third Reich and Japan: A Study in Nazi Cultural Relations." Ph.D. dissertation, New York University, 1956.

Menzel, Johanna M. "German-Japanese Relations during the Second World War." Ph.D. dissertation, University of Chicago, 1957. (The basis for Johanna Menzel Meskill's 1966 book cited above.)

10. Correspondence (initiated by the author)

Baerwald, Hans H.
Chapman, John W. M.
Coox, Alvin D.
Costrell, Edwin S.
Cunningham, James S.
Erickson, John
Farago, Ladislas
Fechtman, Robert H.
Gibbs, Norman
Haruki, Takeshi
Joll, James
Kogan, Arthur G.
Lambert, Margaret
Layman, Richard D.
Liddell Hart, Basil
Melland, Brian

Meskill, Johanna M.
Mink, Jun
Miyake, Masaki
Mushakoji, Kinhide
Nishiura, Susumu
Oliver, John B.
Oshima, Hiroshi
Piggott, F. J. C.
Rohwer, Jürgen
Schmidt, H. A.
Shigeru, Tokuhisa
Tognelli, Vittorio E.
Toland, John
Uwono, Moto
Watt, D.C.
Wolfe, Robert
Yakobson, Sergius

INDEX

Abe, Katsuo, Japanese navy officer, 91, 117n. 21
Abe, Nobuyuki, Japanese Prime Minister, 109, 135
Amau (Amo), Eiji, Japanese Minister to Switzerland, 119n.
  39, 120n. 43
Arita, Hachirō, Japanese Foreign Minister, 39-42, 44, 49,
  51n. 12, 57, 76n. 3, 87-88, 90-91, 94, 96-100, 103-4,
  107-8, 117n. 21, 118n. 23, 133-34, 150n. 13
Attolico, Bernardo, Italian Ambassador to Germany, 96
Auriti, Giacinto, Italian Ambassador to Japan, 64

Baba, Eiichi, Japanese Finance Minister, 46
Badoglio, Pietro, Italian Prime Minister, Mussolini's
  successor, 120n. 45
Baerwald, Hans H., American political scientist, 33n. 25,
  122n. 59
Blomberg, Werner von, German Minister of War, 37-38, 40,
  65, 79n. 14
Bormann, Martin, Chief of the Party Chancellery, 8
Brückner, Wilhelm, Hitler's personal aide, 75
Bülow, Bernhard Wilhelm von, State Secretary of the German
  Foreign Ministry, 51n. 8
Butow, Robert J. C., American historian, 52n. 13, 54n. 34,
  89

Canaris, Wilhelm, German navy officer, head of the Abwehr,
  37, 59, 62, 76n. 3, 77n. 3
Chiang Kai-shek, leader of the Kuomintang and Nationalist
  China, 65, 130
Ciano, Galeazzo, Italian Foreign Minister, 58, 64, 90, 92,
  100, 103-4, 117n. 19, 124n. 79
Clausewitz, Carl von, Prussian army officer and military
  theorist, 22
Coox, Alvin D., American historian, 30n. 14
Craig, Gordon A., American historian, 37

Dewey, Thomas E., Governor of New York, 3n. 3
Dirksen, Herbert von, German Ambassador to Japan, 5, 38,
  50n. 6

239

Index

Dodd, William E., American Ambassador to Germany, 7, 9,
    16nn. 17 & 19, 19, 31n. 18
Dönitz, Karl, German navy officer, Hitler's successor,
    117n. 21

Erhardt, John G., American consul general in Hamburg,
    16n. 17

Foerster, Richard, German navy officer, 106, 124n. 84
Franco, Francisco, Caudillo of Spain, 49, 56n. 49, 129
Fritsch, Werner von, Commander in Chief of the German
    Army, 65, 79n. 14
Fromm, Bella, diplomatic columnist, 7, 19, 33n. 26
Funk, Walther, German Minister of Economics, president of
    the Reichsbank, 142, 144, 154n. 62
Furuuchi, Hiroo, staff member of the Japanese embassy in
    Berlin, 12

Gaus, Friedrich, member of the German Foreign Ministry,
    88, 116n. 12
Goebbels, Paul Joseph, German Minister of Propaganda, 1,
    7, 127, 148n. 1
Göring, Hermann, Commander in Chief of the Luftwaffe,
    8, 61, 74, 79n. 14, 101-2, 112, 144
Grew, Joseph C., American Ambassador to Japan, 82n. 38, 106

Hack, Friedrich Wilhelm, German-Japanese intermediary, 24-
    27, 32n. 20, 33n. 26, 37, 45, 47-48, 140
Harada, Kumao, Baron, secretary to Prince Saionji, 89
Hess, Rudolf, Hitler's deputy, 8-9, 131
Hilger, Gustav, member of the German Foreign Ministry,
    123n. 77
Himmler, Heinrich, Reichsführer SS, 60-61, 62, 95, 112
Hindenburg, Paul von, President of the Weimar Republic,
    7-8
Hioki, Masu, Japanese Ambassador to Germany, 5
Hiranuma, Kiichiro, Japanese Prime Minister, 90, 99, 101-3,
    108, 144
Hirohito, Crown Prince, 21; Emperor of Japan, 10, 99-101,
    109
Hirota, Koki, Japanese Foreign Minister, 39, 46, 49, 51n.
    12, 144

Hitler, Adolf, Reich Chancellor and Führer, 2, 7-11, 26-
    28, 34n. 28, 37-39, 41-45, 48-49, 53nn. 22 & 26,
    54n. 28, 56n. 49, 59, 61, 63-66, 70-71, 74, 77n. 3,
    85-87, 92, 94, 96-97, 101-4, 108-9, 112-13, 115n. 8,
    117n. 18, 123n. 77, 127-28, 130-33, 135-40, 148nn.
    3 & 6, 149n. 7, 151n. 29, 152nn. 38 & 42
Honda, Kumatarō, Japanese Ambassador to Germany, 5
Horinouchi, Kensuke, Japanese Vice Foreign Minister, 66
Hosoya, Chihiro, Japanese political scientist, 148n. 2
Hossbach, Friedrich, German army officer, 63, 79n. 14
Hotta, Masaaki, Japanese Ambassador to Italy, 58
Hull, Cordell, American Secretary of State, 16n. 17

Iinuma, Minoru, Japanese army officer, 20, 29n. 4
Ikeda, Seihin, Japanese Finance Minister, 88
Inoue, Kōjirō, staff member of the Japanese embassy in
    Berlin, 12, 39, 53n. 19
Ishiwata, Sōtarō, Japanese Finance Minister, 90, 99, 108
Itagaki, Seishirō, Japanese Minister of War, 81n. 31, 88-
    90, 99, 101, 104, 107-8, 144
Itō, Nobufumi, member of the Japanese Foreign Ministry, 91,
    96, 117n. 21

Kagesa, Sadaaki, Japanese army officer, 66
Kan'in, Kotohito, Field Marshal Prince, Chief of the Jap-
    anese Army General Staff, 21, 23, 27, 29nn. 7 & 8,
    36, 40, 151n. 26, 152n. 31
Kasahara, Yukio, Japanese army officer, 67, 69-70, 79n.
    19, 81n. 31, 82n. 33, 87, 89
Kawabe, Torashirō, Japanese military attaché in Berlin,
    61, 70, 151n. 29
Keitel, Wilhelm, head of the Wehrmachtamt, 37; Chief of
    the O.K.W., 59-60, 62, 65-66, 76n. 3, 110, 135, 144
Kipling, Rudyard, English author, 10-11
Kojima, Hideo, Japanese naval attaché in Berlin, 70
Konoye, Fumimaro, Japanese Prime Minister, Prince, 82n.
    37, 88
Kuriyama, Shigeru, Japanese Minister to Sweden, Norway,
    and Denmark, 120n. 43
Kurusu, Saburō, Japanese Ambassador to Belgium (also Min-
    ister to Luxembourg), 95, 119n. 39; Ambassador to
    Germany, 138

Index

Lammers, Hans Heinrich, Reich Minister and Chief of the
    Reich Chancellery, 110
Litvinov, Maxim Maximovich, Soviet Foreign Commissar,
    123n. 77

Machijiri, Kazumotō (Ryōki), Japanese army officer, 39,
    42, 107
Manaki, Japanese army officer, 60
Marshall, George C., Chief of Staff of the U.S. Army, 1
Maruyama, Masao, Japanese political scientist, 121n. 52
Matsui, Iwane, Japanese army intelligence officer, 24
Matsuoka, Yōsuke, Japanese Foreign Minister, 109, 154n. 64
Meissner, Otto, State Minister and Chief of the Presidential
    Chancellery, 75
Milne, George, Field Marshal Sir (later Lord), 21
Molotov, Vyacheslav Mikhaylovich, Soviet Foreign Commissar,
    133
Mushakōji, Kintomo, Japanese Ambassador to Germany, 5, 9-
    12, 16nn. 17 & 19, 39-44, 47, 52n. 19, 58, 63, 66, 94,
    119n. 34
Mussolini, Benito, Italian Duce, 58, 88-89, 92, 101-2, 104,
    108, 116n. 13, 120n. 45, 123n. 77, 148n. 3

Nagai, Matsuzō, Japanese Ambassador to Germany, 5-11, 15n.
    7, 63, 94, 119n. 34
Nagai, Mikizō, member of the Japanese Foreign Ministry, 96
Nagano, Osami, Japanese Minister of the Navy, 46, 154n. 64,
    146
Nagaoka, Haruuichi, Japanese Ambassador to Germany, 5
Narita, Katsushirō, member of the Japanese Foreign Ministry,
    67
Neurath, Constantin von, German Foreign Minister, 26, 38,
    65, 79n. 14
Nicholas II, Czar of Russia, 21
Nomura, Kichisaburō, Japanese Foreign Minister, 151n. 27

Obata, Yukichi, Japanese Ambassador to Germany, 5
Ōhata, Tokushirō, Japanese historian, 122n. 59
Okada, Keisuke, Japanese Prime Minister, 51n. 13
Ōkawa, Shūmei, Japanese intellectual propagandist, 154n. 64
Ōmura, Yūrin, Japanese military attaché in Berlin, 24
Ōshima, Ken-ichi (father of Hiroshi Ōshima), Minister of
    War, 21, 85, 115n. 1

242

Ōshima, Tōyō (wife of Hiroshi Ōshima), 119n. 40
Ott, Eugen, German military attaché in Tokyo, 20, 29n. 5,
    36, 45-46; Ambassador to Japan, 65, 70, 82n. 38, 96,
    103-7, 123-36, 151n. 26, 152n. 38

Piggott, F. J. C., British army officer, 115n. 1
Piggott, F. S. G., British military attaché in Tokyo,
    115n. 1

Raeder, Erich, Commander in Chief of the German Navy,
    79n. 14
Ramzai (Richard Sorge's code name), 80n. 24
Raumer, Hermann von, member of the Dienststelle, 37, 43,
    45, 53n. 24
Ribbentrop, Joachim von, German ambassador-at-large, 25-
    28, 31n. 18, 33n. 26, 34n. 28, 36-39, 41-43, 50n. 6;
    Ambassador to the Court of St. James, 44-45, 47, 53n.
    26, 58; Foreign Minister, 60-62, 65-66, 68-71, 74,
    77n. 3, 78n. 3, 80n. 29, 83n. 39, 87-90, 92-94, 96,
    100, 103-6, 112, 114, 116n. 13, 123n. 77, 124nn. 77
    & 79, 128, 132-40, 144, 150n. 18, 151n. 26
Roosevelt, Franklin Delano, president of the United States,
    130, 148n. 6
Rowan, Hugh W., American assistant military attaché in
    Berlin, 23, 31n. 18

Saionji, Kimmochi, Japanese Elder Statesman, Prince,
    51n. 13, 89
Saitō, Makoto, victim of the army mutiny, 26 February 1936,
    51n. 13
Sakamoto, Tamao, member of the Japanese Foreign Ministry,
    96
Sakao, Hideichi, Japanese Ambassador to Poland, 120n. 43
Sakaya, Tadashi, member of the Japanese Foreign Ministry,
    67
Schulenburg, Friedrich Werner von der, German Ambassador
    to the Soviet Union, 123n. 77
Schwerin von Krosigk, Lutz, German Foreign Minister,
    Ribbentrop's successor, 117n. 21
Shigemitsu, Mamoru, Japanese statesman, 39-40, 43, 48-49,
    55n. 36, 95, 119n. 39, 144

Index

Shiratori, Toshio, Japanese Ambassador to Italy, 72, 74,
    82n. 38, 90, 95-101, 106-9, 117n. 19, 119nn. 39 & 43,
    120n. 45, 125nn. 88 & 93, 132, 144
Shirer, William L., American author, 32n. 24, 149n. 7
Shudo, Yosuto, member of the Japanese Foreign Ministry, 67
Solf, Wilhelm, German Ambassador to Japan, 5
Sorge, Richard, spy for the Soviet Union, 47-48, 69, 80n. 24
Stahmer, Heinrich Georg, German Ambassador to Japan, 152n. 38
Stalin, Josef, secretary-general of the Central Committee
    of the Communist Party of the Soviet Union, 61, 77n.
    3, 109, 123n. 77, 140, 150n. 18
Streicher, Julius, Gauleiter of Franconia, 8-9
Sugiyama, Gen, Deputy Chief (later Chief) of the Japanese
    Army General Staff, Minister of War, 36, 151n. 26

Takahashi, Korekiyo, Finance Minister, victim of the army
    mutiny, 26 February 1936, 51n. 13
Tatsumi, Eiichi, Japanese army officer, 91, 117n. 21
Terauchi, Hisaichi, Japanese Minister of War, 39-42, 45-46,
    52n. 13, 151n. 29
Thomas, Georg, German army officer, 31n. 18
Togo, Shigenori, Japanese statesman, 5, 33n. 24, 39-40, 43,
    45, 49, 62-63, 66-73, 81n. 31, 82n. 37, 86, 94, 96,
    119n. 34, 120n. 43, 133, 144
Tojo, Hideki, Japanese army officer (later Prime Minister
    and War Minister), 22, 103, 142, 144
Toscano, Mario, Italian political scientist, 116n. 13

Ueda, Kenkichi, Deputy Chief of the Japanese Army General
    Staff, 20
Ugaki, Kazushige, Japanese Foreign Minister, 69, 71-72, 81n.
    31, 88
Usami, Uzuhiko (Yoshikiko), member of the Japanese Foreign
    Ministry, 81n. 31, 95, 107, 119n. 38
Usui, Shigeki, Japanese army officer, 60-61

Victoria, Queen of England, 21
Voretzsch, Ernst Arthur, German Ambassador to Japan, 5

Wakamatsu, Tadaichi (Tadakazu), Japanese emissary to Berlin,
    27-28, 31n. 18, 36-39, 47, 52n. 13, 56n. 46
Watanabe, Jotaro, victim of the army mutiny, 26 February
    1936, 51n. 13

Weinberg, Gerhard, American historian, 48
Weizsäcker, Ernst von, State Secretary of the German
    Foreign Ministry, 70, 93, 105, 132-34
Wilhelm II, Kaiser of Germany, 64, 85
Woermann, Ernst, Under State Secretary of the German
    Foreign Ministry, 107, 139

Yamada, Yoshitarō, member of the Japanese Foreign Ministry,
    66
Yamagata, Aritomo, Field Marshal Count (later Prince), 21
Yamaguchi, Iwao, member of the Japanese Foreign Ministry,
    57
Yamaji, Akira, member of the Japanese Foreign Ministry,
    51n. 9
Yamamoto, Isoroku, Japanese Vice Minister of the Navy, 104,
    106
Yamashita, Tomoyuki (Hōbun), Japanese army officer, 22,
    83n. 41
Yano, Makoto (Shin), Japanese Minister to Spain, 119n. 39
Yokoi, Tadao, Japanese naval attaché in Berlin, 12
Yonai, Mitsumasa, Japanese Minister of the Navy, 88, 90,
    99, 103-4, 106, 108
Yoshida, Shigeru, Japanese Ambassador to the Court of St.
    James, 57

Zaryanov, I. M., justice from the Soviet Union at the
    IMTFE, 62

Carl Boyd is Associate Professor of History at Old Dominion
University. A graduate of Indiana University (A.B., 1962;
A.M., 1963) and the University of California, Davis (Ph.D.,
1971), he is the author of "The Role of Hiroshi Ōshima in
the Preparation of the Anti-Comintern Pact," Journal of Asian
History 11, no. 1 (1977); "The Berlin-Tokyo Axis and Japanese
Military Initiative," Modern Asian Studies 15, no. 2 (1981);
and "The 'Magic' Betrayal of Hitler," in Selected Papers
from The Citadel Symposium on Hitler and the National Socialist
Era (1982). His various other articles in the field of
military history and strategic studies have appeared in
such publications as the United States Naval Institute Proceedings, the Army Quarterly and Defence Journal, the Royal
United Service Institution Journal, Selected Papers from
The Citadel Conferences on War and Diplomacy, 1977 and 1978,
Microform Review, and the Montclair Journal of Social Sciences
and Humanities.